T0163674

SUCCESS PROFILES

SUCCESS
PROFILES
CONVERSATIONS WITH
HIGH ACHIEVERS

INCLUDING:
JACK CANFIELD
TOM ZIGLAR
LORAL LANGEMEIER
AND **MORE**

BRIAN K. WRIGHT

NEW YORK

LONDON • NASHVILLE • MELBOURNE • VANCOUVER

Success Profiles

Conversations With High Achievers Including Jack Canfield, Tom Ziglar, Loral Langemeier and More

Published in New York, New York, by Morgan James Publishing. Morgan James is a trademark of Morgan James, LLC. www.MorganJamesPublishing.com

The Morgan James Speakers Group can bring authors to your live event. For more information or to book an event visit The Morgan James Speakers Group at www.TheMorganJamesSpeakersGroup.com.

ISBN 9781683506157 paperback
ISBN 9781683506164 eBook
Library of Congress Control Number: 2017908970

Cover Design by:
Rachel Lopez
www.r2cdesign.com

Interior Design by:
Chris Treccani
www.3dogcreative.net

In an effort to support local communities, raise awareness and funds, Morgan James Publishing donates a percentage of all book sales for the life of each book to Habitat for Humanity Peninsula and Greater Williamsburg.

Get involved today! Visit
www.MorganJamesBuilds.com

TABLE OF CONTENTS

ACKNOWLEDGMENTS

A project like this can never be done alone, and for that reason there are some people I want to thank.

First, I want to thank my parents for always believing in me during the good times and the bad, and for always being present. I love you very much.

To all of the wonderful guests who have been on Success Profiles Radio, thank you for being amazing mentors and friends. I am confident I have gotten even more from those interviews than anyone can imagine.

To my inner circle of close friends, thank you for always being willing to listen and help me through this journey called life. Your love and support have been instrumental, and I thank you and honor you.

To you who are reading this collection of wisdom, thank you for your support. My greatest wish is that this blesses you as much as it has me.

To my publisher Morgan James Publishing, thank you for believing in this project. You support and patience have been beyond expectation. Thank you!

And finally, to God my Creator, for giving me life and seeing me through many challenges including a life-threatening illness, and giving me the desire to make a lasting impact on the world. I would not be who I am today without having those challenges in my life. Thank you so much for everything!

INTRODUCTION

What does it take to be successful?

This is a question that many people ask and wonder about. No one would admit to wanting to be average. We all have a deep desire to be significant somehow and leave a legacy worth remembering.

One of the purposes of my radio show Success Profiles Radio is to interview world-class experts and answer not only this question, but discover what they overcame on their journey and emerge victorious.

In this book, I have featured some of the most fascinating interviews that have aired on the show with people you probably recognize if you study business or personal development. When I began this show in January 2012, my ambition was to talk to people I have admired or studied for years, people whose books I have read, and people whose audio programs I had listened to.

I also looked at it as an opportunity to ask these experts the questions I had always wanted to know the answers to, not only for myself but for others as well.

It has been a terrific journey lasting 200 episodes so far, with many more to come.

Without further delay, let me introduce you to the amazing mentors I had a chance to interview:

The first interview I wanted to share with you was with one of my heroes, and whose work I have admired for a very long time.

Darren Hardy is the publisher of SUCCESS magazine, and the author of *The Compound Effect*, and his newest book *The Entrepreneur Roller Coaster*. He made his first 6 figure income at 19, and became a millionaire at 24.

Since he is the publisher of SUCCESS magazine, I asked what it takes to be a successful entrepreneur and what differentiates high achievers from everyone else. We also talked about how successful people deal with self-limiting beliefs and how they view adversity as opportunities instead of wounds that need to be healed.

We also talked about how to sell successfully and how to know when to outsource tasks in our business. In addition, we discussed the concept of having 20 seconds of insane courage to help us overcome the things we tend to fear. Finally, we talked about how to be insanely productive without losing your mind.

This interview was brilliant, as I am sure you can imagine!

The next interview was with **Jack Canfield.** He is the author of *The Success Principles: How To Get From Where You Are To Where You Want To Be*. He is also the co-author of the *Chicken Soup For The Soul* series which has sold hundreds of millions of copies worldwide.

We discussed a few items from the 10th anniversary edition of *The Success Principles*, including accepting complete responsibility for your results, how to handle rejection and feedback constructively, and why the Law of Attraction doesn't always seem to work for everyone.

We also talked about how we create and un-create fear in our lives and how that can sometimes stop us from going for what we want. In addition, we talked about how high achievers think differently from everyone else, and so much more.

Jack was very engaging and generous with his answers. I know you will enjoy it as much as I did.

The next interview I want to highlight was with **Don Green**. He is Executive Director of the Napoleon Hill Foundation, and the author of the book *Everything I Know About Success, I Learned From Napoleon Hill*.

We talked about why many people don't experience success, and one key reason is that they don't have a passion or burning desire for anything in particular. We also discussed the relationship between the thoughts we have and the outward results we get in return.

In addition, we discussed having a positive mindset and being willing to persevere through the tough times. All great champions refuse to give up when having difficulties.

We also talked about developing and maintaining winning habits, being able to identify opportunities when others don't see them, and how to build a legacy that will last beyond our lifetime. It was a great privilege to talk to Don, especially with all of the great stories he told and the wealth of knowledge he has of Napoleon Hill's work.

Next is an interview I did with **Greg Reid.** He has actually been on my show twice, and in this interview he was promoting his book *Think And Grow Rich: Stickability* which had not been released yet. We discussed many ideas relating to perseverance and not giving up.

We also discussed the importance of being flexible about the way that we achieve our goals. Sometimes things don't unfold the way we thought they would, so being open to HOW is important. In addition, we discussed defining and conquering our "cul-de-sac" moments, which means knowing that there is no choice but to keep going once we are in a situation. Greg also talked about some of the amazing people who are involved in this project, including Steve Wozniak, Sharon Lechter, Frank Shankwitz (Founder of the Make-A-Wish Foundation), and more. He also talked about how he organized a 2 day live event around the release of his book and movie, which by the way is a terrific idea if you want to generate buzz around your book release. Greg is a true professional with a servant's heart, and he was a really fun guest.

The next interview was with **Sharon Lechter.** She is the author of the book *Think and Grow Rich for Women.* We talked about her work with the Napoleon Hill Foundation, as well as her previous work with the Rich Dad Corporation. We discussed how women can own their power, the idea behind "having it all", and women's increased influence in business, politics, and more. We also discussed the importance of masterminds, the role of faith in success, and how fear holds us back from being our very best. We also discussed the importance of financial literacy for people of all ages whether young or old. Sharon was really amazing, definitely make an effort to learn more from her as financial literacy is becoming increasingly important in this economy.

The next interview was with **Frank Shankwitz**, who is the Founder of the Make-A-Wish Foundation. He discussed how he and a few others started the organization, as well as the challenges they faced along the way. He also talked about some of his favorite "wish" stories and how Make-A-Wish has grown into an organization that has granted over 280,000 wishes worldwide. Frank also talked about how he was approached about having a movie made about his life. At the time of this interview, the draft for screenplay was done, and the movie is scheduled for release in the near future. In addition, we talked about a couple of books he has written or co-authored including *Once Upon A Wish*. Frank is like your favorite uncle who you could sit around and talk with for hours. It was a really fun interview!

My interview with **Erik Swanson,** also known as "Mr. Awesome", was next. He is the author of *The Habitude Warrior: Quotes and Notes*, and his new book *Sales Habitudes*. He is also CEO of Universal Seminars, which is one of the leading seminar companies in the U.S.A. He has shared the stage with some of the most talented and famous Sales & Motivational Trainers of the world today such as Brian Tracy, Jim Rohn, Tom Hopkins, Jack Canfield, and Tony Robbins, just to name a few. We discussed many success habits that people can adopt, including how to get your day started off right, how to remember people's names more effectively, how to network and ask for referrals in your business, and the power of social media to build personal and professional relationships. We also talked about how to connect with high-profile people and find awesome people to include in your life. Erik is one of the most generous and helpful people I know. You will definitely enjoy this interview a lot.

I also had the pleasure of interviewing **Dr. John Demartini**, who I consider to be the single most brilliant man I have ever connected with. He was one of the featured experts from the book and film *The Secret*. We discussed how he had physical disabilities and dyslexia while growing up, and then became homeless. We also talked about how that led to his interest in personal development, a field in which in he is now one of the top experts in the world. Dr Demartini talked about the Law Of Attraction, what it is, and why it doesn't seem to work for some people. We also talked about how wealth and health are affected by the Law Of Attraction. In addition, we discussed his trademarked Demartini Method, which is a methodology which helps people experience breakthroughs in their personal and business lives. This method has applications in education, business, personal finance, and much more. Finally, we talked about the importance of gratitude and journaling, as well as his book called *The Values Factor*, which had not been released at the time of this interview. The book talks about discovering and honoring your values and living and inspired life.

Loral Langemeier brought an amazing energy to the show, as she discusses money in a way no one else does. She is the author of *The Millionaire Maker*, as well as several other national bestselling books. We talked about how she started by developing an extensive fitness program for Chevron employees, and then working with Robert Kiyosaki and Sharon Lechter in the Rich Dad corporation before striking out on her own. Loral talked about how she has helped people become millionaires in only 3-5 years, as well as the greatest challenge entrepreneurs face in trying to make their first million dollars. We also talked about habits that rich people have that others don't, as well as how to do due diligence when deciding to work with business partners. In addition, we talked about how to have money conversations with our children and why that is important. We also discussed how to make cash fast if we are in a crunch.

Next was **Debbie Allen**, who has been a lifelong entrepreneur, has written six bestselling books, and managed to be interviewed by Howard Stern while keeping her clothes on! We discussed her book *The Highly Paid Expert*. At the time of this interview, the book was close to its release date. We discussed how to take your area of expertise and create a brand and multiple sources of income. We also discussed case studies of clients she has worked with where her step-by-step method of creating an expert empire has worked. In addition, we talked about re-inventing your business when things get very difficult, such as the recent economic downturn, as well as mistakes to avoid when building a business. Finally, we talked about getting major publishers to compete over the rights to publish her book. Debbie tells it like it is and pulls no punches. If you want to create an empire around your topic of expertise, this is definitely for you!

Last and certainly not least, is my interview with **Tom Ziglar.** We talked about what it was like having Zig Ziglar as his Dad, as well as how he got started in the Ziglar Corporation, working his way up from the warehouse all the way to the top of the organization. In particular, we talked about the book *Born To Win* which he co-authored with his father. Tom talked about planning to win, preparing to win, and expecting to win, and how all of those elements are intertwined. We also discussed how to achieve lasting success, how to find a burning desire when you feel stuck in a rut, why people block their own potential, and how to recognize opportunities. Tom was incredibly easy to talk to, and was tremendously insightful. I know you will enjoy this one!

As you can see, there is a lot of wisdom contained in these interviews, and I look forward to sharing them with you now. I am honored to share this journey with you. Let's begin!

DARREN HARDY

THE ENTREPRENEUR ROLLERCOASTER

Brian: Hello and welcome to Success Profiles Radio. I'm your host Brian K. Wright and it is a pleasure to be with you here with you today. I am honored that you chose to spend part of your day with me here, and this is going to be a fantastic show.

My guest this week is Darren Hardy. Let me tell you a little bit about him:

Darren is just like many entrepreneurs. He started out afraid, nervous, and without a clue what to do or what to expect as an entrepreneur. He had no experience, training, or guidance. He did it mostly wrong, which is how he figured out how to do it right. His life has been a living laboratory of trial, error, failure, and success. Darren wrote *The Entrepreneur Roller Coaster: Why Now Is the Time to #JoinTheRide* to help save you lots of unnecessary pain and to significantly accelerate your success by helping you do it right the first time!

Through his first "real" business, Darren was earning a six-figure annual income at age 19. Five years later, he was a self-made millionaire, and by age 27, he had a business generating over $50 million in revenue.

For the past two decades, Darren has been a business leader in the success and human achievement industry. He is the visionary force behind SUCCESS magazine as its Publisher, giving him unprecedented access to interview, study, and draw out the insights of the most successful achievers. This has allowed him to uncover their unique secrets to success, which he shares to empower entrepreneurs around the world. Darren also mentors many of today's high-performing CEOs, advises large corporations, and sits on the boards of several companies and nonprofit organizations. He is a New York Times best-selling author, media contributor, and highly sought-after keynote speaker.

Darren wrote the book *The Entrepreneur Roller Coaster* to prepare you for the wild ride of entrepreneurship. It will warn you (of forthcoming fears, doubts, and the self-defeating conditioning of your upbringing and past), inoculate you (from the naysayers, dream-stealers, and pains of rejection and failure), and guide you (as you build those underdeveloped skills of independence, self-motivation, and self-accountability) safely past the landmines that blow up and cause the failure of 66% of all new businesses. Access your ticket to *The Entrepreneur Roller Coaster* book here: www. RollerCoasterBook.com

We will discuss all of this and so much more on today's show!

With all of this in mind, here is my guest, **Darren Hardy**

Brian: How are you Darren?

Darren: I'm great! I feel spectacular after that introduction, thank you very much for that. That was beautiful!

Brian: You're so very welcome and you deserve every bit of it, you've done so much and I've been a fan of yours for a long time. I've got *The Compound Effect* and now I have *The Entrepreneur Roller Coaster*, both of which are amazing books and if you all don't have it, go to Darren Harvey's website and get those right now—after the show, of course—but get those books and read them, if you have not already.

So, Darren, the first question I ask everyone is: Tell us about your background, your back story. I alluded to some of that in the bio but you've got such a rich, amazing background. I'd love to hear about it.

Darren: Well, Hardy is an English name and so I'm actually a descendant of royalty and one of the high houses from England. I went to nothing but private academies growing up. I graduated top of my class at Yale, I was personally mentored by a descendant of Einstein for the last, but no, none of that is true….

I'm actually from a very dysfunctional family and upbringing, my parents divorced when I was 18 months old. My mother didn't want me so she basically enthusiastically handed me to my father who was 23 years of age when I was born, just moved to the middle of the country that seemed like the middle of nowhere to him away from his support group and family, and it was just he and I growing up together. He was the university football coach father. He really didn't know how to parent. He had the nurturing qualities of a Neanderthal, and the way you got love and attention in our household was to achieve. And so, he did teach me how to work hard, how to be disciplined, how to stay consistent, you know the mantra in our house was *"no pain, no gain"* you know, "suck it up", if you're going to cry, *"I'll give you something to cry about"*—that sort of discipline.

But it definitely instilled this desire to achieve as well as this discipline and hard work ethic which I do attribute to my father, which was just fantastic, but as you mentioned I started out like everybody else started-out. Scared and nervous, without a clue of what to do and with no guidance, and I stubbed my toe and bruised my knees, bruised my ego and bruised my pride many a time. And the other interesting thing is with a single semester of college to my credit, nothing I've ever done that I ended up doing successfully had I've ever done before or had any training, or any experience, or any sort of direct mentorship in order to figure how to do it successfully. So, I say all that to say "Look, if your background is any better than that in the slightest", then "if I can do it, certainly you can do it".

But it really is the pattern of many great people that you might admire today. I mean, Steve Jobs was also abandoned by his biological parents and given up for adoption, and it fueled his drive to prove himself and to feel validated and feel significant, and the world is better for him. Richard Branson was called stupid or lazy by his teachers, and his headmaster said that he'll end up in jail or prison when he left and dropped out of high school, and yet look at what the world has benefited from as result of Richard Branson's success.

So, first message is I always say that your adversities are not wounds that you need to heal from. You know, you don't need to child-regress, get over these childhood traumas. What I see adversities as are great advantages. These were the training ground, this was the emotional and psychological muscle building and development that one goes through that allows ultimately you to do extraordinary things that ordinary people who have not had that muscle development can do themselves. So, really my background is not a factor to my success except for the fact that having to overcome these difficulties gave me greater strength today than people who had that cushy, no adversity laden background. So embrace your adversities and see them as great advantages, is basically of the message.

Brian: That's really awesome! And you had me going for a second because I read your book. And you started talking about your background, and I don't remember reading any of this (laughter). So thank you so much clarifying that. And so, I do want to ask, I did allude to this in the bio, but tell us, when did you know that you wanted to be an entrepreneur because this really set the course for your entire life.

Darren: Yeah! I didn't know that. In fact, my father who didn't really know how to direct a child—the only thing he knew about society was the people who seem to be on the top of the totem pole were doctors and lawyers, and when he saw me faint in the sight of my own blood early as a kid, he knew that being a doctor was off the table. So he focused all his efforts on lawyer so I was supposed to be destined a lawyer. Even the one semester college that I went to was focused on political science, the pathway was to become an attorney. And then I was introduced, just by happenstance by a friend, to this rogue business opportunity of basically buying water-filters and wholesaling door to door, and selling at retail and keeping the difference. That turned into hiring others to it and building a distributorship that turned into a five million dollar business starting when I was 18 years of age.

So entrepreneurship interrupted my path, and if you read *The Entrepreneur Roller Coaster*, the beginning period of that was laden with all sorts of difficulties and problems, but I did get the bug. I got the bug about challenging my skills and abilities, finding some things that I really was great at and then expanding on those, and I never looked back. So, I've been an entrepreneur since 18 years of age, again, mostly by happenstance. And I thank God really that I was interrupted, because I would have been a horrible attorney and the reason is—God love those who are great at it—but I am an anti-conformist. Tell me the rule I will find a way to break it. I truly do have the mindset and the mentality of an entrepreneur, which is in most cases the opposite of the mind of an attorney. Quite frankly, my sister—who is also into the same dogma of my father's philosophy—ended up going to law school. She's tried to take the bar 3 or 4 times and hasn't been able to pass it, and quite frankly because it's really not what she should be doing. She was basically following the definition of success that my father gave her without figuring out the definition of success was for her. And so thankfully entrepreneurship interrupted that path for me and gave me a sense of what my true strengths and skill sets were, my true passions were, and that started at 18. For my sister who is 34 or 35, she is only getting a sense of it right now and 16 years of it have been gone as a result of it.

Brian: I do want to ask for a quick question. How did you decide to write this book *The Entrepreneur Roller Coaster*?

Darren: As publisher of SUCCESS magazine, our mission is to empower entrepreneurs globally and I tried to figure out what causes the 66% of failure rate amongst small business owners who finally get the courage to break away from the herd of mediocrity, or what everybody else doing, because 90% of the population are employees and venture out on their own. What I found was shocking, it wasn't what everybody reports is the reason why people fail as a small business owner—external factors of the economy, or inventory, or technology, or the lack of capital, or lack of talent acquisition—there were more internal reasons. It's the emotional factors that caused people from being able to see themselves through the entrepreneur emotional roller coaster one goes through when they step out on their own and become a small business owner. So, it was trying to correct the major pitfall that most face of why they fail when they become an entrepreneur, and equip them with the skills they need to be ultimately successful.

Brian: So, Darren let's talk about your book, *The Entrepreneur Roller Coaster*. I know there are a lot of answers to these questions, but what do you think it takes to be a successful entrepreneur and can it be learned?

Darren: Yeah! Well, I think that the number one ingredient comes down to self-confidence, because you are going to definitely run into many hurdles, most of which will be emotional and psychological—when you run into self-doubt, when you run into whether you feel like you're good enough, whether you're capable, when you run into naysayers who mock and laugh and try to pull you back into the herd of mediocrity. It is going to be the quality of self-confidence this ultimately going to see you through those difficult stages that you go through as an entrepreneur.

The other quality, I think, is hunger. You really need dogged determination, and the best definition that I ever heard of why you really have to have passion, why you really have to love what are you doing as an entrepreneur, isn't because you need to live this life of great bliss and self-actualization and exaltation and so forth. That is not the reason. It was Steve Jobs who said the reason why you have to have passion for it is because it is so hard, it's so difficult, and if you don't love it, if you don't have a passion for it, you'll give up because it's so difficult. The same person would say it's not worth it, but you've got to be a little insane, and that insanity comes from this real deep down burning desire and hunger to see it through. We know that it's not talent and it's not intelligence that causes and creates success. You could look at many of the greatest successful entrepreneurs of the planet and they certainly are not the most intelligent, and certainly not the most talented, but they went through the grueling 10,000 hours as Malcolm Gladwell pointed out, or as Anders Ericsson pointed out in the Cambridge Handbook of Expertise and Excellence. It takes 10,000 hours to develop what becomes a great skill or mastery of a skill that ultimately people call a talent. So, unless you have that hunger and dogged determination to grind through those 10,000 hours, you're never going to get to the other side of success. So, I would say self-confidence and the sense of hunger.

Brian: You addressed passion just a little bit of ago. I think that is also really important. So, I want to ask, what do you tell someone who says they're not sure what they are passionate about? Where does that fit into the equation for you.

Darren: I actually get tired of hearing this a little bit because it sounds like a whine, *I'm not working harder* or *I'm not more successful because I'm not just passionate about what I do, I'm not just passionate,* like they are entitled to be passionate. You are not granted passion. You're granted an opportunity at life. There are several ways which defines this thing that Steve Jobs talks about where you do have to find your passion, you do have to love it. But it doesn't have to always be what you do.

For the most part, there are a lot of people that do some really not great things but they absolutely love it. We had this house keeper, Latisha, and she just was passion-filled all day long, and she was doing what I thought was really awful work. I saw this stuff she had to do around my own house, but she was just filled with this sense of purpose and passion, and the reason was that because she loved how she did it. She did things with such great care and excellence, and it fulfilled her to see her deliver a result and an outcome that was a standard of excellence. So I've seen toll takers and taxicab-drivers, I've seen CEOs, I've seen accountants, I've seen a variety of different people whose switch is not what they do, it's how they do what they do. And another switch is maybe who you do it for. Maybe you don't love what do you do, or love even the process of how you do it, but you're doing it because you want to financially retire your parents so they don't have to worry about money. Or you want to be sure that your kids can go to the greatest universities that they qualify for. And so you're doing it for their future, or you're doing it for some great charity, or some organization or some disadvantaged group of people that you feel very passion-filled and purposeful helping out, and so what you do and how you go about doing it, is the means to the end of providing for those people. And then last is "What it is for me? Why?"—why you do what you do—the higher purpose or the sense of significance or the contribution or the impact that you're making is been the fuel source for me. It comes down to these Four Switches: "What"," How", "Who", or "Why" it doesn't all have to be "What". In fact no matter what you choose to do—this is one of the things that I write about in *The Entrepreneur Rollercoaster* book—is whatever you choose to do, 95% of the time it's going to suck! You're going to have to do things that you don't want to do. Whether your Bono or Oprah or Richard Branson, 95% of your day is sucked up doing stuff you might not want to do, but the 5% is so amazing and such a great, incredible pay-off that it's worth grinding through the 95% to get to the 5% of true exaltation, true thrill, true extraordinary feeling and experience.

Brian: Exactly, something else you talk about in the book is *find your fight*. I mean, sure, you need to do what you need to do, and know who and what and why and those are all extremely important things. But sometimes we come up against it. Sometimes you just have to pick and choose your battles. How do you do that?

Darren: The reality is that our brain is negative. Our brain is negative, meaning the brain has one job and one job only, and that is survival. That is its only purpose and only desire. It doesn't care about your happiness, it doesn't care about your joy, it doesn't care about your self-actualization, it doesn't care about any of that. It's on alert all day long, looking for anything that might be a threat or to be dangerous. You can find your great purpose and passion in life by figuring out what it is that you love, *"What do I love , what do I want to support, what do I want to contribute to"*. But I'll tell you what, it's not as powerful of a motive and motivation as figuring out what it is that you hate—what you're willing to fight for, what you're willing to defend. Of course, people say, "Oh! You shouldn't hate". Trust me you need to hate, there is good and there is evil. You want to roll through the good and you want to fight the evil. There are both sides, and the way to find what it is that you might hate is figure out what it is that you love and then what is the enemy of that, what's the threat of that? You might love your mother, and you hate the fact that cancer took her away from you too early in life. Or you might love the environment that we have been bestowed to take care of and to be good stewards of it. You might hate what we might have done to influence the destruction of that, or you might love the beautiful mammals that populate our ecosystem. That means you hate the violent injustice of whale hunting. You might love animals and you hate the mistreatment or abuse of animals.

For instance, I love human potential. I love to being able to see the seeds of greatness that are buried inside people that they might not see that is buried in self-doubt. Whereas your fears, if I can break them past that and we can nurture, water, and cultivate those seeds, they will blossom and they will finally live up to the potential that they were bestowed. I love human potential, so what's the threat of that? Well, to me there are a couple of major threats. One is negative, sensational news media that is bombarding our minds, ears and eyes with the worst of what is happening in the world in order to draw your attention long enough to sell you a Crest toothpaste commercial. But it takes 6 most perverted, heinous, lewd, awful, corrupt things that are happening in the world, and then barrages you morning, noon and night with them.

Meanwhile millions of beautiful, amazing and miraculous things happen throughout the day, but you don't hear about it because it doesn't draw your attention, and they can't monetize that attention financially. And so, I hate negative sensational news media. My Goliath in life is Wolf Blitzer and the rest of those on all the different networks, right? But I get out of bed more fired up to fight against that than I do even the joy of human potential. So there is something about being able to hack your primal instincts that drives every fiber of your being. And if you can trigger that brain mechanism that says we need to defend against threat and we need to activate our survival, and you can use that to propel your success—I'm telling you, it is powerful, and you become unstoppable.

Brian: I love that, that's great. And *The Entrepreneur Roller Coaster* is available at rollercoasterbook.com. Is that right?

Darren: Yes, rollercoasterbook.com

Brian: Okay! Fantastic! Let's move to another topic. Let's talk about having a business and hiring people. This is a really interesting discussion in your book. You talked about "A" list people actually being a lot less expensive to your business than "B" list and "C" list people. Tell us why that's true. I think that so interesting.

Darren: Well, as Richard Branson said: "Look, a company is only one thing. If there are planes every airline buys the same Boeing planes. The only thing that makes up one airline over one another are the people that they put in the planes. The team of people that you hire and cultivate, orient, and create a culture for are those that are running your business". Then I interviewed Jack Welch, he said "The bottom line is the organization that fields the best team wins".

The season is determined before the season starts, depending on who you been able to recruit in the key positions, and then cultivate their great talents. Businesses are people serving people, and if you get the people right, the people will take care of the rest. So, the number one job of the leader is to recruit the highest talent possible. So 60-80% of all the operating expenses of any organization is in salary. If you hire the wrong people, it costs 6 - 15 times their annual salary. Not only the time, labor and money that you spent hiring, orienting, and training, or in the money that you spend paid, but also the time and money to repeat that process, the opportunity cost and rehabilitation cost—the chemotherapy you've got to give the rest of your organization once that person has gone. At the same time if you get it right, one great talented person can outperform 2-3 people in business in productive output, and here where it comes down to. "A" players hire "A" players, because "A" players want to work with "A" players and have no tolerance for dealing with sub-par talent. "B" players, on the other hand, hire "C" players because they are threatened by high-level talent. So Steve Jobs called it a "Bozo explosion". If you going to let one "B" player in then all of the sudden you end up with a "Bozo explosion" in your organization. And the last thing I'll say is, the "A" players are free, they always outproduce what you pay them and they come with the 12 month finance-plan.

Brian: My guest this week is Darren Hardy, and he has written an amazing book called *The Entrepreneur Roller Coaster*. So Darren you have rubbed shoulders with some of the world's most successful people. What do you think differentiates them from everybody else?

Darren: Number one is that they are constant learners. The reality is that we are all born with a blank slate, and it's what you do on a constant never-ending basis to grow and improve that ultimately has you rise above everybody else. I mean, you basically stand on the books that you read to get head and shoulders above other people. So whatever that is for you, whether it's books, whether it's audio training programs, whether it's listening to radio programs like this, going to seminars, or hiring coaches. They are learners. And number two is that they also have this sense of resolve, this attribute that "I will do it, or I will die trying". So I think that's a differentiating factor. The last is one that is not that obvious and I just see it every time. They are great communicators. You've got to learn how to communicate. If you look at the Jobs', the Branson's, the Welch's, they know how to communicate to incites people's engagement, whether it be in a factor of influence, a factor of sales, a factor persuasion—they know how to communicate. So, learn and grow a sense of resolve and the ability to communicate.

Brian: I love it, that's fantastic. Something else you do address in the book is the idea of how all of us fight self-limiting beliefs, even the super, super successful people. But the great achievers don't appear to give in to this. How do they do that?

Darren: I'm not sure that they don't give in to it. I have a friend of mine who's a CEO of a two billion dollar company, massively successful, one of the greatest CEO leaders of our time. And he will admit that he wakes up many mornings in a panic then he says, *Maybe, they're going figure me out, maybe they're going to realize that I'm a fraud, that I'm not deserving of the position that I've been given and the responsibilities that I've got*. So, you're human, right? We're all going through this human journey. While as Coach

K said, "*You have to show the face that your team needs to see.*" So you have to show a sense of confidence and a sense of resolve. But that doesn't mean that you're not fighting those feelings inside, right? Whether it's President Reagan when the Space Shuttle blew up in the sky and he had to address the nation—it wasn't that he wasn't scared and wasn't nervous and wasn't dying inside. But he had to show empathy as well as confidence. When George W. Bush stood up in the pile of rubble that used to be the Twin Towers, he might have been scared, nervous and frightened, and he had to show strength and a sense of confidence. I have to tell you, I think they all feel it. But they battle it inside and then show up in a way that gives—whether it be your team or your country or your community—the sense of confidence that they need to see, so that they can get over their own sense of self-doubt that might allow them to ultimately crumble.

Brian: Yeah, Absolutely! I love that. You know, when we run businesses, we all have our ups and downs which is, of course, why you are calling it the "Entrepreneur Roller Coaster". When we are in our down periods or valleys and we have a lot of adversity, some people are much, much better handling that than others. Do you have specific strategies in handling adversity? And how long does it take to get you get going again?

Darren: So when I first got started as an entrepreneur if I was significantly rejected, or was to face some sort of defeat, or had some awful failure or some embarrassing incident, I could be down for a couple of weeks. I realized that being kicked in the teeth and kicked in the gut is part of the process. You can't avoid that. Here is the bottom line. You are going to fail, you are going to be embarrassed, you are going to be rejected. It's going to hurt, you can't avoid that. In fact, I say that *it is not the accumulation of your successes that determines your ultimate success, it is the failure that you go through and how long you stay down in between those intervals*. The faster you get up, the more you exponentially accelerate your path towards success. You can't control getting knocked down, but you can control how long you stay down. So I started focusing on my recovery time. It was two weeks, then I got it down to two days. Then I went from two days to two hours. And even to this day, I've got it between 20 seconds and maybe 20 minutes. Depending how big the failure is, I can either just talk through it and pick up the phone and go again in 20 seconds, or I might need to leave the office—you know, pound my fist on a steering wheel, and shout and cry and moan and gripe in my car for a little while— then come back to the office a little while and get back on the horse. Look, you're human, it's going to hurt and it's going to happen, and don't let that be your sense of failure. Let your sense of success be measured by fast you get back up and get going again. Just know that it's a part of the journey, part of the process and whittle the time down, not the number of times you get knocked down because you want to accelerate your failure rate and you want to shorten your recovery rate.

Brian: Absolutely, that's great. So what do you think is the important thing an entrepreneur should be focused on?

Darren: Well, I would say personal growth and constant never-ending development, really. When it comes down to it, you don't know what you don't know, and it's a learning journey. My mentor Jim Rohn would say *you don't accomplish goals, you can't achieve something that you never achieved before until you become somebody you haven't been before*, and the only way to do that is you grow into your goals. You don't accomplish goals, you grow into them. The one thing that every entrepreneur should do is to really focus on constant never-ending growth. What are your big three goals, what are the one or two key skills that's most important to accomplishing those goals? And then go attack the growth learning curve of those two or three skills that are going to be indicative of accomplishing those big three goals, and then focus on your team as well. Where do their skills need to grow in order to achieve the goals that you have as an organization? Growth is central, it's number one.

Brian: And a lot of people seem to be addicted to the approval from other people. And I've got a coach who's a mental toughness coach and he talks about with me about fighting the addiction of needing to be approved or have approval from other people. How does that really limit us?

Darren: It's a double-edge sword because needing to be accepted in your peer group could be a fantastic motivator. It was my original motivation. The whole motivation that I had in life was to prove myself to my father, to be worthy of his approval and attention. It set me out on a very determined journey of success. One of the stories I love is Michael Jordan, who was cut from his high school basketball team as a sophomore in high school. And then he had this illustrious career, arguably one of the greatest athletes who has ever lived. For his Hall of Fame speech, he took that coach and flew him across the country, put him in the front row and made one of the central themes on his whole Hall of Fame acceptance speech, wagging his finger at that coach, and looking at him sternly, and saying *"See! You were wrong"*, which meant that he was motivated to all those great heights out of trying to be accepted. When I interviewed Anthony Hopkins, I asked him to what he would attribute his success, and he said "anger". When he was growing up his cousins were smarter, brighter, more talented than he was, and he felt ashamed and unworthy. Then he found this community theater and he thought that he might be good at it, and he just worked like the dickens to be great at that so that he can prove himself. For Steve Jobs, it was the same thing. As I told you, he was given up for adoption and spent the rest of his life trying to prove himself. So, I think, in fact, you should use it. It's a fantastic fuel. As a matter of fact, if you're stagnant, if you're complacent—I have an email going out to my Darren Daily group this morning that talks about this—the best thing you can do is get around people who are playing a bigger game than you, because psychologically, we want to be accepted by others. And if somebody is successful right now, it's probably because everybody around them is more successful or at the same level. And if you want to ignite every fiber of your primitive being to level up, get around people who are playing a bigger game, and unconsciously you'll do whatever it takes to be accepted by that new peer group and you'll raise your level of success. So it's an awesome motivation. I wouldn't worry about trying to overcome them. I worry about using it a lever.

Brian: That's great! So let's talk about once we have a team, once you are in growth mode in your business, there comes a point in time where you were to decide whether to hire someone or to outsource things to someone else. How do you know who needs to be on your team? What criteria do you use to determine who do you need to surround yourself around?

Darren: That comes down to what are the vital functions of the organization, and what is in your strength zone and what is not your strength and so on. The bottom line in terms of the process is this: When I interviewed billionaire Ken Fisher, who is on the Forbes 400 list, we talked about this and he says when you first start out as an entrepreneur you're going to have to do everything, you're going to have to do all the sales and marketing and customer service, the accounting, you're going to have to take out the trash. The goal is to start quitting—meaning you get enough sales and marketing going to where you have enough revenue that you can pay somebody else to take out the trash so that you don't have to do that. You get more sales and marketing going, you can pay someone to do the accounting. Get more sales and marketing going, you can pay someone to do the customer service, and eventually, end up paying someone to do the sales and marketing. So all you have to do is strategically think about what's around the corner and over the horizon for the organization, and you want to turn labor into leadership. In the beginning, you're going to have to labor by doing it all, but the goal is to start quitting all of the less valuable activities outside of your strength zone and giving it to other people, and doing it as fast as your cash flow will allow you to do it, and moving as much labor off your plate so that you can involve more leadership onto yours, and labor unto others.

Brian: This is Success Profiles Radio, my very special guest is Darren Hardy and his book is called *The Entrepreneur Roller Coaster*, we are discussing a lot of different topics in this book, and if you want to get this book which I strongly recommend you do, go to www.rollercoasterbook.com So sales is something that obviously drives the machine. Can you tell us two or three of the most successful strategies or philosophies that made it work best for you? What is your philosophy on sales in an organization?

Darren: Most of people sell wrong. They like when they did when they are children, which meant that just push, prod, gripe and complain, and eventually they can wear people out and they will relent. Or they watch movies like *The Wolf of Wall Street*, *Glengarry Glen Ross*, *Boiler Room*, or *The Death of the Salesman*, and they think that's what it takes to be successful in sales—just being this annoying, aggravating, used car salesman-like approach which is exactly the opposite of how sales should be done.

So, the number one rule to sales is stop selling. Stop it and start helping. Turn the four letter word of SELL into HELP, and go around asking people questions about what it is that they are most interested in. And so, stop selling and start helping, stop pitching and start asking, stop focusing on features or even results, and start focusing on what's the ultimate transformation or outcome that people are looking for. For instance, let's say you sell drill bits, and right now you're advertising and marketing and pitching and selling, it's like "I'm a technology guy"—your drill bit has the finest technology polymer, latest greatest NASA science metallurgy, and that's what distinguishes you from your competition. The person who is buying a drill bit does not care. They are not looking for technology. They are looking for a hole, but that's a result, they're still not looking for a hole. What they are looking for is what they can build, and if you focus on what they can build, what the outcome they are looking to create is—it might be that tree house for their kid—you're going do a much better job in providing them the solution of your great drill bit when you focus on what is the actual outcome transformation that they are looking to achieve. Sales is so focused on features and why we're better, all of which the customer-consumer doesn't care about. The only thing that they care about is themselves, and the only thing that they care about themselves is the outcome that they are looking to generate. Those are my three quick suggestions: stop selling start helping, stop pitching start asking, stop talking about features or even results and start talking about transformation and outcomes, and then you can attach your solutions to getting there.

Brian: That's beautiful. I appreciate you sharing that. Something else you talked about in the book which really struck me was the fact that not only is entrepreneurship very scary at times but your solution is to have 20 seconds of insane courage three times a day. Tell us about that.

Darren: You don't have to walk around being courageous all day every day. In fact, you could be completely without courage 99.98 percent of your life and end up killing it and crushing the marketplace with your great success. And the way it is that it only takes 20 seconds to engage in an activity that you find fearful, and it's not the actual activity that you find fearful, it's the anticipation of the activity. And if you can just shut your brain down for 20 seconds and step into the activity that you are afraid of, you will actually engage in that activity, prove to your brain that there's nothing to be afraid of, and your heart rate will come down and so forth. So if you're afraid to pick up the phone, just shut your brain off for 20 seconds engaging in activity of punching the phone number, and you'll find yourself mid-stroke in the conversation. If you are afraid to approach a stranger to introduce yourself, shut your brain off 20 seconds, step up, extend your hands say *"Hi my name is...I've always wanted to meet you",* and then all of a sudden you're engaged in the activity. If you are afraid to speak in front of people, it doesn't require you to be courageous for an hour, it only requires you the 20 seconds to step up to the mic, to start talking, and realize that the people aren't going to attack you or eat you, and your heart rate will descend and you'll be engaged in the activity that you want. The adage *the only thing we have to fear is fear itself* is true because most things that we are afraid of pose no mortal danger whatsoever. And so, it's not the actual activity that we're afraid of, it is the fear and the anticipation of the activity that ultimately paralyzes us. If you did something you were afraid of three times a day I promise you—that's a total of one minute a day—you would scale your success exponentially over your contemporaries who are doing everything they can all day to avoid the thing they fear.

Brian: That is an amazing advice. I love that! That's really fantastic, and again if you have not read *The Entrepreneur Roller Coaster*, go ahead and get that at rollercoasterbook.com. I want to ask something because as millennials are growing up and entering the workforce, and in many cases are crushing it in their own businesses, how does that change leadership in the marketplace?

Darren: It's not just millennials, it's the entire dynamic of the landscape that is changed because by 2020 millennials will hold the majority of leadership positions all over the world. And at that time their kids will be entering the marketplace as well, and at that point we will have five generations working in the workforce at one time. This has never happened in all of human history because their grandparents will still be working and their kids will be working—five generations that were weaned in very different times, and very different cultures, and very different societal inputs. And so, another factor is that the workforce is more female than it's ever been in history as well. There's more women working than there are men, and by 2040 there will be more minorities working than what is considered the majority right now.

So, you got all these dynamics that are affecting the workforce, so everything that anybody knows about leadership right now is wrong. And the reason is you know leadership by what you experience, and what you experienced were 20th century leaders—your parents and the other authority figures that you grew up with, and those people were weaned in the military industrial complex, command-and-control, top-down hierarchy. And all of that is gone now. Instead of financial IQ being the most important skill set that somebody has, it is emotional IQ. How do you manage and lead five generations who are female and minority? You better be emotionally intelligent. The competitive weapon in the marketplace is not financial capital, it's human capital. The competition is for talent, it's not top-down command and control, it's collaborate. It's not hierarchies, it's networks; it's not aligning through spreadsheets and balance sheets, it's aligning through meaning and purpose. You're not trying to develop followers, you're trying to develop leaders because the marketplace is flexing way too fast, way too dynamically. You need to train independently-minded, self-directed people. So, the workforce dynamic is radically changed, and the winners going forward are going to be the ones that can adapt themselves to becoming 21st century leaders and that means that they need to get a mental lobotomy about everything they thought they knew about leadership and become the new century leader.

Brian: Fantastic! We've got four and a half minutes left to the end, and I've two questions that I really want to ask. So, here's number one. How do you talk about becoming insanely productive without losing your mind?

Darren: The most important skill I think we need in the 21st century is learning to prevent distractions and keep our focus. We live in an era of epic distraction, unlike any time we've ever had to experience in human history. All these technologies that open up windows into our existence of constant solicitation on our time and attention has overwhelmed our mind, and frazzled our nervous system. And these tools we created to make us more productive have done just the opposite because they have scaled faster than our ability to manage ourselves with them. So, we've got a "tail wagging the dog" scenario here, and it's the reason why I've devoted so much time and attention to this. I developed a program called Insane Productivity, because if there's a skill you need to scale growth in, it is learning how to manage yourself in these dynamic times and keep your focus and stick to your plan in a very, very distracted world. And so, that's the key skill. I think people need to achieve big things in 21st century.

Brian: That's awesome, and the last question I usually ask everyone toward the end of the show: Who inspires and motivates you?

Darren: It was my father. Unfortunately, he passed a couple of years ago but that's the origin. He was the first to become an entrepreneur in the lineage of our entire family history, and he also instilled as I mentioned before hard work discipline, a sense of dogged determination, consistency and so forth, and that created a level of success that I achieved early in my life. But it was really through brute force. And then the next major influence was my mentor, Jim Rohn, who instead of just achieving things through brute force, taught me that in order to have more I needed to become more. And so, he focused my development on becoming someone, not just achieving something but becoming someone, and then all the finer art of living an extraordinary life—all the tapestry of what it is to weave an extraordinary life—came from the philosophy and mindset that I learned from my mentor Jim Rohn.

Brian: That's awesome and, of course, we can find the book, *The Entrepreneur Roller Coaster* at www.rollercoasterbook.com. Last thing I do want to ask. You talk about ambition toward the end of your book. It can be a double-edged sword, a lot of people think that ambition is really good but it can also be bad depending on what you focus on, right?

Darren: Yeah, It can drive you and it's great because it could become that motor that gets you up hungry. But it can also drive you out of your life, because there's lots of things that you can do, but you have to ask yourself the question "Should you?" So, my capabilities and my ambition could have me conquer great lands and do all sorts of things—build bigger companies, scale of my staff, chase greater revenue—but then you become beholden to all those things that you built. Now I have less time to be a great husband, to be a great friend, to be a member of the family, to be a great community member, to allocate time to charities and causes that I like and appreciate. My greatest challenge is not stimulating my ambition. My greatest challenge is harnessing it, so that I can stay in my strength zone and stay doing the things that I want to do, and staying to the things that I should do based on the life and lifestyle that I have chosen to design for myself. So, that's the double-edged sword of ambition.

Brian: That's great! And we are at the end of the show. Darren, I just want thank you so very much for being a part of Success Profiles Radio this week. It was an honor and privilege to have you here. Go to rollercoasterbook.com to get his book. This has been Success Profiles Radio. Meet up with us again on Monday at 6 p.m. Eastern where I interview the most successful and most interesting people in the world, learn their secrets of success, and how we can derive their lessons and apply them to our own lives. Thank you for joining us. You have yourself a marvelous week. Take care everyone. Goodbye!

JACK CANFIELD

THE SUCCESS PRINCIPLES

Brian: Hello, and welcome to Success Profiles Radio. I'm your host Brian K. Wright, and it's an absolute pleasure to be with you here today. I'm honored that you chose to spend part of your day with me here, and this is going to be an amazing show.

My guest this week is Jack Canfield. Let me tell you a little bit about him.

Jack Canfield is the co-creator of the *Chicken Soup for the Soul* series which has sold more than 500 million copies worldwide. Time Magazine has called this the "Publishing Phenomenon of The Decade", and Jack is America's leading expert in creating peak performance for entrepreneurs, corporate leaders, managers, sales professionals, corporate employees and educators. Over the last 30 years, his compelling message, empowering energy and personable coaching style has helped hundreds of thousands of individuals achieve their dreams. Jack is a Harvard graduate with a Master's Degree in Psychological Education and one of the earliest champions of peak-performance, developing specific methodologies and results-oriented activities to help people take on greater challenges and produce breakthrough results.

His proven formula for success reached global acclaim with his most recent Bestseller, *The Success Principles: How to Get From Where You Are to Where You Want to Be*. This new standard in self-improvement contains 67 powerful principles for success utilized by top achievers from all walks of life and all areas of commerce. The 10th anniversary edition is available in bookstores right now.

Jack is a multiple New York Times bestselling author, and his other books include among many, T*he Power of Focus*, *The Aladdin Factor*, and *The Key to Living the Law of Attraction*. Jack Canfield holds the Guinness Book of World Records for having seven books simultaneously on the New York Times Bestseller List. He also holds the Guinness Book of World Record for the largest book-signing ever for *Chicken Soup for the Kid's Soul*.

We will discuss so many of these things and so much more on today's show. And with all of that in mind, here is my very special guest, Jack Canfield. Jack, how are you today?

Jack: I'm fine, Brian, thank you for having me.

Brian: Oh! And thank you for being here. It's an honor and a privilege. In fact, I bought the original version of this book in 2005 right after it came out in February, and I remembered this is the only book I read for that entire year. That's how much I loved The Success Principles. I was making marks in the margins and doing some of the exercises, and there's one exercise that you recommended called 101 things you want to accomplish before you die. I don't think the term "bucket list" was in vogue yet, but being a man doesn't really want a whole lot, I came up with 50 or 55 and I put that list away. And a couple of years ago, I got that list back out again and was astounded to find that I had accomplished probably a dozen of those without even really giving much more thought to it. So it's a wonderful exercise and I love your book, I'm so glad you're here.

Jack: Oh thank you, my pleasure!

Brian: You're welcome. So let me ask you about your background because that's the first question I always lead off with. Tell us about your background, how you got to where you are now and maybe some of the things you overcame.

Jack: Well, I was born in Texas to a father who was in the Air Force, who was very violent and an alcoholic. And so my mother divorced him when I was 6 because he was beating the children and her, and so there was a little bit of child abuse as a younger child. And my step-father that I then got was an alcoholic, my mother became an alcoholic, so I had to deal with all of that growing up. But I was very fortunate that I got a scholarship to go to Harvard. And while I was there, I began to discover that I really enjoyed Psychology. The civil rights movement was happening at that time, and I decided I want to contribute so I taught in an all-Black inner city school for 2 years. And I became much more interested in on how to motivate my kids when I wasn't teaching history, because they weren't motivated like I was.

That's when I met W. Clement Stone who was a self-made multi-millionaire. He was a good friend of Napoleon Hill who wrote "Think and Grow Rich". And so I ended up working for his foundation for a couple of years training teachers on how to motivate kids all the way from elementary school up to college age to want to achieve more, to go for their dreams, and that's how I got into this work. And I started by training teachers, and I started doing corporate work. And I started doing public seminars and writing books, that was the journey. I can remember graduate school. I talked about my 21-cent dinners, where I was literally eating a can of Contadina tomato paste which was 10 cents and an 11 cent can of noodles, and that was my dinner with garlic salt so I know what it's like to be poor. And it took me a couple of years to move beyond that, but that's when I met Stone. He taught me I could do anything I wanted. He said I want you to set a goal that's so huge that when you achieve it will absolutely blow your mind. And I said "Okay, I'm going to set a goal to make $100,000 in 1 year". And that time I was making $8,000 a year, 8 with 3 zeroes after it as a teacher, and 2 years later I made $92,328.00 so that was a proof to me that the techniques worked. And from then on, I become truth believer and a teacher of all this.

Brian: Great! And how did you achieve that goal? I know you told the story in your book but I would love to hear you share that, how did you get to $92,000 that quickly?

Jack: Well, I wrote book called *100 Ways To Enhance Self-Concept In The Classroom*, and the book had been out for about a year and made $2,000 a year in royalties, which did not get me very far. And Stone said what you have to do—and I teach this to this day—is once you have a goal, you have to visualize it: What would you be experiencing, what would you be seeing, what would your lifestyle look like? How would you know if you were looking out of your own eyes to see you have achieved that goal? So, I started visualizing a $100,000 year lifestyle. I made a $100,000 bill. The biggest bill I've ever seen was a $100. So I projected that on an overhead projector on to some paper, and I traced it on a screen using construction paper, and I put a couple of extra zeroes after so it would look like a $100,000. I put that on the ceiling of my bedroom. Every morning I woke up, and it's the first thing I'd see. And then I close my eyes and I visualize the $100,000 lifestyle. I would then basically go do the normal things: exercise, take a shower, meditate. And I did that for 30 days, there's this thing called the "30 Day Principle" we can talk about it. NASA neuroscientists have come up with. But basically, after 30 days I have my $100,000 idea which was if I sold 400,000 copies of my book, I would get 25 cents a copy because the book back then was $6 now, it's $24 with inflation. But anyway I said, you know that would get me there. I didn't know how to do that. But at least I had a leverageable idea for the first time, it had never occurred to me.

So long story short, over time I started to see all these extra resources in my environment. And I remember being in my grandmother's bathroom, and there was Reader's Digest and it said 8 million readers in 37 languages. I thought, "Wow! If 8 million readers saw my book certainly 400,000 would buy it". So I sent them a copy of the book, and I sent them an article that I wrote, see if they publish it, I tried to find out what the ads would cost. One page ad in the *Reader's Digest* at that time for 6x in a row which what you needed is a $108,000 dollars. I knew that it wasn't going to work; I didn't have that kind of money. But I send them an article, which they rejected. And then my wife said "You know, when we go to the supermarket, there's this thing called the National Enquirer, it's 12 million readers weekly. So I sent them an article and then nothing happened. And then I was giving a talk in New York at Hunter College, and this woman comes up and says "I'd like to interview you". I said "Well, who do you write for?" and she said "for the National Enquirer". And so she interviewed me and we got an article in the National Enquirer, and it started to get the book sales to go up.

And then, my wife and I were sitting around one day and we saw another thing that could help us change. Because once you commit to the visualization, your brain starts to open up the reticular system in your brain which will allow things in to your perceptional awareness. And we had this idea that we could start a mail order bookstore, and have one book—our book. And we'd only have to sell 33,000 copies because we charge the retail mark up for $3.00. So we did that, and then my wife said "You know, why we don't sell other people's books?" So eventually we had an 8 page catalog with 32 products, and we started taking this products to university conferences and counseling conferences. We started making $2,000.00 a weekend. And then the final thing was, I was making $300.00 a day as a consultant to schools. And I talked to this friend of mine who gone to graduate school with me, and I said "Hey, what do you charge people?" He said "$800.00 a day" and I asked, "How do you get

$800.00?" He said, "I asked for it." I thought "Whoa!" So anyway, I upped my fee, and at first I was really nervous, I don't know if you've ever practiced asking for something when you were nervous. So finally this guy calls and he says, "what's your fee?" and I said, "Eeeeeeeeiiiiggghhhh—$600." And he said "Oh! We have $1200 in the budget, no problem." So this guy that called says, "what's your fee?" I said, "$1200", he said "we only have $900" I said, "I'll take it."

So anyway, what happened was as a result of all of that, in less than a year we made $92,327 dollars. And we were not disappointed that we didn't make a $100,000—we were blown away. And my wife said, "Well, do you think it will work for a $1,000,000?" So I put a $1,000,000 bill on the ceiling. It took us a few years but I have a royalty check I show when I do in my seminars for $1,138,000, which represented one quarter of royalties for the first *Chicken Soup For The Soul* book.

Brian: Wow. That's an amazing story. My very special guest this week is Jack Canfield who co-authored the *Chicken Soup for the Soul* book, and his revised edition of *The Success Principles: How to Get from Where You Are to Where You Want to Be* is now available in bookstores everywhere, and I'm sure you'd probably get on his website, too, at jackcanfield.com.

This is one of my favorite books of all time, and I have the audio program, too. In fact I was listening in to it in the car this weekend.

So, Jack, let me ask—you talked a little bit about how you decided to write your first book. How did that the idea for *The Success Principles* come about to you? What inspired you to go ahead and do that?

Jack: Well basically, I was in a place where I had achieved outrageous success when I was making $6,000,000 a year off the *Chicken Soup for the Soul* royalties. I had spoken over 47 countries, our books were in all languages around the world. And then now we've got 500 million Chicken Soup books sold, and that's a half a billion books. And so I was just saying I want to give back somehow. And I have been studying success and teaching success ever since 1968 with W. Clement Stone, and I had never really captured all of that in a book. And so I sat down and decided that if I could write a book, it will be the book that if it was the only one they read in their whole life, it would transform them and give them everything they needed to be successful. Not their professional information like how to be a doctor, how to be a lawyer, but all the psychological and all the actions steps you would need to take just from that level, what would that book like?

So I ended up outlining it in bed one morning, and it was about 114 principles that I'd used in my life, and of course that was way too many for a book. So I cut it down and I worked with my editor, and we got down to the point where we thought 64 and now with the re-issue, it's 67. Because we have a new whole section of success in the digital age because when I originally wrote this book, LinkedIn and Facebook, and crowdsourcing and crowdfunding really weren't known then. And so we added that, but basically these are universal principles that were applied through all time. And so I sat there and said, "OK, what has gotten me to where I am? I'm super successful" and then I said, "But what if this is just unique to me?" And so then I interviewed 75 of the most successful people in North America—everyone from Oscar-winning actors, to platinum songwriters, to Generals in the Army, to top salespeople, to entrepreneurs, bestselling authors, etc—to make sure these weren't just idiosyncratic to me, but they were in fact universal, and it has proved that to be that way.

And then in that first book, all the principles I illustrated with their stories. What is exciting about that the 10th anniversary edition, Brian, is now almost every principle is illustrated by someone who read the 1st book like yourself, applied those principles, and actually created a life of success that's outrageous now. And let me tell you one story, then you can ask me some other questions.

I was in the Manila in the Philippines about 5 years ago, and a guy came to interview me at the bookstore the day before I was going to do a seminar. And at the end of the interview I said, "John, that was the best interview EVER, how long have you've been doing this?" He said, "Oh! You are my first interview." I said, "that's impossible!" He said, "No, it isn't." I said, "What have you been doing up until now?" It turns out that he had a restaurant, the restaurant went bankrupt, and he was couch surfing on friends' couches. He had no apartment, he had no car, he had to sell it for money. I said, "John, how much money do you have?" He said, "I've got $3.28, that's my total cash assets". I gave him a $20 dollar bill so he can buy dinner. I bought him a copy of my book from the bookstore since I didn't have my own to give him, and I said, "I'll be back in a year, I want to hear from you". I came back about 2 years later and in walks John in a suit with a gold emblem on his suit jacket. He's got six guys behind him with polo shirts on that all have the same logo. It turns out that John had read my book, and he is now the #1 motivational speaker in the Philippines who's making over a million a year. He had 2 cars, 2 apartments—one on the beach, one downtown—he had a radio show and a TV show, and he had a book coming out. He was averaging 600 to 1000 people at each of his seminars which he puts on once a week. I said "John! How did you do that?" He said "I read your book! I did everything in it". And I said, "If this guy is so successful, I will do everything he says for 1 year". I don't think I know anyone who did every single principle all year long. And now he is a multi-millionaire and has his own TV show, he's a big guy in The Philippines. And it's all because he read the book and applied this. It's not enough to know this stuff, you have to do it and John did it!

Brian: Yeah…that is absolutely phenomenal! I love that story. And to piggyback off of something you said earlier, your book has been revised to include stories of people who have read the book. I had Heather O'Brien Walker in my show last year, and she mentioned that she was going to be in this new edition, and I thought, "Oh! There's going to be a 10th anniversary edition? That's cool!" And she told the whole story and it was just amazing, she's a sweetheart; I just adore her and wow! What an inspiration she is. And you haven't gotten this, get the book *The Success Principles: How to Get from Where You Are to Where You Want to Be*. Heather O'Brien Walker's story is fantastic, and so are many of the other stories. In fact, the first time I ever heard about Tim Ferriss is when I read about him in your 1st edition. I didn't know who he was, and then I looked him up and realized, "Oh! This guy is amazing!" (Laughing).

Jack: Yeah! He is a great example of Ask! Ask! Ask! He asked me to come up speak at the Silicon Valley Startup Entrepreneurs Association. And the reason he did it was he wanted to meet me, and he knew if he did that I'd have to have dinner with him. And he asked me to be his mentor and help mentor him to do a bestselling book, and of course he's gone on to do way more than that now. But you know, Ask! Ask! Ask! is one of my principles, and he had the courage to just ask me to be his mentor. A lot of people think about it, but very few people ever do it.

Brian: Absolutely, one of the first principles you talked about really early on your book is about the idea of accepting complete responsibility for your life. A lot of people prefer to sit back and blame the world for their problems, so how can doing this change what we achieve? I know there's a very specific formula you share about accepting the outcome we get in life.

Jack: Well, the formula is "E+R=O", and everything in the book, everything in my life is based on this. There are events in your life, it's just what happens. There's your response to that event, the word "responsibility" means the ability to respond, the ability to change my response if it's not working. So E + R is EVENT plus your RESPONSE equals OUTCOME. So, one of the events that happened recently was the recession. A lot of people lost their homes, a lot of people lost their jobs—some people got rich. So it's the same event, but people responded differently, and that produced a different outcome.

When I teach my seminars I'll pick on some woman in the first row, and I'll say, "If I said to Sandy here, 'Of all the people I've ever met my entire life working with millions people in seminars, you're the biggest idiot I've ever met', how many people think I would lower her self-esteem? And everyone raises their hand. And I say, "Well it isn't really what I say to Sandy, it's what Sandy says to Sandy after I stop talking". In response to that event, she might just say, "Oh my God! He's only known me for 20 minutes. How did he figure it out so fast?" Her self-esteem will go down. Or she might say, "Canfield has a perceptual handicap. He doesn't recognize talent when he sees it." Her self-esteem will stay the same. Or she might say, "Wow! He's been looking at me a lot, he's been paying more attention to me than everyone else. Maybe he has little crush on me, he knows I can take this". Her self-esteem can even grow up! So it's never what anyone says or does to you, whether it's the environment, the job, the economy—it's what you do in response. And the only three things you have the ability to be responsible for are your thoughts, the images you hold in your head—that's the visual thoughts—and your behavior, which includes what you say and what you do. And what I do in the book *The Success Principles* is I teach people: What are the thoughts that winners think? What are the images that winners hold in their mind? And what are the actions and behaviors winners do, that other people don't. And that's really all it's about. It's about to having studied successful people, including myself, and then say, "How do they act differently? How do they think differently? How do they image differently?", and then turning that into a program that's basically a system that's guaranteed to give you success. What I promise people if you read the book, within three years or less—most students do it in two, and many do it in one—you can double your income, double your time off and have more balance in your life, and more spiritual fulfillment.

Brian: Yeah, that's great! When I did my list that I was alluding to a bit earlier in the show, one of the things that I wanted to do was to have this radio show. And it's so interesting. I put the list away for awhile. And I came back to it and thought, "Wow! I'm doing this!" So, yes this works. We'll talk about the "Law of Attraction" later on the show, because I know you were in *The Secret*, and I know the "The Law of Attraction" is the huge part of what you teach. So let me ask you this, how do we create fear in our lives and how do we un-create it?

Jack: Well, fear is created by imagining bad things are going to happen to you in the future. You've heard of fantasized experiences appearing real, future experiences appearing real. And so what happens is, most of it comes from the past where we had experiences, or maybe we got laughed at, or where we were giving a speech in school, or we asked a girl to go out and she made fun of us in front of her other girlfriends. And so our ego says, "I never want to have that happen again". So when we see another experience like that we go into visualizing that a terrible thing is going to happen, and then we don't do it. There are a few ways to get through fear. Number one, visualize a positive outcome instead of a negative outcome. Number two, stay in the present moment instead of going into the future because nothing bad's happening now, and the third thing is you can use things like "tapping", which is EFT Tapping where you tap on 9 acupuncture points while you experience thinking about the fear.

I wrote a book called *Tapping into Ultimate Success* with a tapping expert, where we looked at all the issues that come up for people when they read *The Success Principles*—about fear of rejection, fear of failure, fear of taking responsibility, fear of losing face, whatever it might be—and we have protocols for how to tap through those, including tapping through your inner self-critic, your inner judge. So, basically, fear is something that's just in your head, that's the thing we have to remember. It's not really out there, it's in us. You can also feel the fear and do it anyway—the idea that you're afraid, and you just do it. I took Tony Robbins' workshops where you walk on burning coals, and we're all afraid. We learned to look up instead of down, which picks you up into your rational mind not into your fear mind. We learned to say "cool moss" instead of "burning coals", and we learned to believe that were going to get to the other side. With all that going on, we just walked and nobody got burned. So you get off the fire, you think, *"Oh my God, what else have I been scaring myself about?"* And so basically, we just have to think about the positive, visualize what we want, not what we don't want, and the fear disappears.

Brian: Wow, that's absolutely incredible! I love that! Think about what you want, not about what you don't want. It's so absolutely important.

We're talking to Jack Canfield about his book called *The Success Principles How Do You Get from Where You Are To Where You Want to Be*. The 10th Anniversary Edition is out now. It's available in bookstores, it's online, Amazon, Barnes & Noble, and of course go to Jackcanfield.com to find that and any other resources of his that you'd like to partake in. Phenomenal, phenomenal, phenomenal.

And so Jack, I'd like to ask you next, how do high-achievers think differently from everyone else? Because certainly there are certain habits, and certain patterns, and certain things that successful people do that unsuccessful people, relatively speaking, don't do. So let's talk about that.

Jack: Well, one we mentioned briefly—they focus on what they want, not what they don't want. They focus on their outcomes, not their obstacles. When they see obstacles, they don't see them as stop signs, they see them as caution signs, and then as something to solve. I remember interviewing an 11-year old boy who was born with no arms from the elbows down, no legs from the knee down. And yet with prosthetic legs and prosthetic arms, and one of his arms has a cross-stick cage on the end of his arm, which is the little net that they throw the ball back and forth with, he ended up being the pitcher on his Little League team in New York that came in second in the State Championships. And when I was interviewing him he said that it was not an obstacle, it was a challenge he needed to solve. He said you always have to have your eye on the prize and know what you want. That's an 11-year old boy. Now I don't know if he had positive parents or he came in with that attitude, but nevertheless, he was totally clear that whatever he wanted to do he could do it. I meet people all the time with all kinds of physical handicaps who are achieving at much greater levels than people who don't have these handicaps because they believe they can. And that's really the point. You have to believe you can rather than you believe you can't.

I tell a story about a guy named Cliff Young in Australia, who was 61 when he showed up in a race that was a 641 km race. It normally takes about 6.5 days to run. There were all these elite young runners, and he was 61. He didn't dress like a normal runner, he wearing construction boots, overalls, and a baseball cap. (Laughing) I said, "You know, have you ever ran a marathon before?" He said no. "10k?", no. "What makes you think you can do this?" He said, "Well I'm a farmer, I get up early, I'm a vegetarian, I'm healthy. I go to bed when the sun goes down. I often have to chase my sheep. I sometimes I'll run for two days without sleep." They finally let him do it. To make a long story short, he had a secret that no one knew about. That is, he never talked to a runner, he never talked to *Runner's World* magazine, he never talked to an elite coach, he didn't know you were supposed to sleep in a 5.5 day to 6.5 day race. So basically, he ran non-stop for 5.5 days and broke the record by 12 hours. And so the point is, it's not what you don't know, it's what you do know that's wrong. Most us are walking around based on, "Well, that's never been done before, this is the way it's always done." And so, successful people believe they can do it no matter what. You look at Taylor Swift, who was making 50 million dollars a year when she was about 20. And she just had this belief that she could do anything she wanted. She got her parents to move to Nashville when she was 14 years old because she knew she wanted to be in that arena.

And so, the other thing is, most of us when things happen, we say, "Why me?" What successful people do when bad things happen is "What do I need to do to get past this?" They don't complain, they don't blame, they don't make excuses. They're always thinking about "What's my goal? How do I get there? Who can I ask to help me?" and they delegate, they persevere, they never give up. Chicken Soup for the Soul was rejected by 144 publishers, we never gave up. Most people would quit after 50. And we would have self-published if we had to, but we were lucky we didn't have to do that.

But you know, I give you an example of a positive thought. I put this in *Chicken Soup for the Writer's Soul* because I know that you train writers how to write books. Barbara Kingsolver, who wrote *The Poisonwood Bible*, great woman, said—I'm paraphrasing—when you're precious manuscript comes back rejected, it doesn't mean it's no good. It means that the acquisition editor who will love your book does not live at this address, so keep on sending it out. That's the problem, most people give up when they have a few failures. One last thing is that successful people know that everything is a first draft. They know that's it's probably not going to work out the first time. I think Brian Tracy has a wonderful quote. He says "We are try –fail -learn, try -fail –learn, try- fail –learn, try -fail –learn, try-fail- learn, try-fail-learn, try-succeed machines", and many of us, instead of just learning from the failures, we give up because we think we can't do it. We're somehow damaged, we're not smart enough, intelligent enough, rich enough, well-connected enough. And so it's just a matter of believing you can do it, no matter what, and then continuing until you get the result.

Brian: Yeah, that is phenomenal, phenomenal advice. And if you all like to hear that again, listen to the replay when it's available. You can go to successprofilesradio.com and do that. You can also download and subscribe to Success Profiles Radio on iTunes for free anytime you want.

Let's talk about changing our financial temperature and breaking out of our comfort zone. A lot of us are used to making a certain amount of money per year, and you shared an example earlier about how you broke through that. So how do you break through that comfort zone and think: *You know, maybe I actually am capable of making more money than this? I'm not doomed to make whatever this is for the rest of our lives.* So how do you build out breaking out of your comfort zone financially?

Jack: Well, most of us think that our past determines our future. For example, when I work with corporations—let's say they made 10 million dollars last year, or they made a 100 million dollars last year, what most corporations do is say "Well, let's make 10% more next year, 20% more. So they set their goal based on the past. You know, what we did in the past, we'll add a little. Instead of saying: "Well, what do we really want? What would be ideal? What would make our hearts sing? What's our vision of our ideal life?" And so the idea is the same thing with money. If we ask, "How much money do you really want to earn, save, invest, etc.? What you want your network to be? What you want your cash flow to be?" And so, it's just a matter of making a choice, deciding what that is.

Now, for most people, that means you're going to be uncomfortable. When I first moved to Los Angeles, I was buying $38 shirts at Nordstrom's, and a friend of mine took me to a boutique in Beverly Hills and he bought a $120 shirt and I thought "Whoa!" But I didn't want to be a wuss so I bought one too. And then I noticed whenever my shirts come back that was always the first one I wanted to wear. It was better tailored, it looks more stylish, etc. And so, my comfort zones started to change because I got more comfortable with that, even when I was uncomfortable at first. So, many people wouldn't even walk in to a high-end jewelry store because it makes them feel uncomfortable.

So what we have to do is two things. Number one, decide what you want, and then start visualizing again. We said this earlier, affirm. I started affirming "I am easily and happily earning and investing $100,000 dollars a year." That's when I was making $8,000. Then my next one was "I'm happily depositing my million dollar royalty check from my publishing company". This year, I'm happily depositing my 8 million dollars in personal income. Now from my company it will be 25, but for me it's 8 million. It's a little bit above the $6 million that I normally make.

And then the other thing that I have learned that's really cool is called a ten times multiplier. Dan Sullivan teaches this. I remember when I was making $60,000 a year, I never thought I could make $600,000. But when I made $600,000 I never thought I could make $6 million. And when I was making $6 million, Dan challenged to me set a goal to make $60 million. He said when you were making 60 you didn't think you'd make 600, but you did. When you were making 600 you didn't think you'd make 6 million, but you did. And so you can ten times your income. So when I set that goal, about three years later we sold one of my companies for $63 million dollars, so the idea is just a choice. General Wesley Clark, when I interviewed him for the book, said it doesn't take any more time or effort to dream a bigger goal. In other words, it doesn't burn up more calories, you don't have to squint your eyes when you make your brain work harder. You simply add another zero. You don't have to know how.

Just like I don't have to know how to get to where you are, you live in Phoenix somewhere. I can just put that address in my GPS and then my car will figure it out. The same thing is true for your brain. Your brain will start to come up with ideas. You'll start to see things in your environment and with the law of attraction, you start attracting people, ideas, and opportunities to you, that you can then act on. But you have to act on them. And so, we change our comfort zone primarily by visualizing, so we get comfortable experiencing in this virtual reality that which we want to create. So if my goal is to make $8 million, I then visualize $8 million. I visualize my tax return, I visualize what I'm going to be doing with that money. So I visualize it until I get comfortable with it, because the brain cannot tell the difference between a real event and an imagined event. And so if I visualize it a 100 times, my brain begins to think that's the reality. And then it just naturally does those things that it needs to do, and comes up with the creative ideas it needs to come up with. The last thing you can do is put yourself in the places that you visualize. Maybe you can't afford to stay at Ritz Carlton where it's $750 a night, but you certainly go to the lobby bar and have a drink. You can certainly go there and say, "I'm going be have a wedding and I'd like my parents to stay here. Could you show me one of the rooms?"

We were just in the Dubai—Patty Aubrey, the President of my company and myself—and there was this hotel over there called the Burj Al Arab. It's this only 7-star hotel in the world. And we got to go up to the Presidential Suite, which rents out for $20,000 a day, it had gold inlay on all of the tile in the bathroom, beautiful murals everywhere. The furniture is to die for, the doors are all inlayed wood. We got to spend two hours in that room taking videos of ourselves, lying on the bed, sitting in the bathroom, etc. just getting used to what it would be like to spend $20,000 a day for a hotel room. And so you can act as if and do all kinds of things to give yourself that experience. Why not go out to test drive a Mercedes, or a Maserati, or a BMW? They're not going let you not do it. And then you get used to what it feels like.

Brian: Wow! That is absolutely amazing. I love that. Jack, you did mention the Law of Attraction earlier, and you were one of several experts who were featured in the book and the movie called "The Secret" which I love. I've read and watched multiple times. It's about the law of attraction and how you can manifest what you want in your life. And a lot of us who probably listen to this show or pay attention to personal development on a fairly regular basis are probably familiar with the law of attraction. The thing that I want to ask though is sometimes people say that, "This didn't work for me". What are some reasons why the Law of Attraction doesn't work, or what are some reasons why we don't get what we think we're trying to manifest?

Jack: Well, the three things that I've seen that stops most people from getting what they want from the law of attraction is number one, they have subconscious limiting beliefs that are contradictory to their desire. Just to give you an example, there are a lot of women who are overweight, and I mean extremely overweight, and often from my experience—plus, I was a psychotherapist once—also in my public seminars, I find that often they are victims of sexual abuse of some kind. And so when they put on all that weight, subconsciously they feel like they won't be attacked anymore because they are not that attractive. And yet, at a conscious level, they really want to be attractive and they want people in their life. They want to be healthy and wear good clothes. So when they start to lose weight, something takes over and it sabotages them.

So we have to learn how to surface those limiting beliefs. And there are a number of techniques that I teach. One is to just focus on what it is that you want. Close your eyes, scan your body, notice a place of tension or tightness in your body. Invariably everyone finds one, it could be a tension in your stomach, or bar of tension in your back, your neck, whatever it might be. And then we look at really exploring that in terms of how big it is, how wide it is, does it feel warmer, dry. We get to all those different characteristics. And then we say, go back in time, to the earliest time when you can remember feeling that same sensation and that same feeling. And invariably they go back to somewhere between ages 3 and 8 when they made a decision that they are not enough, that they can't have money, sex is bad, relationships are dangerous, I'm not smart enough, whatever it is. Those beliefs can then be healed in that moment by going back as your adult self in helping your younger child internally understand that this was not personal—that your dad was just drunk, or your mom didn't know any better. Or they didn't really mean it, in a sense. And so basically we can heal those. Also there are other techniques, obviously therapy and so forth. Another way to look at it, for example, is if you use Bose headphones on the airline, it's got noise cancellation, and so the sound waves come in and it creates an opposite wave which then flattens out the sound. The same happens to yourself if you have a belief that you can't do something, but you have the desire that you want to. Or it could be, I want to own a car but I don't have enough money. I can't afford it. It cancels it out. And, so we have to surface those beliefs and change them. Tapping can be used, again there are many techniques.

The second thing is that people's vibration does not match that which they are trying to attract. In other words, you need to always be in a state of joy, love, abundance, gratitude—high vibrations states. When you're in a state of sadness, grief, anger, resentment, hopelessness, despair—I don't care what you're trying to bring into your life it won't come because it doesn't match the law of attraction. It says you're going to attract to you that which is vibrating at the same level. So, it's really critical that you learn how to manage your emotional states and keep yourself happy and high. That's things like meditation, dancing, doing things you love, surrounding yourself with positive people instead of negative people, which will also bring your vibration down. As Jim Rohn says we're the average of which are the five people we spend the most time with. So, you want to be with positive, uplifting, goal oriented people.

And the third thing that happens is people don't take enough action. The last six letters in the word attraction are A-C-T-I-O-N.

Interesting enough, it spells action. And what *The Secret* didn't stress enough, although it did mention it, is once you get an inspiration to act, you have to act on it. When you're focusing on what you want, when you vibrating at a high level, and you're visualizing what you want, you're doing the affirmations over and over, you're going to get inspirations to act—call my brother, go to this Starbucks instead of that one, call in "well" today instead of don't go to work, write a book. If you don't do it in the moment that inspiration comes, you lose what they call the vortex of energy that's behind that inspiration. And that inspiration is the information that's going take you where you want to go. And so it's very hard for people, sometimes, to do things that don't make any sense, even though they've occurred to them. When writing *Chicken Soup for the Soul*, everyone on my staff thought it was a stupid title and no one was ever going buy the book. 144 publishers agreed with them. The 145th said "No, we're going to publish it." That's produced over $100 million in income in my life and my partner's life. So basically, you have to be willing to act on the inspirations and trust on your intuitions. For a lot of people, they are afraid, they don't do it.

Brian: Yes, I can certainly understand. I know that I have ton of questions that I could ask, but we have very very limited amount of time left. So, here is the question I ask every single person who comes on the show: Who inspires you and motivates you, Jack?

Jack: Gosh, so many people. You know, I'm still inspired by Mandela, and Mother Teresa, and Martin Luther King, and I'm inspired by people like Tony Robbins who are playing a big game, and I'm inspired by the 41st girl in Africa, where I helped fund a school for 40 girls. This 1 girl walked for three hours to the school and said: "Why didn't you let me in? I want to be in." And all the other 40 girls said: "Please don't make her go. We'll let her sleep in our bed, she can share our desk, we can share our food with her." That level of "I'm going to go for what I want" inspires me, whether it's a big name like Martin Luther King or a little girl in Kenya named Susan Mabet. So I think that everyday there are heroes out there that are taking risks, who are trying to reach their goals and go for their dreams—whether it's a housewife in Peoria, who writes a book that I helped her promote and won a Guinness World Record for 100,000 kids being read the same book in the same moment in the same day—or whether it's someone who goes for an Olympic gold medal. Every day I get inspired by new people. I'll share one more. Asia Ford was a Black woman who lost about 100 pounds and was running in a 10k race in Louisville. An officer, Aubrey Gregory got out of his car. She started to walk and didn't think she could make it, but he took her arm and he walked her for the last two miles. That level of heroism, that level of giving that level of serving. Every day makes me get up and smile, and want to continue to work.

Brian: Wow! Those are phenomenal answers. I just love that, Jack. Thank you so much for sharing that. Now, I know we're going be ending here in the next two or three minutes. I wanted to tease a few topics that we're not going have a chance to talk about. It will help people think about buying this book if they want to. It's called *The Success Principles: How To Get From Where You Are To Where You Want To Be*. If you've ever wondered about how to constructively view rejection, how to effectively deal with it, that topic is covered in this book. If you want to learn more about the importance of feedback, and how to constructively work with that, both positive and negative feedback—we prefer one or the other—but actually, if you do it right you can help someone feel really good about the thing that they didn't do right and help them to do it better the next time. That's in this book. The importance of learning how to ask—there are right and wrong ways of asking for something. If you do it in a way that creates a win-win scenario for both you and the person that you're asking from, you can create wonderful results. So those are three more topics that we're not going to have time to talk about, but those are in the book. Get that book, *The Success Principles*. Here's one more thing I'd like to ask. If you could do thing anything differently, or if you're starting over today, Jack, what would you do?

Jack: I would have started writing books sooner. I would have taken more seminars than I did when I was young because I realize that everything I know and do is because I took a seminar, or read a book. And I would probably hang out with people that I was afraid to approach sooner. I'd overcome my own low self-esteem and fear of rejection, and I know you can do that because that's all in the book as you've said. And I just want to say that if people want to get the book, they can go to thesuccessprinciplesbook.com and order the book through that website at Amazon, they'll get back a receipt, they can send it to us get a bunch of bonuses, including the 1st two chapters of the book they can download immediately. The Instant Income Business planner by my co-author Janet Switzer, a daily discipline of success poster, and also a DVD on how to create a significant life that's an hour long, and an hour long audio on the most asked questions about the Success Principles. That's $100 worth of freebies. If your order through my website and you still go to Amazon.com and do it the normal way.

Brian: That's fantastic! I love that very much. And I know that you do an event, a live event called Breakthrough to Success, which based largely on the principles in this book. In fact, it's a five day intensive that really allows people to work through the examples and really helps.

Jack: Yes, It's a five-day intensive. It's a Monday through Friday event in Scottsdale, Arizona, and if you go to jackcanfield.com, you'll see a button that says Breakthrough to Success. We also have a Train-the-Trainer program now, where we're training people to teach these principles so that they can become a Success Principle Trainer. We've actually certified 500 people from 40 countries. Our goal is to train a million people by the year 2030, so if you're interested in becoming a Success Principles trainer, you can do that as well at Jackcanfield.com.

Brian: That's great. We've got a minute and a half left. Is there anything else that you'd like to share that you haven't had the chance to talk about yet?

Jack: Let's talk about feedback for a moment. Here's a question that everyone can you use to improve your life. Ask your wife, your children, your staff, your boss, every week—ask on a scale of 1-10, "How would you rate the quality of…." It could be our relationship, me as an employee, a product, my service, ask whatever it might be. And everything less than a 10 gets a follow-up question that says "What would it take to make it a 10?" This is where the valuable information is. Most people never ask that because they are afraid of what they are going to hear. But I promise you, you're the only one who doesn't know. I ask my wife that every Friday. If I didn't, the hairdresser would know, her mother would know, her sister would know, but I wouldn't know how to improve the relationship. So whatever it is, feedback is the breakfast of champions. Ask for feedback, then you're going to be able to improve everything in your life, and your life will get very magical. Feedback is so important, and most people have never been taught how to do it.

Brian. Wow! That's great stuff. Once again the book is *The Success Principles: How To Get From Where You Are To Where You Want To Be*. The 10th anniversary edition is out right now, and Jack Canfield thank you so much for being a very special guest on Success Profiles Radio this week. It is has been an honor and a privilege to have you here, my friend.

Jack: Thank you for having me Brian. We'll come back and answer some of those other questions that are asked in the future.

Brian: Alright that's great! We are coming toward the end of our show. And Jack Canfield is phenomenal.

We will come back next Monday at 6PM Eastern. This has been Success Profiles Radio where we talk to amazing experts who have experienced world-class success. We talk to them about how they did it, how they achieved it, what they overcame, and how we can apply those lessons to our lives. Thanks for joining us, goodbye!

EVERYTHING I KNOW ABOUT SUCCESS, I LEARNED FROM NAPOLEON HILL

Brian: Welcome. This is Success Profiles Radio. I am your host Brian K Wright and it is a pleasure to be with you here today. I'm honored that you chose to spend part of your day with me here, and this is going to be a really amazing show.

My guest this week is Don Green. Let me tell you a little bit about him.

Don Green is currently the executive director of the Napoleon Hill Foundation. Graduating with a BA in Accounting and Business at the East Tennessee State University. Don went on to study advanced phases of banking at the Stonier Graduate School of Banking at Rutgers. With banking as his natural flair, Don elevated himself from the bottom rung of the banking industry to become bank president and CEO, a position he served for nearly 20 years.

His meteoric rise in his career was matched by his diverse contributions to community and the commercial fraternity. His public offices spanned a spectrum that included educational institutions, hospital, charitable causes, community service organizations, and arbitration boards. He was the president of his county's Chamber of Commerce and president of the Foundation Board of the University of Virginia's College at Wise, a position in which he still proudly serves. Don is also a board member of the UVA/Wise Board of Trustees.

His memberships include the Hoge Masonic Lodge, the Kiwanis Club, and the Shriners movement. Don also collected the Outstanding Citizen of the Year Award in 1996, the Sam Walton Business Leader Award in 1998, the William P. Canto Memorial Education Award in 1999, and the Volunteer of the Year Award for the University of Virginia System in 2000. Don organized and was successful in getting a three-hour credit course, Keys to Success, included in the UVA/Wise curriculum based on the success principles of Napoleon Hill. Don taught the course for several years, and it is still a very popular course with students today.

We will discuss all of this and so much more on today's show. And with all this in mind, here is my guest, Don Green. Don, are you there?

Don: Yes, I am, Brian. Thank you for having me.

Brian: Oh, thank you and welcome to Success Profiles Radio. I really appreciate having you here. So the first question that I always ask everybody, Don, is to tell us how you got started, what's your background, what did you learn along the way, what did you overcome, and how did you get to where you are today.

Don: Well, I guess, it goes back a long time because I've been around a while. My parents grew up during Depression. My dad was an underground coal miner with a 7th grade education. I lived in a home without running water and without a bathroom until I was in high school. Nobody went to college. They just went to get some education and went to work. But somewhere along the line, I saw a little bit of difference. So I learned to make money at an early age. Having this beginning was a necessity. My mother would tell us when we asked for money, she would say, "Your poor daddy has to crawl around those mines. We don't know when he'll get hurt or when he'll get killed because it's a dangerous profession." So she said, "You've got to take care of our money." So it was much easier to learn to mow yards and pick up pop bottles. I picked up a ton of pop bottles before I went to school. I got a penny a piece. And to make 25 cents, it was a big deal. And it was just a knack. I just kept looking for things I could make money at. And I had a zoo when I was in high school, and made lots and lots and lots of money. I was able, when I was still in high school, to help my older brother buy his first house. He had left home, and was out working. And of course in the beginning, it was all about the money. When you don't have any, it's like you don't have options and you know what you want. And it just seemed to be natural that I could see things that I can generate money from and it just stuck with me and grew. And so, to go into banking was a no-brainer because it's where all the money was.

Brian: Yeah, exactly. You said something earlier just a little bit ago, that really stuck out to me. You said you had a zoo. We all heard you correctly, so tell us a little bit about that, because I've read your book and we'll talk about your book today, of course. But share a little bit about that because I find that really fascinating that you had a zoo.

Don: Well, when it started, we called it a snake pit. My dad and some other men had a hobby of catching poisonous snakes. Of course, they didn't do anything with them you know. They might keep them in a cage or in a box for a while, and show them to others. But they either killed them or they starved to death because poisonous snakes don't normally eat in captivity.

And we had an old building on the edge of our land, there was nothing left but some blocks. So we caught some of the snakes, dumped them over in there and made homemade signs that says "25 cents, see the snakes." And we charged kids 10 cents. I knew a guy that drove what I called it a pop truck, a Royal Crown Cola truck, and they made advertising signs. They had big old signs that say Royal Crown Cola. Down at the bottom, they had a little strip you can put your name of your business on it, Joel's Barber shop or whatever you wanted. I had painted it Indian Mountain Reptile Garden and I nailed them to the trees on each side in the woods. There was a highway that came up to our place of business, and it just took off. People would stop to see them. On a weekend day I was making about $100, which was lots and lots of money. So I started having some other animals. I got skunks and bobcats and monkeys. As I got cash accumulated, I bought other animals and then I started selling souvenirs. I found out you could buy stuff for a quarter, then sell it for a dollar if you put a little sticker on it that said Indian Mountain Reptiles Garden, which made it a souvenir.

Of course, we got a drink machine and sold drinks, and it was just a summer business. But I had it all the way through high school. Then they changed the highway, and that's when I went off to college. But it was a terrific business because then you didn't need a license, and didn't know what income tax was and what sales tax was. You just made money and stuffed it in your pocket.

Brian: Wow. That is a phenomenal story and you do talk about this in your book. In fact, I would like to begin talking about your book because there is so much in this. We could easily spend far more than an hour. But we have an hour, so let me just ask you, Don, your book is called *Everything I Know About Success I Learned From Napoleon Hill*. And now, of course, you are the Executive Director of the Napoleon Hill Foundation. So tell us what the book really is about and why you decided to write it.

Don: Well, of course, we're non-profit and I've done lots of Napoleon Hill books. I'm looking at one across here on a shelf, Napoleon Hill's *Golden Rules*. I put it together and it sold widely about four years ago, got a good advance and it's in 37 different languages. So it wasn't my first venture, but it's my first one that I actually put my name on the book, and it's all my writings. I travel a lot. I've been in Malaysia three times, China three times Singapore and Hong Kong three times, Germany a couple of times. I've been in lots of places, and I was asked even here locally when I would speak to the Chamber of Commerce or to the Historical Society, people kept telling me that I ought to put that in a book. And so I told them, "Well, in the winter time I don't travel as much, I can do that. That'll be a chance to raise some money."

And by the way, all the money—when I say all the money, I don't mean most of the money—every penny of it will go to the Foundation for scholarships. We endow scholarships at the university, and we do a lot of prison work. This is to endow more scholarships here at the university.

So I just talked about some principles and talked about stories on how I applied it, hopefully to get the thing across is if I can do it, a whole lot of people that's smarter than me can do it. Because we know there are some principles that separate people from being successful and others not.

Brian: Right, exactly. And in fact, that is a perfect segue into my next question because there are a lot of things that will determine whether or not someone does succeed. What do you think is really the main reason why some people just don't end up succeeding?

Don: They are drifters that basically don't know what they want. They never have a defining moment or purpose—something to have a burning desire to be successful. Just have something in your mind you want to do so bad that you go to sleep with it, and you wake up with it. You eat with it. And you said something which was absolutely essential. You said choices—we have a little book called *Your Greatest Power*. I put it together and printed it with the rest. It sold more than a million copies. And our greatest power is the choices we make. You either got up this morning and decided you want to work, or you wanted to sit on the sofa and drink beer all day and watch reruns of an NFL game from last season. And those choices we make, they become a habit and the habits make us, either good or bad, it doesn't matter. But the choices we make define what we end up being. I say that we make our choices, our choices make our habits, then our habits make us, good or bad.

And it's absolutely essential. We talked about how planning. You know, most people don't have a plan. It's better to have a bad plan than to have no plan. But you have to take action.

Brian: Exactly. There you go, and I love what you just said. We are talking with Don Green, the Executive Director of the Napoleon Hill Foundation, and we are talking about his book, *Everything I Know About Success I Learned from Napoleon Hill*. Don, I want to ask you something because Napoleon Hill was really fond of saying that "Thoughts are things." So tell us about the relationship between the thoughts we have and the results that manifest themselves in our lives.

Don: Well, "Thoughts are things," and everything originates in our mind, both good and bad. It's the thoughts that we follow-up with, and that we develop a plan for, and put into action that defines who we'll be now and in our future. Most of the people who follow Hill don't talk about it a lot, but he was a great follower of psychology, the study of the mind and so forth. I can go on and on and tell you the people he read and he studied had an influence on him, and it's what separates us from the other animals. That's where creativity comes from is our thought process, that we can take things and create, not necessarily a new thing, but we can improve things. For example, the car, make it into one that runs—as Elon Musk is doing—make it run on a battery, run on a different fuel. Just take a product and make it—or sometimes, create--something brand new that never existed such as computers, or how Martin Cooper made the cell phone.

So that's where the mind comes in. Some guys that were thinking, "If we could just carry that phone around with us." And I never will forget Mark Warner who is a US Senator. I took him around, introduced him when he ran for Governor and Senator, and we became friends. And he showed up at a book signing I did at the one of the local colleges. He talked about how he got a phone franchise for the State of Virginia for car phones. He started out with $10,000 borrowed money and end up with $175 million.

Brian: Wow.

Don: But he went to his uncle to borrow the money. And I'll use his exact words. He said, "Mark, people don't want to drive around in their damn car talking on a damn telephone." He said, "The idea is foolish and I'm not going to let you have the money." So Mark ended up going to the bank and getting a friend to co-sign his notes so he can get $10,000 to get the franchise for cell phones for Northern Virginia, which was the hub of the state. But that's what it grew into because he saw that. He saw that thing through his mind. His thought process told him that, "Hey, people would like to have access to a phone when they're out traveling." And how long did it take the phone booths to disappear? If you see one today, it's an antique.

Brian: Right.

Don: Because somebody thought if we can do this thing better than what we are doing, make it cheaper, make it more convenient and so forth—that's why our thought process is so important. Some people will look at something and can see something better. That's what makes us look forward to the next day, that there's always something out there to challenge us, to make the situation better.

Brian: Yeah. That is a really, really great story. The most successful people have a vision for how to change the world, and we can go on and on and on. Even Gene Roddenberry, when he created Star Trek, had this whole vision of what the future might look like three or four centuries down the road. And I think some of that is definitely going to come to pass. You mentioned the cell phone, that's a really wonderful story. So, I'm sure that he probably didn't succeed the very first time that he tried. Just like Thomas Edison didn't succeed the very first time he tried to create the light bulb.

So it seems pretty clear, Don, that failing your way to success is a really important part of this whole equation. Sometimes people don't enjoy the whole idea of failing, but sometimes we just really don't know how close we are to our big breakthrough. We sometimes tend to give up too soon.

Don: Oh, that's true. You've heard the saying all your life, "It's always darkest right before the dawn."I read Steve Jobs' biography, and his was probably 1000 or so that I've read. If you've seen the movie, you'll get this out of it. He said, "Of all the qualities he had in his life, the one he considered most important was perseverance, which is what our book *Think And Grow Rich: Stickability* is about. If you have a good idea, you stick with it because you don't know how close you are. Hill used to say in some of his talks, he'd ask the audience, "How many times do you think, on the average—the average person tries something before they quit?" And they would holler, one, two, three. He said, "No, I asked you for the average." He said, "The average is less than one because a lot of people never start. They may have a thought or an idea, but they don't do anything with it." So when you factor them in there, almost nobody sticks with anything.

And I think that's what separates us that have an idea. And if we can't do it, he says, the main thing is to have a plan. It doesn't have to be a good plan. It may not work, but it gets you started and you see where the plan is wrong or it needs to be changed.

Brian: Yeah. Yeah.

Don: Or you need a mentor or you need to get help, or you need to get more information. But just because it didn't come out real easy doesn't mean that you quit and say, "Well, you know, I shouldn't have tried that. I should've known better." No. The people that stick with something when they have a good idea and follow it through, they're the ones who are successful.

Brian: That's awesome. I really like that because perseverance is so critical. And I think it's a lot easier to persevere and not give up when you know exactly where you're going. In your book and in *Think and Grow Rich*, of course, there's a huge discussion about having a major, definite purpose. It seems that everyone who excels in anything knows exactly where they are going. Can you tell us a little bit about what that really means to have a major, definite purpose in life?

Don: Well, there's a quote that says it best, "It doesn't matter which road you take if you don't know which way you're going." So many people don't—Hill called them drifters. They just get up in the morning and accept whatever is in front of them without trying to make any changes on it.

Our good friend Zig Ziglar, who I did some fundraising with before—he was just a great, great guy. I was with him a few times and he said, "You just keep doing same thing over and over again but keep hoping for a different result." He said, "That's the definition of insanity."

Brian: Right, exactly.

Don: And so many people live the same life Monday through Friday and start back over on Monday hating their job. Then on Friday, they look forward to the weekend rather than looking forward to Monday. You should look forward to every day. And it's not originally from me but I've heard it said plenty of times, "If you're going to be successful, every day that you go and do something out there, if you're enjoying what you're doing, it's not work."

I absolutely loved every job I've ever done. Don't get me wrong, there were some bad days in banking business—bank examiners, lawsuits, and other things that you have to deal with. But I still loved everything and I saw it as an opportunity, because when something confronts you, that's a problem to someone. It's also an opportunity to someone that takes advantage of it. So when the thing is solved, you're a better person than you were. You can't quit every time something gets in front of you, you know.

You can look at it as a challenge, or you can look at it as a reason to quit and try something else and tell yourself, "I should've never tried it,".

But I was told one time, a long time ago, "If you do a little bit extra one day, it probably won't matter. You do the same thing for a week, it might not matter. But if you do those things over a lifetime, you can be the success that most of the world is only going to dream about."

Brian: Wow. So really, it's what Darren Hardy calls the Compound Effect. You do something a little extra every single day for a long period of time, you are eventually going to experience phenomenal results that maybe you hadn't even thought could possibly happen. I love that.

We've been talking to Don Green about his book, which is called *Everything I Know About Success I Learned from Napoleon Hill.* We talked about how thoughts are things and there's definitely a relationship between the thoughts that we have and the results that we see in our lives. We also talked about how important it is to be sold on yourself, or else no one else will be. Perseverance is a huge quality. The people who succeed do not quit, and they know exactly where they're going.

So Don, what I'd like to ask you next is, times have been tough these last few years and a lot of us have felt beaten up by the world. And so, I'd like to ask, what do you recommend that we do personally to turn things around?

Mindset seems to be a really great place to start. Does that sound like a fair statement?

Don: Yeah. There's a poem we published in a book once by a 14th-century Monk. He said he wanted to change the world, he couldn't. He wanted to change his country and he couldn't. He wanted to change his community, he couldn't. He wanted to change his family, he couldn't. But he said, he discovered if he changed himself, he can in turn have influence—positive influence on his family, who could then in turn have positive influence on his community, then the nation, and then the world. So it starts with us individually from the inside.

If you get 20 people in a room and you tell them I can give you a copy of *Think and Grow Rich*, a few of them probably wouldn't even pick it up. Maybe 3-4% of them would read it and make underlines, and make notes, and not just read the book. You read novels, you find out the girl got the boy or the boy got the girl, or the uncle died and left money, or if he became a medical doctor, or became a missionary, you want to read what the ending is. And these books, if we take notes and we learn what's in them, we can plan our own life. We can write our own life story. We don't have to read somebody's happy ending and somebody's book. We can make our own happy ending by planning our life. You know what? I always thought it's odd, and I know you've seen it before—that people go on vacation, they know more and get back. And they start saying, "Where are we going next year?" "Well, let's go to the beach." "No, we went to beach last year. Why don't we go up to the mountains? We can rent one of the log cabins." So they start discussing it. But they don't sit down and plan their life. Most plan vacations, but they don't plan their life and so things don't just happen. It takes thoughts, it takes planning, it takes action, it takes perseverance.

Brian: It sure does.

Don: But we've all got to start with ourselves.

Brian: Absolutely. That's really great. You know, you were talking about reading and giving yourself some positive input. Well, you can get positive input from other people, too. I'd like to ask you because mentoring and masterminding is such a huge theme in Napoleon Hill's work. Of course, you addressed this in your book as well. How do you think masterminding has been influential and impactful on your life personally, Don?

Don: Well, I was just fortunate to be around people and know what the principle was—and especially when I was in banking—to get involved with people. For example, I developed businesses in cable TV, dry cleaning, spring water, land development for people for Walmart and so forth. And one of the guys, in particular, had been a builder and he does construction in a lot of homes and businesses—and ran businesses. And I don't have a knack for building. But to sit down, or even during a coffee, the three of us would talk about things. And I can remember telling them, I said, "You know, I've been reading all this about water. It seems like people are willing to pay for water, which some people thought was crazy." And I had a guy tell me, "You think people are going to buy bottled water?" I said, "Yeah. I think they will go and buy bottled water. I really do." I said it's starting in places, I think people will buy water.

And so I found out there were 90-some acres of land down in the lower part of the state, close to the Kentucky line in the mountains, and it had spring water coming right out of the rocks. So I ordered a manual about spring water and got all the information. I kept reading and reading and reading and reading. There was an old couple who had the land. They had no children, so we bought it from them and we started developing it. We never actually bottled the water. We were approached by someone else that made us a tremendous offer just to use the water. And we did that and we took a large payment and a lease over a long period of time for them to use the water, and we didn't have to build a bottling plant. So it turned out really well because we were way ahead of what most people out there are doing. But now you know everybody in the world is bottling and selling water from Pepsi to Coca-Cola.

Brian: It sounds like the implementation of an idea was really impactful for you and that worked out really, really well. So let me ask you about establishing meaningful goals and how would you define a meaningful goal? How do you effectively set one, because there's a lot of talk out there about setting goals and taking action, but how do you make it meaningful?

Don: Well, to me for many, many years, I took a legal pad or long sheet of paper, and I do it in the month of December. And I just put it in my mind and think about what I would like to accomplish and compose a long list of things I'd like to do next year, and then five years and years after. And then I would study them and then say, "No, that's not really important." Add some to it and so forth. Then I will condense some down to 3-by-5 index cards, and I would write those goals down. There would be some large ones, but I'd usually write down 10 or so.

I wore a suit for 38 years, I would put it inside of my suit, and if I was talking on the phone with you, as I'm listening, I would get that thing out every day, sometimes, several times a day. I would look at it, it may be June or August or some time, and I'm thinking, "Gosh, there's still three of them I have not done enough on—I'm not anywhere near where I want to be." I always need to refresh myself and know that I've got to do something to move it forward.

Some of it didn't get done during that year, and so they're carried over. One of them was putting up a historical marker for Napoleon Hill many years ago. I wrote the Historical Society and they said, "We don't normally do that." They have to be dead 50 years. So I started writing to politicians, and then my friends who were in politics. One of them put me in touch with the people involved in the Historical Society for the State of Virginia and gave me a list of them. The third one I called said, "You want to put up a historical marker of Napoleon Hill?" And I said, "Yeah." He said, "That's all I need to know." He said, "Man, I read that guy's books, and it meant the world to me." He said, "You tell me what you want to do and I'll see that it gets done." So, you know, I didn't get it done in a year. It was on the second year of when I want to get it done, but that doesn't mean I failed. It simply meant it took longer than what I thought it would.

Brian: Yeah.

Don: So, you just have things in front of you. Another thing was, I wanted to get a course started at the University of Virginia. People asked me, "Do you know how difficult it would be to convince a board at the University to start off with a new course? And you've never taught." I said, "I've taught. I taught accounting." I was told, "Yeah, but it's not the same thing." I said, "Well, I'll talk to somebody that will listen to me. I'd like to talk to them." I put the lessons together, I put some syllabus together, and I met with the guys in the Business Department and I said, "Here's what I want to do." They talked about it, and got back to me. "Yeah, we'll offer the course." And I said, "Who are you going to get to teach it?" And they said, "You. You're the one who knows this material. Who else will we ask?"

Brian: Right.

Don: I hadn't figured on that, but that was part of the conditions for having the course. "Well, it has to be a night class because I got a full-time job in the bank." But I ended up teaching it 12 times until I got somebody else qualified to teach it. So it's been taught 20-25 years.

It's a very popular class. But it was something I had a passion about because I thought I could influence some other young people. No one ever influenced everybody, but for those I did, I think they're much better off. And I still hear from a lot of them today that took the class, even those who took my first class. The stories in my first class were unbelievable. One guy sold his business for $45 million. They weren't all about money. One of the guys—I just got a text from him this morning—he's in Africa doing some work for the government. Another lady I saw at a funeral, and some time back she got a hold of me while I was in waiting in line at the reception. She said, "I've got to talk to you."

And she said, "Do you remember I was in your first class?" I said, "Yeah." She talked about her paper that she wrote, and mentioned that her goal was to be an attorney. I wrote down at the bottom of it, "Don't tell me. Go do it." Now she's a legal representative as an attorney for one of the major companies in the southeastern United States. Last time I saw her, she's driving a $150,000 Mercedes. It's not just all about the material things, but she knew what she wanted, and she went and did it.

Brian: So let me ask you about the importance of habits, because all great champions have winning habits. How do you establish and maintain winning habits, Don?

Don: Well, I think Brian, the first thing you got to do is you got to have something that you care about. I've got a passion for living. You know, I'll be 73 years old on my birthday—and as quick as you and I get done, I'm going to go home and I'm going to put on some shorts and some tennis shoes, and I'm going to go out and walk in the neighborhood until I walk four miles. If I come in at 9'o-clock or at whatever time I want to come in, I do it. And if it's too cold outside or there's snow is on the ground, I go to the treadmill. And so, for me, it's how bad do you want it? And we've established those habits.

At first, it might be like eating right. I don't eat junk. I don't eat sweets. But once you do it for a period of time, it just becomes natural.

Brian: Yeah.

Don: How did you learn your ABCs? Repeat them over and over. You learned your multiplication tables over and over. Someone asked me, "Why do you read more and more success books?" I said, "Well, maybe you're smarter than I am. I won't even tell you how many times I've read Hill's books because I learned my ABCs and I learned my multiplication tables by repeating things like they become part of my subconscious." And if somebody says, "Brian, what's nine times nine?" You don't have to sit there for ten minutes before you come up with 81. Even though you've not been asked years, it's in your subconscious. And that's the reason, and that's how we learn by repeating things.

Brian: And Don, while I'm thinking about it, tell us where we can get this book? I'll ask you again before the show's over, but let's just bring that out right now. How can we find your book?

Don: Well, the first place it went up was on Amazon. It's also on Kindle and Nook, and it's in Barnes and Nobles. It's also in in Books-A-Million—I did some books signing at Books-A-Million. And it would be on audio, I'm told, in a few weeks. It'll be out as an audio book also.

Brian: That's great.

Don: It's in nine foreign languages, and it'll end up being, I would think, at least 30 or 40 within the next year or two.

Brian: That's great.

Don: I appreciate your support. And if anybody gets in touch with me, I'll autograph one and send one to them—I've done thousands of them out of the office. I mean, I've had people buy 200. I've had two different ones buy 50, and I even had one come up and he had 20 copies with him from Florida which is an eight hour drive just for me to sign. I do whatever it takes, because I have a passion of what I'm doing.

Brian: Let me ask you something else, one of your chapters toward the end of your book is about leaving a legacy, everyone wants to be remembered after their life is over. How do we go about doing this in a meaningful way?

Don: Well, I think life is we learn, we earn, and then we share. I'm going through a book on personal finance, and I'll share a little bit with you. Eisenhower once said, "If all you want from life is food, clothing, and shelter, they give all three of those to you in prison." To me, life's a little more about that and we don't get a legacy until we are able to give back, we should be doing it all the time.

But what we need to be successful, one is to provide those three basic things. And the second one is, provide for the future—I call it a rainy day. Brian and Don may not be able to work into their 90's and they need something. And the third one is to lead a good life. If you come home one day and your spouse says to you, "Hey, let's go eat out at that new restaurant", and you have to look at her and say, "Are you kidding? I've not been paid yet."

So if you want to travel and live a good life, that's a reason to be successful. But the fourth one is, which is one where you create your legacy is you're in a position to get back. Now it's your own choosing. Some might choose to help their college, some may help their grandkids, some might be the community, some might be a non-profit like St. Jude, but in the end, your legacy is created not by what you got out of life what you gave back.

They're not going to care how many cars I've got, or how many houses, or how much money I've got in the bank. But somebody's going to look and say, "Can you imagine how many scholarships that guy provided, how many books he give to kids or how many kids he mentored?" In fact, one time I went to a supermarket to pick up some fruit and a guy said to me, "Mr. Green, can I tell you something?" And I said, "Yeah!"

He said, "You know, do you remember financing my house?", and I said, "Yes, I do!"

He said, "You know, I was scared to death and I told my wife we were just wasting our time, they're not going to loan us money to buy that house. We don't have enough money down."

I said "You paid the loan back, that's all I asked for. I just thought you had a decent job and you were the type of person who would appreciate it. I had faith in you, and you didn't let me down."

It will be for what we did for others not what we've done for ourselves.

Brian: Exactly. I love that. Giving back is so important. That theme has come up a lot in this show but I love how you specifically share, first you learn, then you earn, and then you share by giving back. That is really great. Let me ask you about a project that you were heavily involved in, and Greg Reid is going to be back on our show again in a couple of weeks. He wrote a new book called, *Think and Grow Rich: Stickability*, and I know that you were a huge part of the project, talk about that.

Don: Well, I've talked to Greg, I'm going out there to the book launch, and here's what I talk about. I'll give you a clue, the thing is—people ask me, "Why another book?". Well, let me tell you why. When Hill wrote *Think and Grow Rich* in 1937, he wrote about people that he knew. Today, we tell the same principles—we're not changing principles—we're telling stories of people today that people can relate to. One of my business partners taught Sunday school in a Methodist Church, and he said one of the boys came in wearing baseball caps in church, and of course we weren't taught that growing up. So he wanted to give him a little lesson saying, "Now, boys, when you go into a building, you should remove your hat. It's just good manners," and he said, "I've been around Bear Bryant, and Bear Bryant wore a wool herringbone hat, but he would always remove that hat when he went in a building." And one of the kids said, "Who's Bear Bryant?"

You see, we older guys grew up and knew he was the winningest college football coach in history at the University of Alabama. So today, if we were going to tell stories using sports figures, we would use somebody current, so that's what we're doing with Stickability. We're just using new examples of people that applied stickability and became successful—old principles put in a new way.

Brian: Yes, so as we are coming toward the end of the show, once again, how can we get your book, Don?

Don: Well, it's on Amazon. I love Amazon. I talked to them right before we came on. For example, you get the book in two or three days. But if they drive here, I'll sign them. If they get a hold of me, they can buy or 10 or 50, and I'll sign them and send them out. Or they can go to Books-A-Million or they can go into Barnes and Noble.

Brian: We are at the end of the show. I do thank you so much for coming on. I really, really appreciate it. We will be back next Monday at 6:00 PM Eastern. It was a pleasure having you here. Thank you so much for joining us.

GREG REID

THINK AND GROW RICH: STICKABILITY

Brian: Hello and welcome to Success Profiles Radio. I am your host Brian K Wright and it is an absolute pleasure to be with you here today. I'm honored that you chose to spend part of your day with me here, and this is going to be an amazing show.

My guest this week is Greg Reid, who is here for the second time. Let me tell you a little bit about him.

He is a filmmaker and a motivational speaker, and he's a number one best-selling author, entrepreneur, and the CEO of several successful corporations, and he's dedicated his life to helping others achieve the ultimate fulfillment of finding and living a life of purpose. He has published over 42 books in 19 languages, with over a dozen number one best-sellers. I'm sure that number is probably higher now.

He's also a highly sought-after motivational keynote speaker for corporations, universities, and charitable organizations. He's also an award winning filmmaker. He is the creator and producer of internationally acclaimed films *Pass It On*, and *Three Feet from Gold*. I have seen both of those films and they are absolutely terrific. You've got to see them.

In addition, in the coveted *Road to Riches* program, Greg has been gifted the opportunity to follow in Napoleon Hill's famous footsteps by sitting down with leaders of the day to discover how they persevered through challenging times. And his newest project is a book and movie called *Think and Grow Rich: Stickability*. The book will be available on October 10th, and the movie premiere will be a 2 day event in San Diego on October 21st and 22nd. I couldn't be more excited.

We'll discuss all of this and so much more during today's show. And with all of this in mind, here is my guest, Greg Reid. Greg, are you there?

Greg: Of course! I've been looking forward to this. Thanks for having me on again. Thank you for making me a repeater.

Brian: Yes, you are, and I've only had a handful of repeaters. I've got a couple more repeaters scheduled in the future, but I only bring back the best of the best, so I'm so thankful that you're back again. So, here's what I usually like to do, and we've been through this before. The first thing I usually ask, Greg, is for you to tell us how you got started. Some people may not have heard the first show that we did together, so tell us where you got started, what you learned along the way, and what brought you to where you are right now?

Greg: Ah, serendipity, like anything else. What happened is I owned an advertising corporation in the mean streets here in beautiful San Diego, California. One day, someone asked me to go speak at a local university, UCSD, because their keynote dropped out last minute and I literally live down the street.

So I went over there. Being a little successful in business, I gave a talk—just made something up—but it went over pretty well. They asked me to come back, and then I started going to all the different campuses all around San Diego County. It became so good that one kid came up to me and said I should write a book based on this talk. I thought to myself, you know, "That's a good goal," because I never really read a book, you know (laughs), never read books from cover to cover. So I sat down and made it a mission, and obviously, it went through and here we are today.

Brian: That's fantastic. Did you envision when you started that this is where your journey would take you?

Greg: Well, you know, it's like anything else in life. At the end of the day, the road is taking you in a different direction that you thought because I thought I would get in this industry like a politician would. You go in and save the spotted owls, then you realize there's politics. Well, when I got into the motivation industry, I realize it's a business. It's not just only about helping people. You've got to make an income and make it a business as well. So I think I've gone down a different road than most people because I realized that there can be a balance and you can have both.

So when I wanted to become a speaker, I hung out with Les Brown, and Brian Tracy, Denis Waitley, and Charlie "Tremendous" Jones, the leaders of my industry. I ask them for guidance and just watch what they did, and then did the same thing with my own twist, my results. And by doing so, here we are today.

Brian: Yeah, exactly. You touched on something very interesting. A lot of people talk, but they don't walk what they're talking. Do you think it's because they're afraid? Or what do you think holds people back?

Greg: Well, I think that's even in our space, you know. I'll be the one guy to be a realist. I mean, a lot of people even in our arena, they talk a mean game, but they don't live the example that they're out there preaching out on stage and then their public life. And I realized, wouldn't it be cool to go out and start speaking from the heart of who you are as a person.

So we did *Three Feet from Gold*, it's about not quitting. You know why? I'm a quitter. I quit sales, I quit marriage, I quit my business, I quit everything. I'm the biggest quitter in the world. And you know, the greatest leaders study what they need help with the most. So, I sat down with the greatest iconic figures, and picked their brains to find out how they did not quit.

Then, I just started applying the same principles. I've got to tell you, that is the key element of our life, it is the application. People listening in, you need another book, you need another seminar like a hole in the head. What you need really to do is start applying what we know.

Brian: Right.

Greg: Imagine walking by a full length mirror and catching a glimpse of yourself and saying, "Hey, if I was going to mentor and give that person some guidance, what would that sound like?" Give it to yourself and then do it.

Brian: Yeah. And speaking of *Three Feet from Gold*, I've seen your movie for that and also for *Pass It On*, but I think I also told you one day that I went to Barnes & Noble and I bought *Three Feet from Gold*, and I camped out at Subway for three hours, I read it in one sitting. I never read a book in one sitting, and that book impressed me. I was making marks, and it's on my list of things to read again. There's so much in there. If you all have not read *Three Feet from Gold* by Greg Reid and Sharon Lechter, then run, don't walk to your nearest bookstore, or order online, really, really, really highly recommended. So thank you for writing that book, Greg. It's a life-changer for sure.

Greg: Absolutely. So you're the guy who actually bought a copy. God bless you, brother.

Brian: Yes, you're very welcome. Hey, whatever I can do to support you, my friend, I will gladly do that.

Greg: Yeah, in a way it's interesting though, and I know you're going to get to Stickability and I appreciate it.

Brian: Yes.

Greg: You've read about *Three Feet from Gold*. And for people listening, it's about not giving up when faced with adversity.

Brian: Yes, yes.

Greg: And then after that project became such a worldwide phenomenon, people kept saying, "But HOW do you not quit?" You know, having the warm, fuzzy, don't-give-up, leading-the-beat-of-your-dreams is cute, but how do you not do it? So I set myself on a mission to meet the most powerful and influential people to find out the actionable steps they took to not quit. And that's what *Think And Grow Rich: Stickability* is all about and why it's going be such a phenomenal New York Times best-seller.

Brian: Yeah, exactly. We will talk about *Stickability*. That's why I have you on the show. But *Three Feet from Gold* impressed me so much because Greg, your mission is to interview the most highly successful people of your generation, and that's really a mission that I've taken up. So, that's why *Three Feet from Gold* really resonates with me. That's why I do my show, and it's why I am so excited that you're in my circle, because I want to continue learning from you. Having a coach and a mentor is so, so critically important. Let me ask you before we get to *Stickability*, because this next question really sort of lays the foundation for everything you've done, how did you get connected with the Napoleon Hill Foundation?

Greg: Well, it all began with a mentor of mine, Charlie "Tremendous" Jones, who opened up an opportunity of happenstance, meeting with the President and CEO of Napoleon Hill Foundation. He and I hit it off and made a bond. Later on, when the Napoleon Hill Foundation was looking to expand the teachings and help modernize it, my name was thrown in the ring by that same person, by Charlie "Tremendous" Jones. By him giving me that nod, by him vouching for me, actually gave me an opportunity of a lifetime. It's most people's dreams, where we go around and meet these amazing people and actually apply their principles for ourselves. And again, even the rocket scientists that we interviewed aren't rocket scientists. They're regular folks.

Brian: That's fantastic. This is Success Profiles Radio. My very special guest is Greg Reid. He is the author of the new book and movie coming out called, *Think and Grow Rich Stickability: The Power of Perseverance*. And so, that's what we're going spend the rest of this show talking about. So Greg, of course, the very first question becomes, "Where did the idea for this whole thing come from?"

Greg: Well, again, we got so much feedback from *Three Feet from Gold*. It became a worldwide phenomenon in, I believe, over 20 some-odd countries in the first year, in many different languages. People kept asking, "What's the next step?" "How do you not quit?" And Don Green, CEO of Napoleon Hill said, "Well, let's do a new project based on one single word, "Stickability." From there, it just says it all. You will understand what the principles are. It's about actually having a dream, moving toward it, and never letting other people, or more importantly, yourself talk you out of that mission. That's what *Stickability* is all about.

Brian: Hmm, that's really fantastic. I would imagine it took quite a while for a project of this scope to really come together then? What kinds of special challenges or obstacles did you have to overcome when this was happening?

Greg: Well, I might be quite frank with you. It flowed pretty well. It's funny, when we did *Three Feet from Gold*, I invited hundreds and hundreds of people to come meet with me, and to go meet all these incredible people, and no one ever showed up. So I made a little bit different quest when we did this one. I created a mastermind group where we all contributed a bunch of money into a pot. And that way, we had the resources to travel, to fly people in, the camera crews, the whole bit. From there, we created a mastermind of sorts that came together and created something very special. And the same people that were participating in the group also had connections and resources to amazing people that opened the doors. I realized Napoleon Hill's principle of cooperation and not competition was truly in effect.

Brian: That's awesome. That's also the value of masterminding and getting with like-minded people because they have some of the same experiences, but sometimes opposite experiences, and certainly a different network of people that you can collaborate with. So I love that idea. Let's talk about some of the very specific ideas that are discussed in this project. You talk about the three causes of failure. What are those?

Greg: Napoleon Hill in a radio interview back in the 1940s was being interviewed and they were talking about success principles. And Napoleon Hill says, "You know, that's all great. But you know what? If you do these three things, you're guaranteed to fail."

And he called it the "Three Causes of Failure." And we list those, actually, in this project, where you're going to hear right form the horse's mouth what he considered. To me, that's the reason you should buy this book, if anything else, this. Because so many people want to talk about the boom shakalaka, "If you do this, you'll have success," "You do this, you'll have success." But you know what? He turned a leaf and says, "You know, that's great, but do these three things and you're guaranteed to fail." And I wanted to know what those three things are so I don't step in that mine hole. I've got to tell you, it's been some of the impactful information I've ever got in my life.

Brian: Hmm, wow. That's great. So do we have to wait for the book to hear what those three things are?

Greg: You do. It's going to be in the book. I mean, that's the whole principle of writing the book. It is so interesting, when Don Green found this vintage audio, we took that and based the entire project on these things So I don't want to let the cat out of the bag, but I will soon, because failure is the most important project of this book.

Brian: Okay, fantastic. Tell us how important it is to be flexible as we move toward our goal.

Greg: Well, flexibility is the key. In fact, the first interview I did was a guy named Marty Cooper, and people listening don't know who Marty Cooper is, I know that. But you know what he created. He invented something called the cellular phone. And you know, it changed our entire world, how we communicate. I asked him, "What does "Stickability" mean to you?" And he said that, "Stickability has to be parallel with flexibility." He says, "If you're not willing to adapt, if you're not willing to adjust, you'll end up being stuck." Then he told the story about the spider monkey. Didn't we tell that one last time we're on the call?

Brian: I don't remember. We might have.

Greg: Well, the spider monkey in the rain forest is the quickest, nimble creature. You can't harpoon it, spear it, catch it. I mean, you can't. They are too quick and agile. One hunter came up with an idea. He said, "I'll take a giant, heavy log and I'll drill a tiny hole inside and leave it at the base of the jungle." He dropped a peanut inside that hole and the monkey would smell it and come down from the treetop, reach his hand inside the little hole, and grab a hold of the nut. As soon as he does that, his fist becomes so big, it can't pull it back out and becomes anchored, stuck to that log. Now, all he's got to do is let go and pull his hand out to live and fight another day, but that monkey thinks that nut is nutrition that's saving him. And the moral he said was, "How many of us are holding on to our own nut in life right now, but it's in the form of a bad job, or relationship, or fear, or guilt, or remorse?"

And he said, "The whole bottom-line is we have to have the courage and fortitude to sometimes let go, so we can pull our hand out and we can adapt and adjust and live to fight another day."

Brian: Hmm. That can be very difficult to do.

Greg: Of course, it can be. The whole thing is to have, again, a mastermind group of people who are positive, like-minded, that will share what we need to hear and not always what we want to hear. And that is the true blueprint, for me, for success. Like you were talking about mentors earlier, and Lane did.

Here's the reality. You can have multiple mentors in your life, but one mentor that works with me and my speaking is great, but he's not going to teach me backhand in tennis, right?

Brian: Right, right.

Greg: And so, the same person who helps with my financial matters, isn't someone I'm going ask for relationship counsel. So it's very important to understand that we can have multiple mentors in our life. It doesn't have to be just one.

Brian: Okay, sounds great. You also talked about the idea of being forward thinking and just having a vision.

Greg: Well, you know, one of my favorite interviews I did was with the gentleman that started a company called Chick-Fil-A restaurants. His name is Truett Cathy.

Brian: Oh, yeah.

Greg: And he says, the secret for his achievement is to stop planning too much. And I said, "What do you mean?" He said that so many people plan every step and they wonder why they never get anywhere. He has a crystal-clear picture of a goal, and he starts moving towards that goal, and he looks for something called unexpected opportunity. I said, "What do you mean?" He said, "Well, the planners are going to plan where they going to pause, take a break. I'm going look for a skateboard or a bicycle that a kid left out, and make my journey shorter to the end of the street." He said, "If I get lucky, I'll wave down a neighbor and hitch a ride to the end of the street. Either way, I'll get there, I have "Stickability". I'm going to get my goal. I'm just not so caught up in exactly how it's going to happen."

Brian: There you go. It's very important not to be so married to the way that it happens, as long as you're moving in the right direction. Does that sound right?

Greg: That's exactly what it is. It's so funny, like right now. I'm working on a major, major, major motion picture. And I have no idea what I'm doing. So what I do is I start moving towards that goal, and as soon as I do that, all of a sudden, the people that I need to assist come out of the woodwork and start helping me. There's a reticular activator system, RAS, where other people call it law of attraction. And for myself, I realized that everything we need within our sphere is always out there. We have to tune in to it. Like right now, there's country music, and rap music, and more on the airwaves. If we have a receiver and we dial it in to what we're looking for, we can download and listen to it. Well, that's the same thing as the universe. Right now, all of the knowledge, and wisdom, and stuff that's out there—what we have to do is start tuning in to what we need. As soon as we start looking for it and start dialing in for the stations that can help it, all of a sudden, that's what appears. That's where the saying comes from, when a student's ready, a teacher appears.

Brian: Yeah, that's exactly right. And I love that quote. That's a great Chinese proverb, because you don't always know what you're going to encounter. And I think, and I say this all the time, sometimes you want the Red Sea to part before you BEFORE you're willing to put your foot down like Moses did. But, no, Moses had to put his foot in the water before the Red Sea parted. And that's the difficult part, that's where the faith comes from, and that's where taking action really has to be at the forefront of your agenda.

Greg: Exactly. The whole thing is it's about having a picture, having a goal, and then getting off your backside and start moving towards it.

Brian: Exactly. So let's talk about the principle of relaxed intensity in action. What does that mean?

Greg: Well, that's a different one. You know, it's interesting. One of the great interviews from *Stickability* is with a guy named Pem Sherpa. Now, Pem Sherpa fell in love with a woman. See, he was Buddhist and his girlfriend was Hindu and they were forbidden to see each other, it was against the rules. And what happened is, they were in a family who's going to marry out the daughter and Pem couldn't handle that. He didn't know what he was going do. And he pulls this woman to the side and he looks up to the mountain in between both cities and said, "Do we agree that that mountain is our one god, that we all agree to be true?" And she said yes, and he took her by the hand and literally pulls her to the top of Mount Everest. They're the only couple in history to actually exchange their vows and get married on top of there. And the whole concept is he had to maintain this feeling of relaxed intensity, because in all the challenges, all the turmoil that goes with that, between the family and climbing a mountain of such, with somebody who's not even experienced, the bottom-line is he had to be cool under pressure so that he can ultimately reach the achievement that he had for himself and his wife.

Brian: That's great. That's very Hemingway of you. Cool under pressure, I love that. So let me just ask about one more thing. You talk about defining and conquering your cul-de-sac moments. What exactly does that mean? I've never heard that expression before.

Greg: Well, the story came from a good friend of mine, Gary Goldstein. And Gary Goldstein is famous for producing movies like *Pretty Woman, Under Seige, The Mothman Prophecies*, and many, many others. So I asked him, "Was it easy in your industry getting your movies made?" And he says, "Oh, my gosh," he says, "You know, most movies die a thousand deaths before they ever get done." And he said, "Imagine pitching a romantic love story about a prostitute to Disney. It's nothing but rejection."

Brian: Yes.

Greg: And he says his favorite story was *The Mothman Prophecies* because it reminded him of his father, based on a true story. He got a meeting with one of the biggest movie houses in the nation and sat down with these people but they just didn't understand it. And they said, you know, "It's going to be a pass." And Gary says, "Respectfully, I'd like to pass on your pass." They said, "What do you mean?" Then Gary went knees to knees and said, "Look, I've got to explain this to you," and started sharing the idea of this movie from his own perspective, from a humanistic standpoint.

And by doing so, they turn a leaf. As we know, the movie got made and went on to do millions, and millions, and millions, and millions, and millions of dollars.

And he says, at times in our lives, we have something called the cul-de-sac moment. A cul-de-sac moment is basically where you go in and realize there's no way out. Once you're in, you're in, there's not a through street. Most people don't have the courage to go in, they just pass through when the going gets tough. And he says, "For me, I decided to go into that cul-de-sac and set up shop and put a tent and do whatever I had to do, because I wasn't leaving until I got the answer I was looking for.

Brian: Wow…that takes a lot of courage. I'm sure glad that he stuck it out because that was a really fantastic movie.

Greg: Yeah, I agree. And I just find it interesting though, that all these stories over and over and over, everyone we talked about, everyone has these stories. I mean, even people listening in here.

Every single person's got a story about how he had an idea, or a hope, or a dream and—well, everything went against you, you stuck to it, and it came through. Most people wouldn't be married right now if the person they asked didn't marry them. The whole thing is all great things comes to those who are willing to pay their dues, put in their time, and roll up their sleeves and say, "You know what? It's my turn. I deserve this."

Brian: Right.

Greg: Sometimes people will tell us all the reasons we will fail, all the reasons why something won't happen, and we buy into that. And more importantly, we can talk ourselves out of our dreams. The secret is, once you know—not believe, or hope, or wish—when you know in your heart you're on to something, that's the time you persevere against all odds.

Brian: Yeah, that's awesome. So let's talk about a new topic. You also discussed overcoming the ghost of fear. Tell us about that.

Greg: Well, overcoming the ghost of fear is a very interesting topic. Napoleon Hill in Think and Grow Rich, which is the 20th best-selling book in the history of the world, wrote his longest chapter on the six ghosts of fear. He said that there are six primary fears that everyone goes through, and until we face them, we cannot truly be free. Then it goes in deep detail of what these are. Then in *Stickability*, we really dissected them and we brought in Sharon Lechter, co-author of the *Rich Dad, Poor Dad* series and 'Three Feet from Gold". She also got an opportunity to do a new project called *Outwitting the Devil*...

Brian: Yeah.

Greg: ...where basically the devil is saying, "This is how I trick society. Here's how I get you to think differently." And we actually examined what the six ghosts of fear are and go into them knees and knees and pull up our sleeves and say, "You know what? I'm no longer going to let this fear stop me. The false evidence is appearing real and I'm going to forward no matter what."

Brian: Yeah, that's fantastic. That's a great book, too, "Outwitting the Devil". Pick that up if you haven't, by Sharon Lechter. Let's talk about a few more ideas. You also talked about the importance of insight through necessity.

Greg: Yeah, well, insight through necessity is like anything else. Necessity is the mother of all invention. For most people, their greatest ideas come from those that they didn't see coming. And one of the interviews I did was with Steve Wozniak.

And you guys probably know him as the co-founder of Apple computers. I asked him, "What was it like getting started in the early days?" He said it was pretty good because we were broke. And I asked "How could that be good?" And he says, "It's all how you look at it, it's your perspective. For us, when microchips, microprocessors came out, I could afford just one." He said, "Where Hewlett Packard would go from Point A to Point B and have 20 different processors in between, I had to find a way to pull five away and get it still to work. Pull away another five and get it work. Until finally, I could go from Point A to Point B using my one processing chip, because that's all I could afford." He says, "If I had more money, I would've done it like everyone else. I would've built computers the size of a skyscraper. But because I could only afford one, maybe create things so slim, so trim, so different than everyone else was doing." That's how Apple Computers was born.

Brian: Wow. That is a really great story. Yeah, Steve Wozniak is a genius, for sure. So let me ask, how do we develop "Stickability" in our own lives?

Greg: Well that's a great question. I think the bottom line is at the end of the day, people have got to find something that they know that they want to pursue, and then never let other people, or themselves, talk them out of that dream. And again, I keep saying that, but so many people hope, or wish, or pray for something good to happen, but it's the people that go in their heart of hearts and say, "Oh, I know I'm on to something." Those are the people who truly persevere. It's easy to quit when the going gets tough. The difference between "Stickability" and non-stickability comes down to this: People with "Stickability" are committed, where other people are just interested. If you're just interested in something, as soon as there are challenges, chances are you're going to leave. If you're committed, you'll do it no matter what.

Brian: Yeah. That is such a huge point right there, Greg, because a lot of people would say, "Yes, I want to do this. I want to do this." But when you hold them to it, then you meet a couple of obstacles and decide, "Well, do I really want it this badly?" You'll learn quickly the difference between being committed versus being interested. And I really like that point a lot. There's something else that you say and then I've heard it said. Most great people attain their greatest success just one step beyond their greatest setback and failure. When you are in that valley, and you've got all the stuff going on around you and you just don't see a way out, how do you know whether to keep going or whether to stop, because sometimes stopping doesn't just mean quitting. Sometimes, it means changing direction, so how do you measure that? How do you know if you're on the brink of something really great?

Greg: Well, again, you seek the counsel of other people's insight. You know, there's a big difference between opinion and counsel.

An opinion is usually based on ignorance, lack of knowledge and experience, where counsel is based on wisdom and knowledge—they've already paved the way. If we can listen to people's counsel rather than opinion, our lives would change that moment. It's the same way as if I went to someone who's never done a talk show and say, "Hey, I'm going do a talk show." They might say, "You can't do that." 'Why not?'

"I don't know. You just can't." Well, that's their opinion because they never did it. If I go to someone like yourself who is already doing it and say, "Brian, I want to do it like you." You're going to say, "Great. Before you get started, here's what you need to know," and give me counsel based on knowledge and experience because you're already doing it.

Brian: We are here with Greg Reid. He is the author and filmmaker of the new project called, *Think and Grow Rich: Stickability*. And we are learning some really amazing things. In fact, the book comes out, I believe, October 10th. The movie premiere is on October 21st and 22nd in San Diego. We will send some time during the final segment discussing all of that. But I do really encourage you to pick this up and anything else that Greg has written. *Three Feet from Gold* is absolutely phenomenal, *Pass It On* is a really, really great film. I've seen that. Just a lot of wisdom there, and Greg is definitely someone that you want to learn from. But I'll tell you what, perseverance is so important. In fact, people who know me, know that when I was in graduate school, I did not pass my comprehensive exams the first time that I went through them. And I realized, it wasn't just that I wanted to give up. I decided that I really was more interested in finishing the degree than I was in what course of study that I graduated in. I ended up changing my major. I end up doing very, very well because I had passion. I found something that I love, something that I was very, very passionate about. And really a lot of times, that's where really true greatness come is you have to know what you want. You have to be absolutely passionate about it because you're not going to be motivated to take the action that you want, unless you absolutely believe in your heart that what you're doing is exactly the right thing you need to do. So let me ask, Greg…

Greg: Before you even ask, I've got to just tell this thing because you hit the nail in the head. You know, one of the interviews I did was with the guy who took NASCAR and turned into what it is today.

And he said something so brilliant. He says, "You know, it's not the degree that hangs on your wall, it's the degree of the passion that's in your heart that matters most." And again, it goes down to that commitment and that desire, that knowing—and that's the difference between those who succeed and come out on top and those who just think about it and wonder what happened.

Brian: Yeah, exactly. What I was going do is just throw out some names, people who were involved in this with you. But maybe just share a story or two about what specifically they contributed. We've already talked about Steve Wozniak and Sharon Lechter. I want to ask you about Frank Shankwitz. He is the founder of the Make-A-Wish Foundation. How did he get involved in this and what did he contribute for you in this project?

Greg: Frank has completely transformed my life. I mean, Frank and I became great friends, allies, associates. In fact, that's the major motion picture. He ended up giving me the rights to do his life story, and we're working on it right now with some of the biggest A-list celebrities in Hollywood and tell them the story of the Make-A-Wish Foundation. So many people want to participate because it's such a great message. I appreciate you bringing that up. That guy truly is a champion. He is so selfless. It's all about making a difference to other people.

Brian: For those listening, this is a project that you definitely want to dive into very, very deeply. The book and the movie are going to be amazing. So tell us the cool story about him.

Greg: Absolutely. And we also talked about Pem Sherpa, the Mount Everest guy getting married and Gary Goldstein.

Brian: We did. Yes.

Greg: You know, we had a three-time gold medalist, Leah O'Brien-Amico in here. We had Peter Diamandis, the founder of the X Prize of how it changed the way that space exploration is done in the future.

We have the founder of Word Press. We have some of the most incredible people participating in this, and I realized a great lesson there. The most successful people are also the most available people. People don't understand that, but it's true. The most successful people are also the most available. And if you're brand-new at something, you're pretty happy-go-lucky, you're fresh, you're cool, and you're new. If you're at pinnacle, happy-go-lucky, you have nothing to prove. It's the people that are in the middle that are a pain in the neck. So I realized for myself, I would just go to the front of the line. I want to go meet the inventors, the visionaries that have changed our planet. And before we talk about Frank, I've got to talk about Ron Klein who will be at the *Stickability* release event October 21st and 22nd, San Diego.

You do not know his name, but he changed everyone's world. He completely changed our society. He invented the credit card magnetic strip. What would your life be without an ATM machine or buying anything over the internet without a credit card? Imagine one guy changed this all and his name is Ron Klein. He'll actually be with us at the event. Talk about a visionary who invented the MLS, multiple listing service for realtors and automated the New York Stock Exchange. This guy is a genius.

And I've got to tell you, he's just one of the most incredible human beings you'll ever have the opportunity to go knees to knees with.

And when you're out there, if you're an inventor, you've got to be here. If you're a movie buff and you want to create your own movie, you've got to be here. If you're an author, or an aspiring author, and you want to be around New York Times best-selling authors, you've got to be here. If you want to start a non-profit, we've got the best people. If you want to be a business tycoon, we're bringing *Undercover Boss*, Dina Dwyers, who owns Mr. Rooter, Glass Doctor—ten different major franchises. You're going to have a chance to meet people that most people only talk about.

Frank Shankwitz, he's a legend. You see, he was a cop for forty years, always serving, always giving back. And one day, this is all again, serendipity, he got an opportunity to meet a young man names Chris who has had terminal leukemia. That relationship, completely inspired Frank and made that little boy's wish, his dream come true. Afterwards, he said, "Man, if we can do it for one child, why can't we do it for all the children?" So he started something as we know as the Make-A-Wish Foundation that has gone over to impact, literally, millions and millions of people across this world. That guy has got to be not only a champion in life, but he's got a place in heaven because he is truly a selfless human being.

Brian: Wow, that is fantastic.

Greg: I know.

Brian: And we talked about Don Green a little bit ago. He was on my show a couple of weeks ago. He's the executive director of the Napoleon Hill Foundation and he certainly added a whole lot to this project, too.

Greg: Well, it's his brainchild. It's his thing. He didn't add to it, it's his idea. You know, Don Green is just a legend. I've got to tell you, he is an incredible human being because, he has history of being in the banking business, understanding how money and how prosperity flows. Then being connected to *Think and Grow Rich*, where he says, "It's not just about thinking and growing rich, it's about acting and growing rich." He has instilled some of the most incredible words of wisdom and insights and helped expand the teachings of the 20th best-selling book in history. Don is just a saint. He's gifted me and Sharon and a few other people a golden opportunity to carry on these teachings in a brand-new way. So I owe him everything.

Brian: That's fantastic. So let's talk more specifically about the actual event and the movie premiere. We mentioned that it's going be October 21st and 22nd?

Greg: Yeah, October 21, October 22, San Diego, California in the most beautiful area called La Jolla. We rented out the Marriott Hotel and we've got only 400 people coming in for this. This is not a giant event. It's a very intimate event, and we keep it that way specifically. There is no website, there is no phone number, there is no way to go. You have to be invited. You've got to sit and say I want to go. That's the only way you can even attend. Here's the thing, we've got a two-day event where you're going to not only listen to these amazing people, you get to hang out, meet with them, mix, and get to know them on a very personal level. On the evening of the 21st, we rented out the movie theater, ArcLight, right across the street, where we're walking across and having a red carpet movie-studded premiere, where we have the world's first showing of the film *Think and Grow Rich: Stickability*. Everything, altogether, is only 199 bucks. That's just to cover the cost of doing this venue.

If you want to go VIP, spend the $695 sit up close and have super turbo access. But I've got to tell you, for $199, you'll never have an opportunity to be with this quality of people in one place at one time ever again in your lifetime.

Brian: Wow. That is absolutely is phenomenal and really very generous, too. I mean, the fact that you're pulled the price down to that is really amazing and just serving people that way. That's really fantastic. I am looking forward to this event and I'm looking forward to meeting all these wonderful people. Some of the people, like yourself, we've still not met in person but we're going to. You've been on my show twice. Don Green has been on my show. And there are some people on that list that I would love to have on my show, and what a wonderful opportunity. Is there anything else that you'd like to tell us about what we can get from this experience moving forward?

Greg: Well, yeah. I can sell it, but I really don't need to. This one sells itself. So many times people say, "What's the one thing I could do differently to change my life today?" And I will tell you this, we are a reflection of the people we hang around the most: our attitude, our income and lifestyles, the average of that group. When you change your association, your life changes accordingly. What I'm doing is putting together the most powerful, positive, like-minded people all in one place at one time. There is no excuse. If you want to change your association, if you want to step up the game, this is the place to do it, and I've done it all for you. I've made it so ridiculous that it just covers the cost, so we can get together. And it's so interesting, because so many people want to do events where you run in the back of the room and you got to buy their stuff. We're not playing that. Nothing is even going to be sold at this event. It's for you, it's for us. And here's another thing, if you're listening to this show, I might not know you, but I know this about you. For years, you've been taking care of your family, your friends, your peers, your co-workers, and enough is enough It's time to draw an imaginary line in the sand and say, "It's my turn. I'm going to find a way to come to this place, I'm going find a way to get through this thing, because you know what? I watch other people that aren't as smart as me, have more success than me. And it's my turn now."

"It's my turn to start taking the first steps to create a life of sustained abundance that other people already out there have. And it's my turn to start having the associations and the opportunities that other people seem to have fall in their lap." You know why? Because they put themselves in the situation to have those opportunities, and that's what this is all about. "It's my turn to start changing my association and start asking the right questions." Look, if someone's listening to this, you've got an idea for the next book, or the next movie, or the next play, or the next inventor, the next non-profit. Guess what? This is your opportunity to step up, step out, put on the big boy shorts, show up, and start participating in life. This is your chance to do something that most people only wish that they can be part of.

Brian: That is fantastic. I am so fired up, Greg. Let's go, let's do this right now.

Greg: Well, the thing is, it's cool and people, listen in. Brian is going be working the red carpet. In fact, he's going be showing up with the camera crew, the whole bit. And as the celebrities are walking down the line, he's actually going be interviewing them face to face, eye to eye, and get to know them. One of my favorite people who is in my next project coming out is also going to be there. His name is Sir Bruno. He just became knighted and he's the CNN Hero of the Year. And I've got to tell you, this guy is an amazing human being. If I started going down the list of the who's who of who's going to attend, it will just blow you away. But the realities are, we've talked it out, we got the cat out of the bag, this is time to step up. This is the time to take action.

Brian: Yeah, there you go. That's great. We've got less than three minutes until the end. And so, I know I asked you this last time, but this is the question I ask everybody at the end of the show. Greg, who inspires and motivates you?

Greg: Right now you do. Man, I'm telling you. I'm watching the way you're doing stuff and being in action, in person, somebody who lives in integrity, somebody who's reaching out, grabbing content, information, and then sharing it with others in a selfless way. I've got to tell you, you're doing what most people only dream about. And I admire and I acknowledge you, and if there's anything I can ever do to add contribution to your life in return for you're doing for mankind, Brian, I just want to you to know that I'm here to serve you back, all right?

Brian: All right. That is a deal. I am so fired up. Thank you so much for that, Greg. That was not what I expected you to say, but I'm so happy and grateful that you did say that. I appreciate that. Less than two minutes until the end. You got one final story, or case study, or words of wisdom that you'd like to share with my wonderful audience?

Greg: Yeah, I'd like to end with one of my favorite interviews. I think I did last time, Evander Holyfield.

I asked him, "How did you win more championships than anyone?" And he says, "I have a higher standard. I showed up early, I left late, I invented exercises. I had a higher standard and I won more championships." He says, "Where could you be outside the ring, if you're a pet groomer, stock broker, or insurance sales executive and have a higher standard?" And I said, "But did that hurt being in a fight?" He says, "Yes, it does. But when you're in a fight, you don't focus on pain, you don't focus on the blows. As soon as you do that, you end up on your back." He says, "That's what people do outside the ring. They focus on the gas prices, war, economy, all the other excuses and they wonder why they never become a champion." And he pulled me in tight and says, "You know what the funny thing is? When you do win the championship, everyone comes to their feet, they chant your name. They raise your hand in victory and a guy puts a big, shiny, belt around your waist. And at that moment, you don't feel even one of the punches you took along the journey."

"But the guy in the losing locker room will feel every bruise for the rest of their life wishing they had a higher standard." This is your chance, this is your opportunity, you listening in right now, to change your standard, to raise your association, to do something special. And again, thanks, Brian. I appreciate you having me on the show and if there's anything I can do, you let me know.

Brian: Thank you, Greg. You are amazing, and awesome, and phenomenal, and thank you so much for being a return guest. And for everybody else, we will be back next Monday at 6:00 PM, Eastern Time. This is Success Profiles Radio. You can link up with me on my Facebook fan page, Success Profiles Radio. You can find me on LinkedIn, you can find me on Twitter @MrBriankwright, and I look forward to reconvening with you all next Monday at 6:00 PM, Eastern, where we will have another phenomenal guest and another amazing show. Take care, everyone. Have a great week. Good bye.

SHARON LECHTER

THINK AND GROW RICH FOR WOMEN

Brian: Hello and welcome to Success Profiles Radio. I'm your host Brian K. Wright and it is a pleasure to be here with you today. I am honored that you chose to spend part of your day with me here, and this is going to be a fantastic show.

My guest this week is Sharon Lechter. Let me tell you a little bit about her.

Sharon Lechter is the founder and CEO of Pay Your Family First, a financial education organization, and YOUTHpreneur, an innovative new way to spark the entrepreneurial spirit in our children.

Sharon was appointed to the first President's Advisory Council on Financial Literacy. The Council served both President Bush and President Obama advising them on the need for financial literacy education.

Sharon is an entrepreneur, author, philanthropist, educator, international speaker, licensed CPA, Chartered Global Management Accountant and, most importantly a mother and grandmother.

In 1997 Sharon co-authored the international bestseller, *Rich Dad Poor Dad*, along with 14 other books in the Rich Dad series. And for over 10 years as CEO she led the Rich Dad Company and brand into an international powerhouse. In 2008 she was asked by the Napoleon Hill Foundation to help re-energize the powerful teachings of Napoleon Hill just as the international economy was faltering. Her bestselling books, *Three Feet from Gold* and *Outwitting the Devil* were both written in cooperation with the Napoleon Hill Foundation.

Her new book in conjunction with the Napoleon Hill Foundation is called *Think and Grow Rich For Women*.

We will discuss all of this and much more on today's show. Here is my guest, Sharon Lechter. Sharon, how are you?

Sharon: I am fantastic Brian. I'm thrilled to be with you.

Brian: I'm very glad to have you here, I'm a big fan of your work, I've got several of the *Rich Dad* books. And I've told Greg Reid this, but *Three Feet from Gold* is one of my favorite books ever, ever, ever and when I met both of you at his *Stickability* event, you both autographed the copy of that book for me. That book has a very near and dear space in my heart for sure. So I'm very glad you were here, too.

Sharon: Well I am delighted to be here with you, and *Three Feet from Gold* is my first book with the Napoleon Hill Foundation, so it was really a huge honor when they asked me to step in and work on that project, so it is near and dear to my heart as well.

Brian: That's fantastic, so the first question I normally ask everyone Sharon is, tell us a little something about your background, your back story. How did you get from where you were and to where you are now? What is your path and what did you overcome to get from where you are now?

Sharon: Well you covered a lot of it in your introduction. But I started off with the normal going to school. I wanted to become a CPA, which I did. I had a rising career, at that time, with a Big 6 accounting firm. By the ripe old age of 26, when I knew everything, I ended up realizing that I was working really, really hard for other people. And so the entrepreneurial bug bit me at the age of 26. I started to launch my career by going into a company with a new investor, it was probably the worst business decision of my life. But it was when I met my husband, so it was the best LIFE decision of my life. I started building companies at that point of time. We had three children, and they didn't like to read, so I met the investor of first children's talking book— the kid's book with the sound strips down the side and you make noise. We joined forces with him and we built that industry from 1 million in sales to 23 to 51 million, and we sold it in the 3rd year. Then we moved to Arizona which is where we've lived for 22 years. At that time our oldest son was going off to college. In 1992 he went off in the fall and came home at Christmas time and said, "I'm in credit card debt, Mom and Dad". And then I was pretty mad at him, but I was even more mad at myself because I hadn't taught him about money. I hadn't taught him the things that my parents taught me. He was with me when I use my credit cards, but he just wasn't with me when I paid them off every month, and he got caught in the gauntlet of credit card offers for new students on campuses. That was December of 1992, and that's when I dedicated the rest of my career and the rest of my professional life to financial education and financial literacy.

That was the beginning of all of it, and fast forward a few years that's when I met Robert Kiyosaki. We wrote *Rich Dad Poor Dad* and released that in 1997, and started 10 years owning and building that company. Then when I decided to leave the Rich Dad organization in 2007, it was a very difficult decision for me but that's when so many other doors opened for me. President Bush asked me to be on the President's Advisory Council, then getting the call in March of 2008 from the Napoleon Hill Foundation asking me to help re-energize the messages of Napoleon Hill. It really brought it full circle for me because I had read *Think and Go Rich* when I was 19. So we were honored and thrilled to have built an international powerhouse brand like Rich Dad, the number 1 personal finance brand. But then to be asked to step into the largest personal development brand in the world, this was an incredible, unbelievably huge honor—one that I cherish and honor—and I do everything in my power to make sure that everything I do as it relates to the foundation is to honor Napoleon Hill and his original messages.

Brian: That's really fantastic, and I love the idea that financial literacy is your big major cause. I know that you are in Arizona just like I am. It's where you're from. You have spent time lobbying the school system to put financial literacy education into their curriculum. Correct?

Sharon: Oh, absolutely! When people ask me about highlights of my career—I have a lot of them because I'm so old—but one of my most recent highlights of my career is certainly in 1992 was when I dedicated myself to financial literacy. But it was in June of 2013, we finally got there bill passed in Arizona that requires financial literacy education for high school graduation. It doesn't have enough teeth in it for me, so we're still lobbying it and we have to get it put into the school system. But it was a huge major accomplishment. We ended up with unanimous votes from both the Senate and the House. And now we need to see it implemented and take that same message to share to every other state in the Union.

Brian: That's really great, when I was in Nebraska I taught in a two-year business college and I remember teaching a business math class. And one of the lessons I remember teaching in that course was about writing checks, balancing checks, how to identify your account number on the check, how to identify the routing number, and I found it odd that this was in a college course. Why is this not taught much earlier? And it wasn't. So I'm so glad that you helped to bring this about in Arizona. This is so necessary. I really appreciate that message for sure. So you were asked to be co-author the book *Three Feet From Gold*. How was it exactly that that opportunity came about?

Sharon: Well, because we're both in the same field I got to know Don Green, who's the CEO of Napoleon Hill Foundation, while I was still in Rich Dad. My husband and I own a company called Tech Press, which is a publishing company. It was the original publisher of the *Rich Dad, Poor Dad* book, and we help the foundation get some of their international translation work done, so we had known each other for several years. And when Don learned that when I made the decision to leave the Rich Dad organization, he reached out to me immediately and said, *you know we need* you... I think everyone listening knows about what happened to the economy in 2007-2008, and so they really wanted to bring the messages of Napoleon Hill to the forefront because most people under the age of 50 at that time had never even heard of Napoleon Hill, let alone the incredible lessons that he teaches about the personal development, personal responsibility, and to be tapped on the shoulder by them was an incredible honor.

Brian: Don Green has been on my show. He was amazing, and you know how amazing he is. So do I, and so do my listeners remember hearing that show. And Greg Reid, who was your co-author for *Three Feet from Gold*, has been on my show for a couple of times too. I know he has a book coming out soon. I hope to have him back in the show shortly too. What a great legacy to be a part of! That is just absolutely phenomenal, so you've worked on *Three Feet from Gold* and also *Outwitting The Devil*.

Sharon: Definitely! It's a pretty exciting book. It made a huge impact of my life.

Brian: Let's just talk real briefly about that book *Outwitting The Devil*, is that basically a metaphor conversation with the devil or a real conversation with the devil? It is basically the devil teaching us how he trips us up, right?

Sharon: I know you know this but for your listeners, *Think and Grow Rich* was a lifelong effort by Napoleon Hill. He worked on it for 25 years, and he released it in 1937. When he released it he was actually frustrated. Even though people know what they're supposed to do to become successful, they don't do it. That probably hits home to a few people listening. I know it did for me. So, he sat down and in just a few months he wrote this book called *Outwitting The Devi*l, and it was about fear—the power of fear, all types of fear and how fear either motivates or paralyzes—and most of us are paralyzed by fear. In *Outwitting The Devi*l, he says you can believe that I was talking to the real devil, or you can think I must talking to the imaginary devil. It doesn't really matter. But you as the reader can determine if you're going to get any value from what I share.

Brian: My very special guest is Sharon Lechter, author of the new book *Think and Grow Rich for Women* which came out very recently. So, let's finally talk about *Think and Grow Rich for Women*, Sharon. You initially resisted the idea of writing this book and why was that? Why did you finally decide to do it?

Sharon: Well, it is a great question, Brian. In fact, I lead off the book by saying "Why *Think and Grow Rich for Women*, why now?" Why a book just for women? For most of my career I felt that way. I felt that the steps to success were the same for men and women. I started my career in the mid-1970s, and at that time we didn't think about glass ceilings. We just figured women had to work harder than men and so we did. We didn't really have a chip on our shoulders. We were pre-feminist movement, we just got out there and do what we need to do. The steps to success are the same for men and women, but as I get closer to the twilight of my career, I realize that certainly in the last few years it has become very evident that women approached those steps to success very differently than men do. As we see the changing world of business, we went from the Industrial Age, which is very competitive dog-eat-dog world, to today where the world of business is much more collaborative and cooperative. You grow your business through strategic alliances and strategic partnerships. All of that is very important, and it is a wonderful fertile field for women because women are great collaborators. In the last couple of years, particularly right now, we really had a tipping point for women and that was really brought it home to me. I wanted to stop the complaining, stop the criticizing, and start celebrating the progress that women have made, and let's focus on the accomplishments and celebrate what good has been done instead of continuing to focus on the things that needs to be done to happen.

Brian: That is really fantastic! There is definitely a need for something like this. In fact, you're interviewed over 300 women for this book and you put a different twist on this which I really appreciate. So, let me ask how did you decide who you wanted to be a part of this project? Did you have a special criteria in mind? And talk about some of the people that you had in your book.

Sharon: Well, the criteria for me was the book *Think and Grow Rich for Women* follows the same chapter outline of the original Think and Grow Rich. I wanted to start each chapter with a synopsis of Hill's message, and then look at that message through the eyes of successful women who had applied that principle in their own success. So over 300 women are highlighted and celebrated in the book. Many of them I interviewed personally, many of them I found as I researched each principle of success to see women out there who had created success using that principle. So for instance, the founders of the international organization called Childhelp who have helped save millions of children lives. Sara O'Meara and Yvonne Fedderson helped me with the chapter on faith which is an incredible chapter. They are very close personal friends, but yet there is no one better to write and contribute to the chapter. I had other people that I highlighted in the book.

I talked about Oprah's commencement speech to Harvard where she talks about having lost that confidence in herself when she started the O network and how she had to re-tool into her burning desire, and those are all elements. There are also other women in the book I have never met, but I researched and I found information about them, about how they created success. I did further research to make sure that each woman in the book is an embodiment for the principle that I share. And then I talk about how I've used that principle in my life, and then I end each chapter with what I call The Sisterhood Mastermind. I wanted to create the body of quotes for women that are consistent with the philosophies of Napoleon Hill.

At the end of each chapter, I bring it back to the reader because the most important woman at that point in time is the one reading the book. And I also have this section called "Ask Yourself". How have you used this principle in your life? Let's celebrate what you've already accomplished and what are some things what you can do today, tomorrow and next week to deepen the impact of that principle in your own pathway to success.

Brian: That is great. So let me ask you this. Earlier we have alluded to the fact that men and women tend to think differently about a lot of things. Do you think success looks different for women than it does for men? What is your experience and your findings on that?

Sharon: Well, the subtitle of *Think and Grow Rich for Women* is *"Using Your Power To Create Success and Significance"*. One of the things that I found when I was starting to pull this book together is, I've read *Think and Grow Rich*, the original book, probably 200 times and I always pale when he talks about determining the amount of money that you want to earn or create in a month. Even though he didn't really believe that success equaled money, that is what came across when you actually read the words on the book, and I think there's an element. Women want success, but success is not necessarily in terms of money, and so that's why I said success and significance. A lot of times women want to make money, not to buy something but to do something, to create an impact. And so I think it's really important—women want to make a difference. So their success is in the results that are created by their success, not necessarily the fact that they are successful.

Brian: Wow! That's really great. So, in terms of creating significance and success, what we're talking about is women owning their own power, as they should. I mean, men have owned their power for generations. Let's talk about the idea of women owning their own power.

Sharon: It is so important. Another reason why I wrote this book, when I talk about changing the dialogue from negative to positive—men don't usually have a problem saying that they are in an expert on something. Women have a horrible time saying "*I am an expert.*" They will say, "*Well, I'm pretty good at that*" or "*Well, I'm OK*". Most of us have been raised in that maternal environment where we are supposed to take care of everybody else. And far too many women put themselves last, and I speak from painful experience because that's something that I definitely deal with every day. We want to make sure we are the best mother, the best wife, the best leader, but we forget to take care of ourselves. Part of owning the power is understanding that if you take care of yourself first—if I'm a better Sharon, then I will be a better mother, I'll be a better wife, a better entrepreneur, a better author. And that is something that's truly is hugely important in getting across. One of the top issues today for women is a lack of self-confidence, so I talked about how you deal with that. Let's admit that that's an issue. So instead of me just relying on myself, let me get together with a couple of other women leaders and we'll be each other's greatest advocate until we get that self-confidence where it needs to be. And when you're using your own power but also combining your power with other powerful women, watch out.

Brian: I will tell you what, that's a really great answer. I was thinking as you were talking—society tends to really have this concept of having it all, having balance. Is it possible or desirable? Or should we be defining success differently than "having it all". What's your take on that?

Sharon: Well, you hit my other hot spot. Not only do I not want to change the dialogue I want to get rid of the word *balance*. I often joke that my next book is going to be Balance BS. It doesn't stand for what just came to your mind. It stands for "Before Sharon". There's only one chapter in the book that was not in the original *Think and Grow Rich* book, and it's the last chapter. That chapter is called "One Big Life" because when someone is balanced, they're not moving, and women are never still. We're always doing something, and what's happening is when you try to achieve this work-life balance, it becomes that unachievable goal. You're constantly upset with yourself and frustrated that you are not balanced. So what happens is you get into a constant feeling of guilt, shame, and worry, and it's a real bugaboo for me because again I own it. I feel it all the time and I fought it all my life. I am a champion warrior.

About 7 or 8 years ago I found a definition of the word worry, it's to pray for what you do not want. And it cripples us, we end up using precious time today—taking up time worrying and feeling shameful about something that happened in the past. Each and every one of us, when we get up in the morning, have the ability to choose how we spend that day. As soon as we start thinking about X hours here, X hours there, we have one big life. And if you spent too much time at the office yesterday, spend more time with the kids today. But don't allow yourself to drag that crap forward with you because it just ruins your presence today. And understand that each and every one of us has every morning the opportunity to say *I'm going to be the best mom today*, *I'm going to be the best business woman.* My kids are going to be proud of the fact that I'm in a business meeting because I'm going to tell them why I'm going, and it's going to be one big life. Just get rid of the concept of work-life balance because you have only one life and your life is a one big life.

Brian: Exactly. I am talking to Sharon Lechter. We are talking about her book *Think and Grow Rich for Women* and we've been talking about why she wrote the book and how she interviewed and talk about over 300 women in this book and what success really looks like, and really talking about women owning their power which is so, so important.

Certainly you've pointed out in your book that women are starting businesses at an increasing rate and I would like to ask: Do you think that women have inherent advantages as business owners and their place in the global economy?

Sharon: Well, there are essential. Warren Buffett said the number one impact on investing in the next decade is going to be women entering the workforce and having their own businesses, and the economic power of women. Women already control 60% of the personal net worth in the United States, so we already are the major economic influence. We make 85% of all consumer decisions, 2 out of every 3 new businesses in America are started by women. So there's a huge influx into entrepreneurship. A lot people think that it's because women get frustrated with the glass ceiling and go out and start their own business. That's certainly a part of it. Women are great problem solvers, Brian, and the greatest way to start a new business is to solve a problem or serve a need. And there are certainly a lot of problems out there. So women have a way to get out there and start solving problems, and then start making money doing it. And those women who are very much dedicated to wanting to have their children as part of their businesses and they want to have flexibility over their time—they don't want to have a job. They want to have that ability to control their own time. So by having their own business, they have more control over the one resource we can never get back, which is our time. Certainly today there are fewer brick and mortar type businesses and so many more that are online, or women can work from home. So you have a move to a much more viral, flexible work environment with people starting businesses. So it's conducive to women who want to try and make sure that they can have their family, have their business, and make sure that they are present at all times.

Brian: That's fantastic! Whether women are in business or not, I'm sure they tend to feel stuck because of the gender roles they've been placed in. I'm sure you can relate to this. I love how Napoleon Hill talks about the idea for mastermind, and you have a chapter about this as well. So, how can women apply this principle whether they are raising their kids at home or whether they have a business. How can that work?

Sharon: Well, women naturally form masterminds. They're called girlfriends. I've tried to break down the concept of masterminds, and I have been involved in several of them. I'm a member of the Women's President's Organization on the National Board of Directors, and I have the same group of women that I can get together with once a month. There are 15 to 20 of us, and we help each other because when you are the President of your company, it can be sometimes be lonely at the top. So this is a group of women Presidents who are from unique industries, but we are there to support each other. When one of us has an issue, everything stops and we address that issue. And more than likely, if it is an issue that I have, two or three of the other women have the same issue. They can tell me what they did that worked, but also more importantly, they can tell me what they did that didn't work. And by doing that you have the opportunity to find a solution much quicker for your own issues and that camaraderie. Some of my closest friends today have come from that group. So that's a mastermind of peers.

There's also a mastermind of working on your business where you have your strategic advisors. You may have your mentors, you have your attorneys, your accountants—industry specialists who are there to help guide you in the direction your business is going. So that is a mastermind working ON your business. Then I talked about a mastermind IN your business, where you have a mastermind of your employees or the team members that are helping you within the business. They are on the front lines, they can help educate you about what's happening in the business. And then there's a personal mastermind—if you have some workout buddies, or just girlfriends or boyfriends, or just a group of people where you are invested in each other's spiritual, emotional, and physical health. So think about what you're doing. What circles are you in where you are working on supporting each other to get to the end goal? As Napoleon Hill says, it's the power of when two minds come together, you get exponential results.

Brian: Wow. I love that. Let's talk about something you have mentioned early in the book. It's about having a burning desire, and he talked about this in the original book, too. Do you find that people get going because they're fed up with where they are? Or do you find that because they have this dream that they want to accomplish? Talk about that idea and the importance of having a real burning desire as a starting place of success.

Sharon: The number one principle of success, chapter 1, is burning desire. I ask people "What's your passion?" Well, my passion came from anger. It's not what I love, it's what I was mad about. My passion was the lack of financial education. So, my passion today is as strong as it was 22 years ago, but it's very important that each and every one of us knows what gets us out of the bed in the morning. That passion is what helps keep you going when the going gets tough. It's what gets you through the down times—that combined with faith in yourself and faith in what you are doing. So most of us have a burning desire to be good parents or to be good spouses. We need a burning desire to accomplish our goals within our business and professional lives as well if that's what keeps us moving and keeps energizing us. If you start feeling fatigued a lot, then you are probably allowing something to interfere with your desire, or you're not focused on the energy where you're burning desire really lies.

Brian: Yeah! That is so important, if someone does feel stuck and they are not sure what they want, what recommendations do you have for someone like that?

Sharon: Great question! We talked about that in the Ask Yourself section of the book *Think and Grow Rich for Women*. We talked about it in *Three Feet*

From Gold as well. A lot of times people are saying, "I just don't know what I'm passionate about, I don't know what rings my bell". Have you ever been told that you're stubborn or you're focused on something? Typically that's probably something you're pretty passionate about. I've said a lot of times you can have a group of your closest friends together, and start talking and they can identify what they think your burning desires are. Sometimes we can't see the forest for the trees, so it's very important that we allow ourselves to get input from others so that we can identify those elements that are most important to us.

Brian: Yeah! That's a great idea because if you're talking to your friends and they say to you, "This is something that you keep talking about over and over again, and have you thought about doing something with this?" And that will actually became the big "a-ha". I've have that happen for me in my path, too. I love that idea, that's really great.

Let's talk about that concept of faith, and you alluded to this a little bit earlier. Faith is very important. Desire and faith really go together. Do you think that there are unique challenges women go through that allow them to apply faith differently, or is faith important in a different way to women that is for men?

Sharon: Well, in *Three Feet from Gold*—and I appreciate you mentioning it at the beginning of the hour—we talked about the personal success equation, and we interviewed many of today's successful people. We talk to them not just about their success stories, but also how they got through their deep, dark moments. And the success formula is your passion plus your talent times having the right associations, the right people on your team, times taking the right actions. We almost went to press for the formula and I thought, you know, there is still something missing. And underlying it all, what got them through the difficult times when other people quit and they often thought about quitting but they didn't, was their faith—faith in themselves, faith in their business, faith that it was necessary and needed to make a difference in the world, and that faith is what gets us through that. Faith in ourselves, faith in God, faith in the business, faith in the need for what we are doing that helps you stay focused and sometimes we get all physically tired, but it's that faith and that burning desire that keeps us going in the right direction. So faith is vitally important in reaching your goals and creating success.

Brian: Yeah, absolutely I can certainly understand that, and when things get really, really tough, what kinds of recommendations do you have? We all hit that point where we say "Well, here is a big wall. Do we go through it, should we go around it or go home?" What recommendations do you have when we feel like we're at that point that's we are absolutely stuck and not sure what to do next even though we are passionate about something?

Sharon: Well, The first thing is take a step back and say, "Okay, I'm feeling a lack of faith". But then ask yourself, is it really a lack of faith, or is it that you are allowing fear to become stronger than your faith? When you step back and look at it, you can usually identify the fact that, wait a minute, *I'm allowing fear to impact me,* because right now you can't have fear and faith simultaneously, and that fear will probably paralyze you. When you're paralyzed by fear, you insulate, you isolate, and you draw within yourself. And when that happens it's almost self-fulfilling prophecy. So what you want to do is look at the fear and say "Okay, wait a minute let me stop, let me think about what I'm grateful for". If you concentrate on the things that are going right in your life and in your business, the people that you care about, start focusing on the things that you are grateful for. Then that faith is going to start rebuilding, and it's good allow to you to get past the fear. I talked about courage. The definition of courage is it's not the absence of fear. Courage is acting in spite of the fear, so you're not taking a leap IN faith, you're taking a leap WITH faith, and that faith is what's going to help you passed through that fear.

Brian: That's great. We are talking with Sharon Lechter, and we are talking about her book *Think and Grow Rich For Women*. While I'm thinking about this, where can I find this book?

Sharon: Well, thank you so much Brian. Of course it's on Amazon.com, barnesandnoble.com, it's in your local bookstores. You can also find it at sharonlechter.com, and we'll be happy to support in all those arenas, and we're very happy and have been so thrilled with the responses that we had in Amazon, all 5 star reviews

Brian: That is wonderful. I want to go back to financial literacy. I know that this is your biggest passion, and we think about teaching financial literacy in schools because young people just have no idea how to handle money. But on the other end of this spectrum, there's a whole generation of women who were never socialized to know what to do about money because it is always a man's job to take care of the money, and some of these women find themselves stuck. They're not really sure what to do because they have never really taught to handle it. So, let's talk about the importance financial literacy really for everybody. How is your work impacted basically all generations?

Sharon: Well, I think it's so important. Each of us is either a master of our money or a slave to our money. There's not much in between. We either know how to control ourselves financially, or we are controlled by our lack of ability to control. What I see so often, particularly for young people, is they are not being taught. When we are young, we end up learning the hard lesson while we are out in the real world, but also a lot of women tend to give up that power. They might be more successful in their own right, but when they get married they turn that power over to men. The good news is we outlive men typically by 7 years for the same age, even longer if we're younger. The bad news is we outlive men and if we don't understand money, then we're not going to know how to control it and take care of it ourselves. And so for women, when we get divorced, we tend to drop our standard of living because of our lack of income. So, it is really important that women understand that they need to have their own identity, they need to have their own credit rating, they have to have their own credit, and they need to understand where the money is coming from. And I start with something really simple. Do you sign your tax return without understanding what's in it? It's so important that you understand where your money is coming from, and before you sign that return, you need to understand what's in it. By doing that, just by understanding where the money is coming from, you start gaining power and knowledge and comfort and more confidence. A lot of times women are fearful about learning about money and investing. So form a mastermind, get a group of girlfriends, or group of friends together to start understanding, do an investment club. By doing that, you start educating yourself literally on the terms of money. By understanding the terms of money, you start having that confidence built.

Brian: Yeah. Do you have any online games or board games? I know in the Rich Dad Corporation, there's Cash Flow 101 which people play to learn more about handling money. Do you have anything similar to that when you educate people for financial literacy?

Sharon: Absolutely! As you know, I co-created Cash Flow 101 and Cash Flow For Kids. When I started my new company, which is Pay Your Family First when I left the Rich Dad organization, we created a game called Thrive Time For Teens because it was so important to have a game that was fun, had humor, and really addressed young people where they were and where they are, so they feel respected and valued and understood. And so we won all kinds of awards on it, Brian, and we also have that same game, Thrive Time for adults and for women that's been in production. We've got several companies that are looking at taking our concepts and games online, and I think it's also so important that everything I do, all the books that I write, are very experiential in nature. I talk through stories, through parables, because that makes the book experiential, and the best way to learn is through experience. So when you're just teaching through a textbook, you look at the words that goes to your eyes to your brain, but when you share experiences and involve emotions which goes from the page, to your eyes, and to your heart. Once it goes through your heart, it makes an imprint. The best way to learn is through experimental knowledge. I've also just completed a college curriculum called Your Money Mastery, and that college curriculum is going be available in universities across the country that's basic financial education. It covers all aspect of money and your financial life to give young people in college the understanding of what they are going experience when they get out into the real world. So whether you get it in high school or in college, I'm covering every base to make sure that everybody gets an opportunity to understand money before they become a slave to money.

Brian: It's such an incredible mission, Sharon. I love this! I think it's so great you're creating educational tools that people of all ages to understand money better so that we could be a master of money instead of a slave, so I think that's fantastic. So let me ask you, going back to the book a little bit, we talked about how you interviewed a whole bunch of women for this book. Are there any 1 or 2 favorite interviews or stories you found especially impactful you'd like to share with us?

Sharon: There are so many! There are 3 different stories. One is Margie Aliprandi, one's Donna Johnson, and third one is Kimberly Schulte. They are all in different chapters of the book, but the 3 of them were married and successful and ended up going through divorce, and they lost everything and found themselves with small children, facing bankruptcy—penniless. It just tugs on your heart to see each one of these women, and they found that courage and they found that strength to say "I am going to take care of my children". And they all three found the ability to recover from the worst situation whether it was a divorce or abusive situation. All of them went through tremendous struggles. One, Margie Aliprandi, talks about having to drive away from her home and seeing her children crying because she was leaving, knowing that she didn't want to leave her kids but knowing that when she focused on what she was building as a business, that she would be able to take care of them the way she wanted to. And now she can travel the world with her children because she built a multi-million dollar business. All of that feeling and experience and what these women went through, gives you the hope that if they can do it, so can I. I have women in the book that are very well known, of course. Sandra Day O'Connor and Oprah Winfrey, Sarah Blakely who created Spanx—all of these women have incredible stories. But then when you read the story, you understand they're just like every other woman. They just had an idea and the passion and followed through on it, and they were able to create great success. Every woman who reads a book, every man who reads a book, will see some stories that don't relate to them. They will see others that are like mirrors, and say *Wow, I've felt that way!* That was the whole purpose. I wanted this book to be a celebration of women, and I also want it to be a celebration of those men who are champions for women.

Brian: Wow! That's wonderful! You just emphasized women who read this book and men who read this book. I think a lot of people are automatically assuming that this is a book for women. But do you find that men are reading this book and giving feedback about it, too?

Sharon: I'm getting great feedback from men. They're talking about how it helps them understand their wives more. So many men buy the book for their daughters, and say *I want to make sure my daughter gets this wealth of information.* It's so important to have them not listen to all the negativity, but to really understand there so much for us to be proud of. There is so much opportunity to stop the complaining and criticizing, and start celebrating. It's a way to create and paint the picture you want in your life and go for it.

Brian: Absolutely! And while you're talking I think this is such a great, great message, and I know that you're currently speaking and talking and promoting this book. If there are any meeting planners out there who want to book you, or any organizations that want to buy more than one copy are there ways for them to do that?

Sharon: Absolutely! Contact me at sharonlechter.com, my personal email sharon@sharonlechter.com I have a team that will absolutely pick up the phone immediately. My office number is 480-607-1940. I absolutely would love to come speak to your group and have the opportunity to share the message and to answer any questions I can.

Brian: And I have spoken to your staff on several occasions and they are amazing and you have a good team, Sharon.

Sharon: I am so so lucky! Yes!

Brian: So here's the last question of the show as we start to wind down. I have to ask who inspires and motivates you?

Sharon: I would tell you the one person in the book, and somebody that I've always admired and had the incredible honor meeting several times, is Sandra Day O'Connor. She was a trailblazer, she was tough, and she was grace—pure grace. She was the first female Supreme Court Justice and mother, passionate about her family and successful attorney, successful judge, the height of success—and yet there was never any arrogance. She and her whole mission now that she's retired is to bring back civility to politics, to our society again, to lead as a woman, not because she's a woman—but to lead with grace and dialogue, and trying to get rid of the combativeness and the impasse that we have in politics right now. And I think the way that she lived her life is exemplary, and the fact that she has made such an incredible impact on the reputation to women, and create such opportunity for women who have followed her.

Brian: Wow! I love that yes! Sandra Day O'Connor is amazing and I think the fact that she was the first Supreme Court Justice, I think it speaks a lot to her character. She broke barriers. So tell us one more time, Sharon, how can we find you? How could we find your book?

Sharon: The book is available through Amazon, Barnes and Noble, and at your local bookstore or at my website sharonlechter.com You can contact me at sharon@sharonlechter.com, please do email me. I would love to hear from you we've a got a team of people there willing and ready to support and help you. My number again is 480-607-1940 and I thank you, Brian so much and I really applaud you for what you're doing. Your show is incredible, I think you said this is your 108th or 109th show. I'm honored to be on your list, thank you.

Brian: Alright. You bet! And thank you, Sharon for being on the show. Success Profiles Radio is on every Monday at 6pm Eastern, where I interview the most successful people in the world and draw out their secrets on how they achieved. Come back next week. Thank you everyone! Goodbye!

FRANK SHANKWITZ

THE MAKE-A -WISH FOUNDATION

Brian: Hello and welcome to Success Profiles Radio. I'm your host Brian K Wright and it is an absolute pleasure to be with you here today. I am honored that you chose to spend part of your day with me here, and this is going to be a fantastic show.

My guest this week is Frank Shankwitz. Let me tell you a little bit about him.

In 1972, Frank started his career with the Arizona Department of Public Safety, assigned to the Arizona Highway Patrol as a car officer assigned to Yuma, Arizona where Frank's interest in working with children began as a coach for the Special Olympics program. In 1975, Frank was transferred to the Phoenix area to be part of a new 10 man Motorcycle Tactical Unit designed for work throughout the state. For the next 10 years, whenever assigned to small towns, Frank would visit local grade schools and talk about bicycle safety and let the children sit on his motorcycle.

Frank was one of the primary officers from the Arizona Highway Patrol who was responsible for granting the wish of a 7 year old boy with leukemia, who wanted to be a Highway Patrol Motorcycle Officer like his heroes, Ponch and Jon from the television show, "CHiPs". He and his wife, Kitty and several others, founded the Make-A-Wish Foundation in November, 1980, with Frank being the first CEO and President.

Now 32 years later, the Make-A-Wish Foundation has grown to include 63 chapters in the United States, 36 International chapters, covering 5 continents, and has granted over 280,000 wishes worldwide, with a wish being granted somewhere in the world on an average of every 38 minutes, all because of a boy named Chris who wanted to be a Highway Patrol Motorcycle Officer. Frank has received civic honors from President Bush, and from the U.S. Military Academy at West Point.

He retired as a Homicide Detective from the Arizona Department of Public Safety, and has 40 years of service in law enforcement. In 2010, Frank was featured in award winning author Brad Meltzer's book, *Heroes for My Son*, identified as one of 52 people who have made a difference in the world. Frank has been featured in USA Weekend Magazine and The Huffington Post, as well as numerous television productions. Frank is also featured in several books; Greg Reid's, Universal Wish and Lisa Heidinger's, *Wishes in Flight*. Frank has also co-authored, with Rachelle Sparks, *Once Upon A Wish*, which was a book released this year. Frank is currently involved in the making of a movie about his life called "Wish Man".

With all of this in mind, here is my guest, Frank Shankwitz. Frank, are you there?

Frank: Yes, sir good afternoon. Thank you for inviting me to be on your show.

Brian: You are welcome! So, here is the first question that I normally ask everyone. Tell us a little bit about your background, your back story, how you got to where you are now, and some of the things that maybe you overcame and we can learn about.

Frank: I was actually born in Chicago, and my mother divorced very young, and she was a *Harvey Girl*. For people who don't know, *Harvey Girls*—this is 1938, 1940—the Santa Fe Railway and several high-dollar hotels that were built along the Santa Fe Line from Chicago to Los Angeles. She applied at the age of 18, wanting to go to Arizona, was accepted, and moved to Arizona and just fell in love with the state. Unfortunately, she had to go back to the Chicago area because of an ill mother. And while there, married, I was born, but she divorced when I was very young and wanted to make her way back to Arizona.

We lived somewhat in poverty in those years, living in everything from tents to boarding houses, but she eventually made her way back to Arizona—and again, very poor during that time. People in a little town called Seligman, Arizona took us in. And for listeners, if anybody ever saw the Disney movie, *Cars,* that was based on Seligman, Arizona. Radiator Springs was Seligman, Arizona. So that was a little notoriety years later.

But people took us in, they fed us, and at the age of 10, I got a full-time job washing dishes. It wasn't unusual for young kids to work. Everybody in that town did everything they could to help their family.

Then fast forward a few years. In 1972, I started my career with the Arizona Department of Public Safety, assigned to the Arizona Highway Patrol.

As you mentioned, in 1980, I was introduced to a little seven-year-old boy named Chris. Chris had leukemia. We learned that Chris only had a few weeks to live, and that his heroes were Ponch and Jon from the TV show, CHiPs. He told his mom, "When I grow up, I want to be a motorcycle officer just like Ponch and Jon." And through contacts through our department and friends of his, they asked if we can do anything special for Chris, which we did, with the permission of our commanders. They had flown in our helicopter to our headquarters building, which was the first time I met him.

I expected our paramedics to help this very ill little boy. I can't imagine, seven years old, leukemia, and Chris knew he only had a few weeks to live.

But instead, here comes this little boy full of energy, out of the helicopter, running up to me, high-fiving—"Hi, I'm Chris." And as far as he's concerned, I could be either Poncho or Jon. He was just ecstatic. He was having so much fun as a 7 year old boy you would imagine would be. Chris and I bonded immediately. We went on that day to visit our armory to get his own badge, his own uniform, and was made the first and only honorary Highway Patrol Officer in the history of Arizona Highway Patrol to this day.

Brian: Wow.

Frank: He wanted his motorcycle wings and that was a humorous little story. We went to his house and we just mentioned, "If you had a motorcycle, Chris, I could test you in your driveway," and explaining, "To test him, there's instructions we had to go through for motorcycle officers." Chris was a step ahead of us. He ran inside the house and came riding out on a little battery-operated motorcycle that his mother had gotten for him in place of a wheelchair.

And he had on his uniform that we had made for him and a helmet and he was as serious as can be. We set up some cones in the driveway, he went through them.

"Did I pass my test? Am I a motorcycle officer now?" "Yes, you are, Chris." He wanted motorcycle wings that we wore on our uniforms which were custom-made, and I told him that I would order those, and I did. A couple of days later, I picked them up. As I picked them up, I learned Chris was in the hospital, in a coma and was not expected to survive the day.

When I went into the hospital, his uniform was hanging right by his bed. And as I pinned the wings on his uniform, Chris came out of a coma.

He looked at me, he looked at his uniform, and he just started giggling and laughing—"Am I a full motorcycle officer now?" "Yes, you are, Chris." He reached over, got his uniform, showed his mom. He was just happy as can be. Unfortunately, Chris passed away later that afternoon.

Brian: Oh, my goodness.

Frank: And I said, "They gave you those wings to get to heaven."

So, we had lost a fellow officer, and he was buried with full police honors. But then I started thinking, there's this little boy, he had a wish, we made it happen. Why can't we do that for other children? And that's when the idea was born for the Make-A-Wish Foundation, right there in 1980.

Brian: Wow, that's great. So what were some of the special challenges you faced along the way? Did you envision this blowing up as big as it has gotten? What was it that you were wanting to do with this, and what kinds of challenges did you face along the way, Frank?

Frank: The biggest challenge was I was working full-time. I was still a police officer and as most police officers, you're working secondary jobs. Then the other challenge was finding people that were interested in the idea. By the charter, I had to find four other people, and that was very difficult. They just didn't think it was a good idea, it wouldn't work. But when I did find those other four people, we went to work. You asked, did I ever feel that it was going to blow up to the size it was today? Not to sound egotistical, yes, I did. After we granted our first official wish, I mentioned to the people, "Someday, we're going to be national or international, granting wishes all over the world." They kind of laughed at me, but they stuck with me on it.

Brian: Yeah. I love that you said that, because really anyone who achieves greatly has to have an enormous belief in who they are and what they're about, and where they're going. So I love that you did think this big so early on. Were there some challenges or issues that you had to encounter along the way? Something this big doesn't grow without its growing pains.

Frank: Well, the biggest thing is after we were two years into it, I had to make a decision—now we were becoming big, we were getting national attention all over. We were getting calls from different states. They wanted to develop chapters. I had to make a decision, am I going to be a police officer, or am I going to run the foundation? I liked what I was doing. And by the way, none of us in the beginning ever took a salary, and I've never taken a salary from Make-A-Wish in all the years that I've been involved because I had a job. But we made a decision to start hiring the professionals in the non-profit world, which I think, was our best decision ever.

Brian: That's wonderful. And I love the fact that you didn't ever take a salary. So let me ask you this. It sounds like you kept your job as a police officer while you were doing this, so your employer was really, really supportive of this big mission that you had then, correct?

Frank: Very supportive. I'm working full-time and I get called into the Director's Office and I thought, "Oh, I'm in trouble now." And he told me, he says, "I know what you're doing, I support you 100%. Sometimes you're going to do a lot of this on duty time, just give me eight hours a day. If it takes you 15 hours to give me 8 hours a day, you work 15 hours, but you give me

8 hours a day." And I respected him for doing that, and I honored that little verbal contract, making sure that I did give I'm that full eight hours a day.

Brian: Wow, that's fantastic. So let me ask you about how you built this organization. Obviously, no great thing, such as this, happens by one person being an island and trying to do it themselves. I would imagine you had to be a really good networker, I imagine that you had to learn how to make really great, authentic connections, right?

Frank: Yes. Luckily, nobody had ever heard of anything like this nationwide and the press picked it up immediately and we started getting great press coverage. The major networks, NBC, ABC, for example. And a big breakthrough is a relationship that we started with Disney. That really gave us the boost, so it all really fell together. It was constant of networking, but we had a good mission.

Brian: Yeah. And I've heard you talk about the story, and I think I might have read about it in Greg Reid's book called *Think and Grow Rich: Stickability: The Power of Perseverance*. I met you at his event, his movie premiere, and I interviewed you on the red carpet. I read the book, and the chapter about you talked about how you developed a relationship with Disney. A lot of people might ask, "Well, how do you get in with a company like Disney?" So what is it that happened that gave you such a great relationship with them?

Frank: Well, it's a funny story and our very first official Wish Child, a little boy nicknamed Bopsy—again, 7 years old, again, leukemia. In those days, in the early 80s, there were very few children that survived leukemia. For now, about 70% of the children, thank God, and through modern medicine and God, are surviving these illnesses. His wish was to go to Disneyland. I called Disney several times asking if they could maybe give us reduced fares, free entry, knowing that this child is in a wheelchair, to go to the head of the line just to try and establish this relationship.

Brian: Right.

Frank: And one of our other board members kept trying to do the same thing. Disney had never heard of us. They really didn't respond. I called one day over there and I said, "This is Officer Frank Shankwitz, Arizona Highway Patrol, and I need to talk to the Director of Human Relations." And I think they misunderstood why I was calling because right away, they think I'm calling on an official business.

And I'm just trying to use that title to talk to somebody. That little misunderstanding led to Disney people listening to me, and learning about our organization, giving a first-class treatment to our little boy named Bopsy, and starting that whole relationship with Disney which has been a major supporter for Make-A-Wish now for 33 years.

Brian: Wow. So they thought you were calling to bust one of their employees about something?

Frank: Right. Maybe a warrant or maybe a problem going on in there. When, in fact, it was the farthest thing from the truth. But that little misunderstanding led to that great relationship.

Brian: Yeah, that's great. I think that's just a great lesson in just taking what comes and making the most of it, I love that. That's a great, great story. So let me ask you something. The whole idea of starting an organization like this is going to involve a huge level of commitment, and as a leader, it's very important that we learn how to instill our vision into other people, so that they want to own it, too. Was that a difficult process for you, helping or getting other people to really commit to your big vision for this?

Frank: It was. In the beginning it was difficult, but everybody just right away grasped the idea, especially with the children. To watch the results of a wish and these children, it was just amazing. People just gravitated to that immediately. We call it "the power of a wish, now a popular term within the organization. Some of the children that we have is what they call a "rush wish".

A doctor would notify us that this child is not going to survive their life-threatening illness. If you're going to do something, it's got to be in the next month or two. The child does the wish, whatever it might be—travel, meeting a celebrity, whatever it might be.

Brian: So if someone wants to give to the Make-A-Wish Foundation, how can they go ahead and do that, Frank?

Frank: The best contact is on the website which is www.wish.org and that will get you to the national website, and the anybody who's in the United States, they have a locator on there that you can put in your ZIP code, your city, your state, and it will direct you to your local chapter throughout the United States.

Brian: That's fantastic. My very special guest this week is Frank Shankwitz who is the Founder and CEO of the Make-A-Wish Foundation, one of the largest and one of the greatest charitable organizations in the entire world, in my opinion, doing fantastic work. And we've talked a little bit about how he got started and the challenges of growing an organization like that. If you do want to give to the Make-A-Wish Foundation, please do so. Go to www.wish.org. You can look for your state, your local chapter, and give where it makes a difference wherever you are.

So Frank, I'd like to ask, and this is a question that maybe other people out there may be wondering: Make-A-Wish is a huge organization, and it's something that a lot of us have heard of. But what makes the Make-A-Wish Foundation different from a lot of the other organizations that do something similar? There are other organizations that grant wishes to people, and what makes Make-A-Wish Foundation different?

Frank: I think our credibility and the integrity of the foundation. And again, there are several—you could say—copycats. I'm not saying that in a derogatory term whatsoever, because a lot of those organizations are doing fantastic jobs.

Brian: Exactly. So putting together a non-profit organization today would be very, very different and perhaps a lot harder than it was when you started. I mean, I'm sure it's a lot more highly regulated now. Does that sound right?

Frank: It is. And obviously, with IRS, the 501(c)(3) status, they check very close to make sure that everything is above board. It wasn't as difficult 33 years ago as it is now. Now, it's just a lot more time consuming a lot more paperwork, a lot more scrutiny of the non-profit. And it should be.

Brian: Yes.

Frank: Just to make sure we're not taking somebody's money and put it in somebody else's pocket instead of what the charity is trying to go for.

Brian: Right. Exactly. So say for example, if you were to start a non-profit organization in the state of Arizona, because that's where I'm at, you have to file your papers in Arizona, and how do you comply with the standards and regulations of other states? I mean, is that all taken care of when you file in one particular state?

Frank: For example, with Arizona, you file with the Arizona Corporation Commission—and then your IRS for Arizona, and then you would have to file IRS and corporation papers in each state that you want to branch out to.

Brian: That's time consuming...

Frank: And that's right. Now, it's also very costly compared to years ago because each state is requiring the fees along with the IRS fees of that individual state.

Brian: Sure, absolutely. So let me ask, I know that you love to tell the stories of the people you've granted wishes to. How about another favorite story someone's dream coming true because of Make-A-Wish Foundation?

Frank: We have several celebrities—and a lot of times, you won't read about a lot of wishes because—let us say a celebrity, or the Wish family itself. We never ask that they allow publicity. We ask them if they would, if they don't, we understand the privacy of what they're going through in this life-threatening situation with their child. It's very private for the family. A lot of times, let's say it's a celebrity wish, the celebrity would say, "I would love to interact with this child, but I don't want the publicity because this is between the child and I."

Brian: Yes.

Frank: I'll give you an example in San Francisco area, a few years, a very major motion-picture celebrity, the child wanted to see the Beauty and the Beast, the stage show of Beauty and the Beast.

Frank: They had just left the tour in the San Francisco Area. This celebrity heard about that, arranged for the whole production to come back to San Francisco. The celebrity picked up this little girl, again, 7 years old—why most of these children are 7 years old, I don't know, but escorted just him and her to this theater and explained to her, this is where the production was, took on stage, and just started talking about how the whole production was. All of a sudden, some music started playing from the theme of the Beauty and the Beast. He asked if he can dance with her and she started dancing. All of a sudden, some stage lights come on, and here comes the Beast now dancing with her. Further stage lights come on, the full orchestra is there, the theatre lights come on, the whole theatre is packed, and the whole production is playing special for this girl, and this celebrity arranged for the whole thing.

Brian: Oh, my goodness. Wow, what a great story.

Frank: I know. If you can imagine this little girl all of a sudden dancing with the Beast and the whole stage production was there.

Brian: Wow. That is fantastic. So let me ask, Frank, how do you identify sponsors and organizations to help you with your outreach? I imagine the wish comes first and we can talk a little bit later about how you screen the wishes and how you get the wishes that you get to work with. But how do you identify the organizations and the people that can help you?

Frank: Well, the marketing team will reach out to several major corporations. Also, major corporations will reach out to the Make-A-Wish Foundation within the local chapters, or the national, and international office because of the integrity of the foundation.

It is a good marketing and charity tool for them, and probably the best example is the Macy's Campaign that happens every year. Take a letter to Santa and put it in the mail in the store, and for every letter delivered Macy's donates one dollar up to million dollars. It's great for Make-A-Wish, it's a great marketing tool for Macy's. They have the child and Mom and Dad in the store, and, "While we're here, let's do a little shopping." So it's a win-win for both of us.

Brian: Wow, that's great. So I would imagine that in any organization's mission such as yours, there are probably several components that have to come together. One of those would be the funds, the money that you have to work with. I suppose, another of those components would be finding volunteers that can help you, and finally, the connections that need to be available. And, of course, the sponsors that you're talking about certainly are connections. So let me ask, how is it that you find out about these wishes? Maybe the better way to ask this is if someone out there has a child that has a special wish, how can they reach out to you and see if their wish can possibly be granted?

Frank: A lot of our referrals come generally from the hospitals, from the children's hospitals. There are pamphlets in children's hospitals throughout in the United States explaining about Make-A-Wish. A friend or a neighbor may hear of a child or about a child and tell the parents or contact the foundation. Up in my area here in Northern Arizona, several times I'll pick up a newspaper and just read about this child within Northern Arizona somewhere battling this particular life-threatening illness. I will politely reach out to the family and ask if they know about Make-A-Wish Foundation. If they don't, give them the information, and then the referral will go to the local chapter.

Brian: That sounds fantastic. How many wishes do you grant a year?

Frank: I believe last year, nationwide, was in the area, 4,500 for the US chapter. I don't have the information of the international chapters. In Arizona last year was, as I recall, 350 wishes.

Brian: Okay. That sounds great.

Frank: And it's a shame—it's great we could do that, and it's a shame, there are so many children that are battling a life-threatening illness just in one state.

Brian: So let me ask, and we visited this topic a little bit ago, if somebody wants to be part of your mission, if they want to give or donate, what can they do?

Frank: The best thing is to go to www.wish.org, which is the national website, and it will allow you to click on to your local chapters, wherever state that you're in.

Brian: Okay. My very special guest this week is Frank Shankwitz, who is the founder of the Make-A-Wish Foundation. We've talked about the mission of his organization, we've talked about how Make-A-Wish is different from other organizations. He's shared some amazing stories of some of his favorite wishes that have been granted, and what it's like to put together a non-profit organization.

And Frank, you have been abundantly blessed lately. There is going to be a movie made about your life and it's called *Wish Man*. Tell us a little bit about how that got started.

Frank: It was very flattering and very humbling. During a speaking event, I was introduced to a director out of the Hollywood Area named Theo Davies. He just started saying he's followed a little bit of my career and he said, "This is going to be a fantastic movie because we need more motivational movies like *Blind Side* and *Rudy*." He asked me if I would be interested. I was very flattered, of course. I just started listening to his ideas and his thoughts on the screenplay, and Greg Reid happened to be involved in this also. He wanted to get involved and I like his credentials, so I said, "Yes, let's do this. Let's see what we can come up with."

Brian: That's great. So somebody approached you about this and you decided that this might be something worth doing.

Frank: Right. And I think it would give great inspiration not only for Make-A-Wish, but for people also. I am always interested in giving back somehow.

Brian: Absolutely. So I've been reading your posts on Facebook lately. It sounds like the screenplay is about done, is that right?

Frank: Yes. We've been working several months on the screen play, for the draft of the screenplay, and I get a kick out of the writer on this. Sometimes, he makes me work what I call a midnight shift. Around 2:00 in the morning, he's calling me, he said, "I'm sending you a draft. Look at it, correct it, tell me what we need to do." So we've got a lot of work put in this together and I like the way he's putting it. And he's giving me control on this script so that nothing is getting out of sync. We're sticking to the true story, and I respect him for that.

Brian: That's great. In fact, that was going to be my next question is how true to the story is this going to be, because I know a lot of biopics—at least in Hollywood—they take what we'll call creative license in the interest of "making a better script."

Frank: Right. Exactly.

Brian: That's not going to happen. Well, your life is interesting enough that there shouldn't have to be that much creative license necessary. I'm sure they'll probably cover your career in law enforcement, they'll cover how the first wish came about. They'll cover the difficulties of how the organization got started. There's a lot of stuff there, so I think it's going to be great.

Frank: Yeah. It'll be mostly—and again, like you've mentioned, it's from the events of my life from childhood up to the years I started the foundation that inspired all of this. And the sad parts, the humorous parts, the downright funny parts, he's put it all together.

Brian: Yeah. So let me ask you this, is there a timeline or an estimated time on the release date for this?

Frank: The release date as, I understand, will be the end of 2014 or beginning of 2015. The screenplay—the draft—is being finalized, it goes for review, and after that time, it will go for script writing, then casting. The schedule right now for filming—they told me it is April, May, and June and then also October of next year. But I'm thrilled because lot of them we filmed right here in my own town of Prescott and in Northern Arizona.

Brian: That's great. And I know that a lot of the details are still pretty hush-hush, but have you thought about casting and where you're going to get your actors from?

Frank: That is still hush-hush right now. I can't reveal some of the people I've already asked for cameos in the movie. We got some major names that we will have for cameos to be in the movie.

Brian: Oh, that was my next question—is while you can't reveal their identities specifically, will some of these people be people that we all know?

Frank: Oh, yes, definitely. You'll know who they are. There won't be any hesitation on it.

Brian: Yeah. In fact, it's interesting. I've seen the poster—Greg Reid has posted on Facebook what the poster of the movie is going to look like. At first I thought, Marlboro man. It looks a little bit like the Marlboro man image. I also think that if someone like Wilford Brimley was about 20 years younger, he could play the current version of you. So there's probably going to be several actors playing you. A younger version and a current version, is that right?

Frank: Yes. For my mid-30s, when I was the motorcycle officer, and then current age, and then along with my wife also, in her mid-20s and current age, and then some young actors to play as my grandson and the Wish children. So I'll be quite involved with casting.

Brian: Yeah. So when you assigned the parts of the Wish children, will you be using real Wish children then?

Frank: That will be strictly up to the—let's say, a local chapter and the family. And we will also seek permission from the national office if we're using Wish children. I can understand. Again, the families don't want that exposure because again, it's a very private thing.

Brian: Absolutely. Before we move on to our next topic, is there anything else you'd like to say about the movie Wish Man, as it is going into production here in the next few months?

Frank: Yeah. You can follow us on Facebook right now or on the website www.wishmanmovie.com, and it will give you all the information. They're developing a blog. This is all new to me. Obviously, I'm a novice in all of this. This is also led on to another possible TV show on another topic, but one thing has led to another here.

Brian: Wow, that's really great. We've got probably five or six minutes until the end, so I'd like to ask about your career as an author, because I know that you were part of the *Think and Grow Rich: Stickability* project. That's how I met you. There's an entire chapter about you in that book. There also have been other books that you've been involved in, one that was released earlier this year, I believe, called *Once Upon A Wish*. Tell us about that.

Frank: Yeah. *Once Upon A Wish*—a young reporter here in my local hometown of Prescott, Arizona, started doing articles on local Wish children where we're granting wishes, and she became very interested in the Foundation, wrote quite a flattering feature article about me in the local newspaper, which got picked up by The Associated Press. And then she came to me with the idea. She said, "We need to write a book about Wish children…about 8 to 10 different wish children throughout the United States. The whole experience of the life-threatening illnesses they're going through, the wish, the power of the wish, the effects on the total family, the child." I thought, this is a great idea and she asked me to help her write it. So between the two of us, we spent about a year and a half not only interviewing these children and the family, beginning with getting the permission of the family, then put together this book which is released in March of this year, *Once Upon A Wish*.

Brian: Wow, that's fantastic. It's just so interesting, once you keep putting yourself out there, how opportunities start to gravitate toward you. Do you find that things are just coming to you now from directions that you don't even anticipate and what do you attribute that to?

Frank: Well, it is. I did my final retirement with the Arizona State Police, just October 1st, because I was still doing a lot of follow up work from my own side. All of a sudden, this whole new career path is becoming available. Because of Greg Reid, I'm speaking at his Secret Knock and the *Stickability* event. The book has been out, another one we just finished that Greg wrote, *Universal Wish,* was just released during the last month. And now I've been contacted by another publishing company to write my life's story which we'll start working on that after the movie is finished.

Brian: That's fantastic. So as we are coming toward the end of the show, I'm going to ask you, Frank, the question that I ask everyone who comes on my show, and it's simply this, who inspires and motivates you?

Frank: Who inspires me and motivates me right now are the children, without a doubt. I get to meet these children that are eligible for a wish. I'm still a wish granter with the foundation, so I get to go out and talk to these children, talk to the families. My biggest thrill at events around the nation is meeting Wish children that have survived illnesses that are now adults, and come up to me and just say, "I'd like to meet you, I'd like to shake your hand.

I'm a Wish child." And that just almost brings a tear into my eye. But that is my biggest motivation, to keep taking care of these children.

Brian: That's great. So one more time, how can we make a contribution to the Make-A-Wish Foundation if we'd like to go ahead and do that?

Frank: On the national website, www.wish.org, and that will lead you to your local chapters throughout the United States or international countries. And everything from volunteering to a dollar donation, whatever you can do to help, a sponsorship, any kind of help, anything that could help the foundation would be helpful.

Brian: That's great. And how do we get a hold of you if we want to connect with you. I know you're on Facebook.

Frank: I don't mind giving out my personal email address. I'm getting flooded with that anyhow. And that's frank1091@att.net.

Brian: Okay. So if you want to email Frank and ask him a question or talk to him about anything, Frank is really responsive and I really appreciate that. So we are coming to the end of the show, and Frank, I am so thankful that you are on the show today. Thank you so much for being here, my friend.

Frank: And again, thank you very much. I enjoyed talking to you.

Brian: That's fantastic. And we will be back next Monday at 6:00 PM, Eastern. This is Success Profiles Radio. I really appreciate all of you. Thank you so much for listening. Have a wonderful week everyone. Good bye!

ERIK SWANSON

THE HABITUDE WARRIOR

Brian: Hello and welcome to Success Profiles Radio. I'm your host Brian K Wright and it is an absolute pleasure to be with you here today. I am honored that you chose to spend part of your day with me here, and this is going to be an amazing show.

I want to introduce today's amazing guest, and I've been waiting for this guest to be on my show for a while and I'm so glad that we're finally able to do this.

My guest this week is Erik Swanson. Let me tell you a little bit about him.

As a Speaker, Motivator, Coach, Mentor, Best-Selling Author, and a Corporate Trainer, Erik Swanson has been an influence and mentor to tens of thousands throughout the years since his early start in the industry over 16 years ago. Having been in sales since the age of 21, he finished his studies at the University of Vermont and started working with an advertising agency in the North East.

He broke every goal put in front of him and was eager to move to the next step. At age 27, he was soon noticed and picked to share the stage with some of the most talented and famous Sales & Motivational Trainers in the world today such as Brian Tracy, Jim Rohn, Tom Hopkins, Jack Canfield, and Tony Robbins, just to name a few. These real life experiences molded him into the amazing "Connector" and Speaker that he is today. His style combines step-by-step tactical teachings with humor and vivid story telling.

Nicknamed 'MR. AWESOME', Erik's energy, warmth and enthusiastic nature, engages each audience member and allows participants to not merely observe and listen, but rather they will enthusiastically participate and be driven to action. He has developed his own unique and super rewarding system in which he calls "Secret Habitude Warrior" Training. He is the author of the book *The Habitude Warrior: Quotes and Notes*, and his upcoming book *The Sales Habitudes*.

In addition, he is the founder of Universal Seminars, which is one of the leading seminar companies in the entire country. We will discuss all of this and much more on today's show.

And with all of this in mind, here is my special guest, 'MR. AWESOME', Erik Swanson. Erik, how are you today?

Erik: Hello. I feel great, man. What's going on?

Brian: I am so super excited to have you on the show. It's been a long time coming, my friend.

Erik: I know. It's been a couple of years since we've been talking about this, so I'm glad we can make our schedules work.

Brian: Yes. A lot of our common friends have been on the show, and a few more scheduled in the future. It was about time to get you on, so I'm so happy that you're here. So here's the first question that I ask everybody, Erik. Tell us a little bit about your background, your back story, how you started, what you learned and accomplished, what came along the way, and what brought you to where you are right now.

Erik: Wow, this can be a long answer. Well, I'm originally from Washington, DC area. I live in San Diego now and I got started with Brian Tracy, actually, as my mentor. I'm sure a lot of your audience members know Brian Tracy. So he was the catalyst of my success journey, really. One of the first things that he told me was to diversify myself and to learn tons from him, but also learn from other individuals, other authors, other speakers, and surround myself with the other successful people out there. So I started really just diving in and meeting as many people as I could, and became a Senior Trainer with Brian Tracy and worked with his group for a while. Now I share stages with him, it's an honor and it's pretty fun, so that's where I got my start. What was the second part of the question?

Brian: Oh, what have you done, what have you overcome, what brought you to where you are right now?

Erik: Well, I got into sales and sales training with Brian. And for that, I did about eight or nine years of just sales training throughout the nation. Really, I was into just teaching people how to close, how to handle objections, and how to prospect which is great. It was a lot of fun. But about seven or eight years ago, I started seeing a change in me and also noticed a trend that was changing, where it wasn't all about closing skills and handling objections. It was more about relationship building and habit training.

So I really got into working on myself. I shared stages with Jim Rohn, and I'm sure a lot of you know Jim Rohn before he passed. It's all about working harder on yourself than your job. So, I started working more diligently on myself and my habits. And that's actually the genesis, that's where "habitude" came around.

I invented something called Habitudes, which is combination of your habits and your attitude put together. And I go through a whole systematic way of keeping yourself in check and in tune with your habits and your attitude on a daily basis. So I had a lot of challenges just getting out of my own way, really. That's the biggest challenge I had, and I think a lot of people out there in today's world—we have competitors out there in our marketplace, in our certain industries. But our biggest competitor is usually ourselves and getting in our own way and limiting belief factor. So I started working on that and that's part of my Habitudes Training.

Brian: That's great. So how do we get in our own way and how do we get out of our way?

Erik: I like this. You know, Brian, you just go right to the meat of it, I love it.

Brian: Absolutely.

Erik: We get in our own way because of many reasons. One would be fear. The second reason is just we develop this habit of sabotaging ourselves—not managing our time more efficiently or asking for the sales and orders for business. A lot of us don't actually do the things that we're supposed to be doing and we don't hold ourselves accountable. So what I have done is I put together my Habitudes book which has about 50 different training habits in there to get you out of your own way and into the success quotient, if you will. I can share are a few of them with your audience, if you like.

Brian: Absolutely.

Erik: You read my book the other day, is that correct?

Brian: That's right.

Erik: Awesome. Which ones resonated with you a little bit more?

Brian: Oh gosh. There were several of them, actually. I love the idea of remembering people's names. That's something that people tend to take for granted, but it's so important and sometimes, that's a little bit of an issue for me.

Erik: Is it really? Yeah, recalling people's names is critical. I think it's does two things. If you develop the habit of recalling people's names in an amazing way, what it does is it not only makes them feel good, but it builds up their attitude as well—and it also builds up yours and your confidence. So you don't have to worry about, "Oh my gosh. Don't forget his person's name." When you're worrying about that, then you're actually not focusing on something else that you can be focusing on to build up that relationship. So, here's what I find. Often we go out there, we meet people and I hear this all this all the time. "Well, I remember people's faces, I just don't remember names." Right? I've got a dog named Jackson. He remembers people's names and faces. He remembers everybody, so why can't we? So what most people do is most people get out there, we meet somebody, and we say, "Now, don't forget their name. Don't forget their name. Don't forget their name." Well, you and I both know, Brian, we're using the Law if Attraction against us.

Brian: Right.

Erik: And we're actually giving ourselves an embedded command to say to ourselves, "Well, go ahead and forget that person's name." And you're not focusing in on something that you really should be focusing on. Here's a scoop, I've seen this before. A lot of people take those memory courses, memory training and so forth, and they're great. If you find a great memory trainer or a course that resonates with you, use it. It's awesome. For me, it got me confused. I was putting different things in different sections and different areas. Putting glue here, putting this there and it's still didn't work for me. So I had to really simplify it for myself. So what I do is I use what's called bracketing, it's a three-step process. I'll share it with the audience right now, if you want. The first step is this, your first word out of your mouth should be their name. That's rule number one. By the way, I highly recommend writing this down. Don't rely on your memory for the memory training, right?

Brian: Right, right.

Erik: So the first word out of your mouth should be their name. So if I'm going to meet somebody named John, let's say, I'm going to come up to them. I'm going to say, "Hi, my name is Erik. What's your name?" And they're going to say, "John." My first word out of my mouth in that next sentence is going to be his name. So I'm going to say, "John, great to meet you today." Then rule number two is I'm going to place his name at the end of the next sentence. So I'm going to say, "John, great to meet you today. Hey, let me ask you a quick question, John." And then rule number three is I'm going to repeat their names three to five times while I'm looking at them. But not aloud though, okay? So make sure your audience doesn't do that. It's really embarrassing when you're saying, "Hi, nice to meet you John, John, John, John, John." Don't repeat it out loud.

Brian: Exactly.

Erik: So that's the three-step bracketing system, Brian. And it really, really helps people remembering people's names.

Brian: That's wonderful. So Erik, your nickname is "MR. AWESOME." So let us know how that happened. Where did that come from?

Erik: Great question. Well, my peers have been calling me "MR. AWESOME." Actually some people you've mentioned, Erik Lofholm, Jeffrey Gitomer, Loral Langemeier, Les Brown, Sharon Lechter, the list goes on, Bob Proctor—I share a stage with all these friends of mine. And it's really cool because when I walk in, I realize that the authors and speakers out there, we're just like anyone else. Sometimes we have doubts. Sometimes we need that little push. Even eagles need a push. So what I do is I give people high-fives. I walk up to them and I bring them a cappuccino or something, just do anything to make somebody smile. So I used to do that, I still do. And my nickname came around from all the rest of the speakers saying, "That's 'MR. AWESOME'." Because I like to bring the awesome to the party, if that makes sense.

Brian: Yeah, absolutely.

Erik: I was thinking why not? Either way, something's going to happen. Why not make it awesome at the same time.

Brian: I love that. And you've got this thing where you'll just high-five random strangers without them expecting it, right?

Erik: Exactly, yeah. I get a lot of business that way, actually. It's one of my habitudes.

Brian: Really? Tell us about that.

Erik: Yeah. It's one of my habitudes. That's actually how I met you, Brian. I met you at a conference—somewhere in LA, I believe. I think I came up to you and high-fived you in the hallway or something.

Brian: I think you did. Yes, I was thinking, "This random guy is high-fiving me. This is cool. I'm down with this. That's fine."And then we started a conversation. We've seen each other a couple of times since then and we've struck up a great friendship, so I really appreciate that. In fact, we've already talked about a couple of the things that are in your *Habitude Warrior* book. In fact, you have 50 items. We aren't going to have time to go through all 50 of them today, but we've already talked about the Art of Remembering People's Name and we've talked about How You High-Five Random People. In fact, you challenge people in this book to high-five—how many people before noon—five people?

Erik: Exactly. Yes, five people before noon. And the reason why I came up with that is I needed to get out there and meet different individuals. I was in direct selling, get out there, meet people, prospect and so forth. I really wasn't getting any business while sitting at home, on the computer with Facebook. So I decided to commit to myself to getting out of the house and meeting five new people by noon. And I say by noon because most people want to make a million dollars, yet they still want to sleep till noon. So I decided, "Hey, I'm going to get out there". Another one of my Habitudes is take a different route. So I go to different places and I force myself to look for different environments, so that I can meet different people. I did that all the time, and high-fiving people by noon gets my juices going. My goal is to go out and to meet different people. And most of the time, 98 to 99 percent of time, people will high-five you back. Every city I've done this in, except New York City.

Brian: I love the fact that you say take a different route because that's another one of your habitudes. Sometimes, people get stuck in the same rut and they go the same way to work, or they go the same way to the grocery store, or wherever they're going. There's more than one way to get there, and sometimes just taking a different way there exposes you to a whole different set of scenery…and possibly a whole different set of circumstances. I love that idea very much.

Erik: Oh, yes. Actually, what I do, Brian—this is going to sound silly, but I'd rather be silly and successful than not.

Brian: Right.

Erik: I don't fill up my gas tank full all the time. I always fill up my gas tank half full. So I'm literally adding new gas stations twice as much as other people. I assume that nobody has butlers that fill up their gas tanks. So everyone's out there, and what I do is I just strike up a conversation when I'm sitting there pumping my gas and somebody is next door. This happened the other day. I'm over here in Miami today, and over here in the East Coast, I drive a Mercedes out here, and somebody had another Mercedes next to me. So I just struck up a conversation. I said, "Is that the new S-class?" And he said, "Yeah, yeah, it is." And we're comparing our Mercedes against each other and we're just striking up a conversation. I said, "Wow, you have nice car. You must be the mayor of the town." And he said, "No, no. I just own it." He turned out to be a big real-estate mogul out here and sure enough, I got a little appointment with him and now we're working together to do some meetings and things for his association. So it's just striking up conversations with people, taking a different route. When I'm not traveling, I have three different dry cleaners that I go to. It's inconvenient but what it's convenient for is meeting different people. So I drop off things to different places. I actually go there and meet different people this way. So again, it sounds silly but, it really makes a big difference, and it actually builds up business for me.

Brian: Yeah. Well, there's a greater purpose to it all, so who cares what anyone else thinks about it, right?

Erik: That's true.

Brian: Well, you talked about high-fiving five people before noon. Prerequisite to that is starting your day off on the right foot, and that's also another one of your Habitudes. So let's talk about what you do to start your day off on the right foot. What makes you ready to take on the world in the morning, Erik?

Erik: Great question again. So what I do is this, and let me preface it by saying my mornings were character building. They were not that fun, okay? So, I had to change it around. I decided one day, I was going to use affirmations and self-talk. And at the beginning of doing this, I was really apprehensive about using it. And literally, Brian, I would say to myself, these affirmations don't work. Sure enough, I was affirming that they weren't going to work. So I said to myself, "All right. You know what? I'm going to give this a 21 to 30-day trial. It takes 21 days to make a good, new habit and 30 or more to make it stick. So I said, "All right. I'm going to do this myself." So one day, I wrote down about ten different things that I was going to say to myself. I actually put it on my bathroom mirror. It's just very simple. It's just a saying that I say to myself, and here it is:

I am the best, I am focused, I will succeed, I believe in myself, I have the will to win, I set high expectations, I visualize my perfect future, I don't let others bring me down.

How many of your audience members could use that?

Brian: Yeah.

Erik: I surround myself with winners and I will learn and grow every day. Those are my ten things that I say to myself, and I know it by heart. I say it every morning. But it affirms it to myself and it's my creed that I say, and it takes me through the day. I also put it on my refrigerator in my home in Texas, and a friend comes up and says, "Hey, what's that?" I said, "Well, that's my creed." And he said, "Oh, that's awesome, man. You should print that up and give it out to people." I said, "All right. Well, I'll do that." So I went to Kinko's. For $50, I bought 1000, and I just started handing them out. And he comes back about a couple months later. He said, "Hey, how's it going?" I said, "It's going great. I'm handing them out there." He goes, "Any business from it?" I said, "No, not really." So I realized that I didn't have anything to contact me with it. There was no email or phone number or anything. So I thought, "All right. Maybe I'll re-do this." So I re-did them and, I've got some numbers on the back and a QR code.

So then I was in Hoboken, New Jersey, doing a program over there, and I was walking out of the Best Buy parking lot. And this woman and I were walking towards the same direction, so we struck up a conversation. I think I high-fived her, then we started talking. She said, "Oh, do you have a card?" And I said, "Yeah, sure." I gave her my creed, and it was the printed version of it. Then she said, "Oh my gosh. This is awesome." I said, "Oh, thanks. You know, they call me 'MR. AWESOME.'" She goes, "Wow, we can really use you for our company." And I said, "Really?" She says, "Yeah. How much do you charge?" And I'm not sure why I said this but I said, "Oh, I'm not sure that you can afford me." So that's what I said to her. I don't know why, but it just came out. Then she said, "Oh, I think I can." Brian, she turned out to be the HR Department for a little company called Johnson and Johnson.

Brian: Oh, okay then. Yeah, she can afford you.

Erik: Yeah, yeah. You know, she said, "How much do you charge?" Back then I charged $7,000 for the 30 or 60-minute talk. So you know, what I told her is $12,000, and so that's what came out of my mouth. I don't know why.

Brian: Yeah.

Erik: And you what she said back? "That's all?"

Brian: Nice.

Erik: No, I charge a few less. So I'm not saying use this for evil. Use it for good, right But that's my creed. I say it to myself during morning.

Brian: Erik, we have so much to talk about. There's no way we will plow through all of these in only one hour. So let's move on to something a little bit different. You have a training program, Habitudes Training. Tell us a little bit about that.

Erik: Oh, sure. Yeah, it's called Secret Habitudes. What I do is I put together a combination of online training and coaching. We put together this awesome package. So what it is, is it includes about 10 years worth of our past seminars. I'm one of the founders and the CEO of Universal Seminars. So what we do is we put together these seminars for all the great speakers from Brian Tracy, Les Brown, and all the greats that we just mentioned. A lot of your guests, actually. I see you got pretty much all of our speakers that have spoken to your audience as well, which is fantastic. So what we've done is we put together a 10 years worth of live, unedited seminars that we record, whether it's audio or video, and that's included in this.

We also have something called "Conversations with Experts". It's really what you're doing right now with the radio show. We have experts in different fields that we interview, and it's a very conversational hour. It's a teleseminar that we do once a month. So we include that in it. Also, it also includes a whole year worth of Secret Habitudes Training that I go through with them in each of these 50 different topics of the Secret Habitudes. Then the second year will be actually the *Sales Habitudes* which is my next book that's coming out, and will be published in about three more weeks. So I'm really excited about that. And then lastly, is it includes a ticket to one of our events throughout the nation, whatever event you want to go to. I'm sharing the stage with Loral Langemeier from *The Secret* and *The Millionaire Maker*, and Sharon Lechter, *Think and Grow Rich for Women*. Her new book just came out. Les Brown is sharing the stage with me, as well as Kevin Harrington, one of the original Shark Tank cast members and myself.

Brian: Right.

Erik: We'll be in Miami at the end of the year, so I'm really excited about that.

Brian: That's wonderful. So let's talk a little bit about the *Sales Habitudes* book that's going to be coming out in just a few weeks. Tell us about that.

Erik: Absolutely. What I've done is I took all of the trainings that I've been doing for years in sales for sales organizations, where I speak to big organizations and companies—we help them with their sales teams. We also go through ideas on goal setting techniques, time management skills, prospect and closing skills, handling objections, attitude, the whole nine yards. So we go through all those things, and the book is a combination of all that training. We call them *Sales Habitudes.*

Brian: One thing that you talk about that I love, and was actually very profound, is the rule of 30. A lot of people can't even adequately give 5 or 10 reasons why someone should work with them. You advocate that someone should have 30 reasons to tell someone why they should work with you. That just builds a lot more confidence all the way around, doesn't it?

Erik: Absolutely, yeah. and it's a habit. We're all habitual, and what habit is bringing you either up or down? So we need to identify those. One of the things that I needed to go work on was to convince myself before I convince somebody else to use my product or service. So years back one of my manager's challenged me to come up with 5 or 10 reasons why someone should work with us, and I just kept on going. I said, I'm going to produce 30 reasons why someone should work with me. Then it expanded into 30 reasons why someone should use that product or service, in general. I took a bank page and wrote all of those reasons in the first column. The second column was 30 reasons why they should use our company to provide that product or service. Then the third column was actually why they should use me as a representative. So I had literally 90 major reasons why—some of them overlapped, of course, but it was really cool. Then I started asking my clients to give me their answers. So that was really profound all on its own, because what I did, Brian, was I combined that into a referral gathering and testimonial gathering experience in that appointment. So let me explain that if I have time here.

Brian: Sure.

Erik: What I would do is this: I wanted to build my 30 lists, so 30 reasons why someone should work with me. So I simply emailed and called some of my existing clients for the last year or two or three.

And I would call them and say, "Hey, Joe, it's Erik Swanson. I wanted to touch base with you, first of all find out how you're doing and just do a little follow up. Maybe I can swing by next Thursday. Would that work for you?" "Sure. Come on over, Erik. No problem."

So I go over there, we sit down, and I literally blamed the whole appointment on the fact that I'm producing these 30 lists and I would love to have his or her information as to why they love working with us. So right there was the testimonial. Then I would turn to them and say this, "Wow, Joe, that's amazing. I really appreciate that. I never thought about that one area that you're talking about as a benefit of using our services. That's fantastic. I'd love to share that with other prospects and clients of mine. Do you mind if I do that? In fact, would you mind if we did maybe a 30 or 45 second quick video testimonial where we will highlight you and your company, XYZ company here. Then, you introduce yourself, your company, and then who you are, and then introduce the fact that you went through us and you really loved us and the reasons why." And they said, "No problem."

So we did that, and then I would always ask for referrals. I always start off by saying, "By the way, I wouldn't be doing my job if I didn't ask you for some referrals. Then I would highlight them right there and compliment them right in front of them. I would say, "Joe, you being a progressive thinker that you are obviously, you know a lot of people that we can work with and we could assist just like we're assisting you. Could you think of maybe two companies?" I always ask for two. That's the key that I always do because I figure they will say, "Oh, yeah." Sometimes they'll give me two or three but for the most part they'll at least give you one.

Brian: Sure.

Erik: So I got a 50/50 chance right there. So that's what I would do.

Brian: That is really clever. I love how you spin that around. Anyone listening, please, go ahead and use that strategy. That is really, really great. You're asking someone to help them by asking them what you like about working with us. Then you spin that around and say, would you be willing to provide a testimonial, and then you ask for a referral. Of course, pre-requisite to all of these is that you did a really great job with them in the first place. That's one thing that Jeffrey Gitomer talked with me about on my show is that people tend to ask for referrals at the wrong time. They tend to ask way too soon before they have a chance to experience what you would do for them.

Erik: Yeah, Jeffrey Gitomer—you definitely have to ask the right way and in the right time. You know a lot of people ask too soon. Timing is huge, Jeffrey is awesome in all of that.

Brian: Yeah. Absolutely.

Erik: It's ironic to bring up Jeffrey's name because he just sent me over a testimonial for my new *Sales Habitudes* book. So I'm really excited about that too.

Brian: That's great. He did a really awesome testimonial for my show, too, so I'm very excited about that. Let me ask you about how you use social media because I know you are very active on social media. In fact, in your

Habitudes book you make it a priority to introduce yourself to seven new social media contacts every day, is that right?

Erik: Absolutely. What I do is I connect with a minimum of seven social media contacts per day. I get out of the copy and paste situation. So I just want to make that clear for your audience that I'm not talking about just doing a blanketed email to seven new people and just send it out to everyone. You have to actually take 15-20 minutes each day, and introduce yourself. Find out a little bit more about them, stop trying to sell them, but actually ask them how you can assist them in building up their business, and that will just help you out tremendously.

Brian: Yes, and come to it from a point of service, how can I help you in your business? I know that both of us have been around Greg Reid. That's one of the things that he is so huge on is asking, "So how can I serve you?" And anytime I meet someone who's connected with him, that question always comes up. And I think "Okay, I know who you're hanging around with", which is really cool. That just validates everything. When you know that people are associated with other people that you are already good with, that just makes everything better. I love that.

Erik: Without a doubt. Greg's one of my close friends and he's just tremendous. If you don't know Greg Reid you need to know him. And by the way, I always tell him that he should work for missing persons because he knows everyone.

Brian: Yeah. He's referred some really great guests to my show and he's been on here twice. Let's talk about the power of rewards and awards. You do something pretty interesting in your company. You reward your employees in a pretty unique way.

Erik: Yeah, actually, can I back up and tell you just another thing about what we we're just talking about a second ago? I've got another technique.

Brian: Yeah.

Erik: So, this is a great technique I have for your audience. Look for what I call the elephant list, okay? The elephant list is those people that you actually want to meet and you want to get to know them. Maybe you're an acquaintance somewhat but you really want to get to know them, for example, in our world it's always great speakers, Les Brown and Greg Reid, even Jeffrey Gitomer and so forth. So what I do is this, without them even asking me, I go ahead and I read their book or I take a look at their blog, or look at their company and see what they've done. Then I'll do a video testimonial for them without them even asking me. Then I'll send it over to them and I'll say, "Hey, I just wanted to highlight you. I'm really excited about, what you're doing out there and how you're serving others and I wanted to serve you by just letting you know that." So do a really nice, professional two-minute or three-minute video highlighting them and giving them a huge testimonial. That's what I've been doing, and it's awesome.

Brian: Wow. It's really amazing.

Erik: And then what I did, I trained one of my coaching clients. I told him to do this. He's been asking how he can get literally on stage at certain places at certain events. So I said, "Well, you know, what you should do is make an award for that person." Another really unique way that I reward employees, for example, is I literally make a special day for them. So if they've done a great job and so forth then we will surprise him, and everyone say, "It's Joe's day" today. So we're all high-fiving Joe, we're sending him pizza, we're taking him out to lunch. We're doing all these things for Joe. We've got balloons that say Joe. Every single parking spot out front is Joe's parking spot. He can park anywhere. It doesn't matter. We'll actually valet park his car for him.

Brian: Wow.

Erik: And if that's the first year that we do that, then that day—let's say it's May 12— that day every year is Joe's day. So actually, Joe was our first employee that we did this with in Houston, Texas. He was really excited about it, so we continued it with a lot of other people too.

Brian: That's really great. Let's talk about Universal Seminars. This is your seminar company. You get really amazing speakers and you have really great events. You speak all over United States and Canada and you get amazing people. So tell us how that all got started.

Erik: Sure. I was not getting on the stages that I wanted to be on, so I decided to build my own baseball field. That's it. Did that make sense? It's called positioning.

Brian: Yeah.

Erik: And I decided if I'm not able to speak on that stage or this stage, I said, okay, well, you know what, I'm going to bring together a bunch of audience members who want to hear from these speakers, and then I'm going to call the speakers. So eventually, I had—now, please don't tell anyone this, okay? And stop recording this because it's a secret.

Brian: All right.

Erik: I had about 500 individuals already signed up for an event and I did not actually have the speakers yet. So I said, look, we put together this event and I said we're going to have some amazing speakers and they had no idea who it was. Then I called all the speakers. Then I said, "Look, you know, here are the 500 people, they've already signed up, they're excited to see you, will you come over?" And they said, "Okay, Erik, let's do it." So that's how we started. This is a good 10 years, 12 years ago. And ever since we've been doing it throughout the nation, usually in a new city every month or two. We're in a different city each time, and we've been doing it for years

and years. We do this in Canada as well, and that's how I decided to set up Universal Seminars, so that I could share a lot more stages with the people that I really wanted to share stages with. Now the way we pick our speakers, we've had that kind of flip in a positive way. We're now speakers, major speakers, are looking at us saying, "Hey, how do I get on your stage?" So we've got somewhat of a waiting list now. As you do too, man. Do you know how hard it was to get on your show here, Brian? It took me two years.

Brian: Yeah, I'm booked out for quite a while, so that's the power of getting something going and having the word spread. So I really appreciate that, and I'm really glad you're here and you're welcome to come back any time for sure. You definitely are someone that I want to repeat up here on the show for sure.

Erik: Oh, thanks, man. Well, we got a lot to talk about too. I want to chime in and say this as well, Brian, that positioning yourself with what I call lateral referral marketing is huge. That's what you and I are. Meaning, I've got the live, in person 500-600 people show up in each of our event throughout the nation, right?

Brian: Yeah.

Erik: You have the live audience that's on your radio show. So what I do is I love connecting with people like yourself when I put on my promoter hat on right now, let's say. I say to myself, "Okay, well, I want to work with you and you want to work with me. Let's go ahead and refer back and forth." Where if you say, "Hey, I want— "and I call it the elephant list or the 30 list as well. Give me 30 people that you would love to interview and that have already shared my stages and I'll introduce you to them. It's just like Greg Reid when he passes referrals around. I'll do the same for you and you do the same for me, you know.

Brian: That's nice. That's perfect.

Erik: It's really, really a win-win.

Brian: When Greg was on my show I had mentioned during a break that I had this wish list of people that I'd love to interview. He says, "Send it over to me." I said, "Okay, that's great." He's referred a few people from that list. So, yeah, I'll definitely do that for you. That's great.

Erik: I want to just mention something. The reason why I mentioned that to your audience right now is not because of you and I, but for them to take that same principle and use it in their industry.

Brian: Absolutely.

Erik: So it's huge.

Brian: Yeah, align with someone whose interests are the same as yours, but whose referral list may have some overlap and just exchange referrals with each other or exchange contacts with each other. You never know where that's going to go. That's excellent, so glad you brought that up. So let me ask you this: You are very well connected to some really amazing people as I am, how do you go about meeting and connecting with high profile people?

Erik: Just call me or call Greg, we know everyone. But I just call them. I send out a quick email introduction and letting them know that I'd love to touch base with them and we have a lot of audience members who would absolutely love hearing from them as well, so always give them that compliment. That's what I do. I can't give them all my trade secrets, by the way.

Brian: Right.

Erik: But actually, if you have a wish list, send it over my way as well and I'll do the same thing that we were just talking about a second ago. What I do—and I want to share this idea if I have time still.

Brian: Yup.

Erik: What I do is this. I have that same principle whenever I'm in front of a group, when I'm training them one-on-one, or one-on-two, or one-on-a-thousand. If somebody comes up to me and says, "Wow, I just read this book, you know. I absolutely love Bob Burg". Let's say, somebody just told me that the other day. And I said, "Oh, really?" And I hear them out, they say, "Yeah, he's changed my life." I said, "Wow, do you know him that well?" And they said, "No, no, I don't know him at all. I've read all of his books. The referral marketing book is great. Then I said, "Wow, let's introduce you." And they said, "Wow, that would be great."

Brian: Yeah.

Erik: I say, "Great, do you have a second?" And I called them right there, and with speakers we always answer each other's phone calls, and introduce him, right there. You make that person's day completely. I've done this with so many different people and it just really, really resonates with them and, you know. You send somebody else out of that meeting, they're on cloud 9.

Brian: I love how easy and straightforward your answer was, I just call them, I just email them. Some people have this real mystical woo woo about meeting someone that they would deem to be very, very important or very, very high profile. It's almost like some people think these really high profile people are unreachable, untouchable. It's not the case. In fact, I've heard it on some of my show several times, I think Greg is probably the one who said this most—the people who are the most successful are actually the ones that are the most accessible. They make themselves available because they want to share.

Erik: Exactly. Yeah.

Brian: And I love that.

Erik: I got a buddy by the name of Steve Schiffman. Steve answers his phone calls, 100% of the time, he answers his phone calls. He doesn't let the assistant grab it. He's a famous speaker as well. These people are very approachable, if you will.

Brian: Exactly.

Erik: And here's another thing that I've started doing. I'll share this with you. It's a secret, by the way, Secret Habitudes, right?

Brian: Right.

Erik: They're secrets because nobody does them. It's so weird but what I do is this: I send thank you notes in advance. You can use this in so many areas of your business. So, I send a thank you note in advance. I sent one to Frank Shankwitz, the founder of Make-A-Wish Foundation, pretty huge, right? Huge association. I never thought that I could get in touch with this guy, but I sent him a thank you note in advance, just saying, "Frank, just wanted to thank you so much for this nice lunch that we had over there in Arizona and what a tremendous gentleman you are and I'm really excited about working with you in the future. P.S. Lunch is on me. When can we meet?"

Brian: Nice.

Erik: And it works. This stuff works.

Brian: We've got three minutes till the end. So let me ask you the question that I ask everybody. Who inspires and motivates you?

Erik: Brian Wright. That's who inspires and motivates me. So, I will answer the question this way. This is good that I have about two more minutes to answer this way because it's really important the way I'm going to preface this. There's a guy name Matthew McConaughey. He's an actor.

No, he's not the one that inspires me the most. But he said one time at an award ceremony—now, I don't care if you love Matthew McConaughey or you don't like the actor. It doesn't matter to me. But he said something very poignant one time as a thank you to an award, he said, "I aspire to be me in five years, in ten years. I can't wait to meet that mentor that's going to inspire me. And what I mean by that is I cannot wait to meet me five years from now because of the combination of people that I've been meeting and learning from their journey, and serving them and them serving me as well. It's just going to be an amazing mentor when I'm me five years, ten years from now." So I aspire to be myself in a better, better, better way.

Brian: All right. You're looking forward to meeting the new and improved version of you down the road. That's awesome.

Erik: Exactly.

Brian: So one last time. How can we get your book? How can we connect with you, Erik?

Erik: Sure. My book *Sales Habitudes* is coming out soon. You can go to universalseminars.com for the book, and that has a lot more information there. If anyone wants to have me speak to their association or group, I'd love to. I'll even give you a huge discount because I know Brian. So they can go to my personal site which is speakererik.com. And I just locked down one new site called mrawesomeworld.com. I thought that will be catchy.

Brian: Okay. That's great, and we are at the end. Thank you so much, Erik, for being on the show. I know you've got a busy evening ahead of you. You're speaking at an event right after the show is over with. So I'm so thankful that you took the time to speak with me and my audience today. Take care everyone. Goodbye.

DR. JOHN DEMARTINI

THE LAW OF ATTRACTION

Brian: Hello and welcome to Success Profiles Radio. I'm your host Brian K Wright and it is a pleasure to be here with you today. I am honored that you chose to spend part of your day with me here, and this is going to be a fantastic show.

My guest this week is Dr. John Demartini, let me tell you a little bit about him.

Dr. Demartini is considered one of the world's leading authorities on human behavior and personal development. He is the founder of the Demartini Institute, a private research and education organization with a curriculum of over 75 courses covering multiple aspects of human development.

His trademarked methodologies in human development, the Demartini Method and the Demartini Value Determination are culminations of over 44 years of cross-disciplinary research and study and utilized in all human development industries across the world.

Dr. Demartini travels 360 days a year to countries all over the world where he shares his research and findings in all markets and sectors. He is the author of 40 books published in 31 different languages. He has produced over 70 CDs and DVDs covering subjects such as development in relationships, wealth, education and business. He has created over 75 different courses; the most advanced of which is a 21-year correspondence course. Each program is designed to assist people to activate leadership and empower all seven areas of their lives including financial, physical, mental, vocational, spiritual, family and social.

Dr. Demartini was also one of the featured experts in "The Secret" which I referenced earlier.

I am so excited to introduce as my guest this week, Dr. John Demartini. John, are you there?

Dr. Demartini: I am, and thank you for allowing me to be on today.

Brian: You are welcome, it is an absolute pleasure! The first thing I do with all of my guests is I ask them what their background is. Certainly you have had an amazing journey. I've read about it on your website. So tell us what your journey was like, what you've learned, what you've overcome, maybe some things we can take from that.

Dr. Demartini: Well, without too long a response I would say that I was challenged as a child with learning problems. I ended up dropping out of school at a young age and living on the streets for a few years—about 4 years—and then nearly dying when I was 17, almost 18. I was blessed as a result of getting through that ordeal, meeting an amazing teacher named Paul C. Bragg, who truly inspired me one night at a little talk, and inspired me to believe that just maybe I could be intelligent and that I might be able to return to school. That night in that one hour with that one message by that one man, my life turned. I had a dream that night to do what I am doing today, and now that's 45 years later. And here I am getting to fulfill that dream, which is traveling the world and researching, and doing what I love most to teach and to inspire the people to do something amazing with their lives.

Brian: That's wonderful! Now if I read correctly on your website, were you born with a physical disability, or were you dyslexic, or had some learning challenges like you alluded to before?

Dr. Demartini: Yes, I was born with my hand and foot turned in, and had to wear braces as a child. I begged my Dad to let me out of those when I turned 4. He said if I promised to keep my hand and foot straight, he would let me try it. But if they go crooked again, you've got to put them back on. When I got out of those braces, I felt free for a moment. I just wanted to run and be free. I guess I've been on the run ever since.

Then when I got into 1st grade, I was told by my teacher in front of my parents, "I'm afraid your son's got learning problems—dyslexia—and I don't think he's going to be able to read or write or communicate, go very far, or do very much or amount to anything in life." So I had a challenging start, but I was fortunate enough to learn how to ask questions to the smartest kids and I picked up enough information to make it partly through elementary school. It wasn't until we moved from Houston, Texas to Richmond, Texas that I didn't have a smart group of kids, and I started failing and then dropped out of school.

Brian: There's a really important lesson there. You made the choice to ask some of the older smarter kids, so you were seeking mentors at a very early age.

Dr. Demartini: Well, I would say that the quality of your life speaks to the quality of the questions you ask, and if you ask extraordinary questions you lead yourself to an extraordinary life. I was blessed! It was just like Richard Branson in that he had the same kinds of learning challenges. He ended up asking other people to help him, and now he runs 300-400 companies because he gets other people to assist him. He realized his strength, and he delegated other strengths. I guess I've been blessed to do the same.

Brian: Exactly, and one thing that comes up over and over again on this show is that if you know what you're good at and what you're not good at, delegate the stuff you're not good at. That just makes you look smarter and makes your organization run a lot more efficiently. Does that sound accurate?

Dr. Demartini: Absolutely, you are right on the money! I would say the key is to identify what's truly most important, most inspiring, and most meaningful to you and prioritize your life in such a way that if you fill your day with high priority things it doesn't get distracted by low priority things. Then delegate and give yourself permission to do something extraordinary while assisting other people in doing the same.

Brian: Yeah, and it's OK not to be the smartest person in the room.

Dr. Demartini: Well I know that in certain areas I may have some degree of intelligence, and in other areas I'm quite ignorant, and those areas I delegate. I haven't driven a car in 24 years, so I have delegation to other people to drive. I've found that's a lot smarter.

Brian: Wow, that's great! So what got you interested in human development? This is such an amazing field, and there's a lot of work being done, and you're right there at the forefront of it. How did you get interested in this?

Dr. Demartini: When I met Paul C. Bragg, who was the gentleman I met when I was 17 years old, a week before my 18th birthday. He was such an inspiring individual. His life impacted many people from Steve Jobs to Luther Burbank to William Kellogg to Donald Trump, even Jack Lalanne. The list goes on and on. I was blessed to meet him, and he said we had a body, mind, and soul. The body must be guided by the mind, the mind must be directed by the soul to maximize who we are. He said that whatever our innermost thought, our innermost dominant vision, our innermost dominant feeling and affirmation is what our life becomes. We must set goals for ourselves, our family, our community, our city, our state, our nation, and our world for 100-120 years and beyond. He gave me some great gems that really shifted my life. So I guess I'd have to say you have to put your hand in the pot of glue of a great mind. That was very instrumental in inspiring me to do what I'm doing today. If it wasn't for a woman who found me sick in my tent and for him, I might not be alive today.

Brian: You said that you've learned some very important lessons. How about giving us one? What's one of the greatest lessons you've learned that you've carried with you throughout your life that maybe we can implement?

Dr. Demartini: Well, every human being lives by a set of priorities, a set of values—things that are most important to least important in their life. Whenever they are doing things that are high in their values, they tend to excel. Whenever they are doing things that are low in their values, they tend to not excel. Identifying what is truly most important—that highest value—and organizing your life, and you might say structuring and strategizing your life to fulfill that, you don't need any outside motivation to do that. You're inspired from within to live the fulfillment of the highest value. But you need motivation, too, from without to do anything lower. So identifying what that is is crucial, and that very highest value is called "telos" by the ancient Greeks, and is the foundation of teleology, meaning and purpose in life. It's also the foundation of ontology, the study of our own being, and epistemology, the study of knowing. So any time we are living by our highest values, we know ourselves and give ourselves permission to be ourselves, and we will end of loving ourselves.

Brian: I love the idea of giving yourself permission to be yourself, and giving yourself permission to live to your highest values. We're with Dr. John Demartini, one of the world's leading experts in human behavior and personal development.

What I want to do next is talk about Dr. Demartini's work in *The Secret*. He was in the book and the movie. For anyone who is not familiar with this project or has lived under a rock for the last few years, it's about the Law Of Attraction, like attracting like. So Dr. Demartini, tell us about the Law Of Attraction and what it really represents and what we should be getting from that.

Dr. Demartini: I ask people in seminars around the world, how many of you have gone to pick up a telephone and call somebody, and right as you are about to dial, they found that they were on the phone? Most people put their hand up, and they've had these synchronicities. I commonly say that your innermost dominant thought becomes your outermost tangible reality. But there is a factor that I think is wise to include. As I said earlier, we all have a set of values, and whenever we set goals that are aligned and congruent with our highest values, we have the highest probability of seeing opportunities with our senses, and acting on those opportunities with our motor functions, and having a higher degree of synchronicity. But whenever we set goals that are not ours, but are injected goals and values from other people that we may be subordinating to, we have a decreasing probability. So one of the variables that I think are important is, how important it is to set goals that are truly ours—truly meaningful to us—to increase the probability of the synchronicities where people, places, things, ideas, and events are more synchronously brought into our lives to help fulfill what is most inspiring.

Brian: That's great, now some people think about the Law Of Attraction, and if they read the book they think about attracting money but they think there is something Zen-like about it, or they believe that if you just think it, it will just happen. You HAVE to take some action to do that. So, what is it that causes some people to do very well financially and others maybe not so much?

Dr. Demartini: I ask people also as I travel how many of them want to be financially independent, and I can be in front of 1000 people or more, and they will all put their hands up. And then I'll ask how many ARE financially independent, and most of the hands will go down unless I'm in an executive leadership program. What I explain is I have them write down the 10 things that they would do if they had $10 million cash, and most people will write down that they would spend their money on consumables and depreciables, and use up that money. Very few people will write down that they would put it into certain investments and double it. So what happens is each person has a set of values as I've said, and the hierarchy of their values dictates their financial destiny. And if they don't have a true value on serving people— which is a source of income—and learning about managing money, and the art of saving and investing money, then the probability is that they will be consumers and depreciable buyers, instead of appreciable investors. The key is to make sure you really value serving, value money, and value living and having wealth. Many people think they do and have a fantasy about doing it, but they don't have the true value that it takes. Money circulates through the economy from those who value it least to those who value it most. Money circulates through the economy from where it is managed with the most disorder to the most order. So whoever has the most value on it, learns about it, studies it, manages it wisely brings order to it, and invests it so it works for them instead of them becoming a slave to it.

Brian: So it's really about respecting money and respecting what it means to you, and actually having a really good handle on what it means to you—if it's something that you use to serve other people instead of using money.

There's a slight shift but there's a real profound difference there. Does that make sense?

Dr. Demartini: Yes, whenever you're living consciously according to your highest values, you feel the most fulfillment. When you do, you embrace pain and pleasure in the pursuit of a great purpose. Whenever you're NOT fulfilling your highest values and attempting to live somebody else's values, because of the unfulfillment you seek immediate gratification, and immediate gratification costs people money, but long term vision builds wealth.

As Warren Buffet did literally before he was 11 years old, he read every book in the Omaha, Nebraska, Library on wealth building and financial matters. That means he had a really high value on building wealth, and people who truly are going to be wealthy are going to study it and learn the art and science and philosophy of wealth building. But most people will live in a fantasy that they're going to get wealthy by miraculously going to their mailbox and expecting a million dollar check. My experience is the people that I know who are very wealthy—and I've been blessed to meet many multi-millionaires and billionaires—is that they work. They're dedicated to serving a vast number of people. When I ask multi-millionaires, and I've never met anyone who was a multi-millionaire who didn't have the ability to build a business that served vast numbers of people, that they also work at managing that business to make sure it made profits. Then they make sure that they saved and invested their money, and then they learned the art of accumulating it so they could do great things with it, and they had a cause for it—a cause that they could contribute to society for. When they put those 6 things into operation, they increase the probability of building wealth. The hierarchy of your values dictates your financial destiny, and if you truly don't have a value on wealth building, the probability of you building wealth is pretty low. The key is to make sure you're not lying to yourself about what's really important, and not confusing the desire to live a fancy lifestyle of the rich and famous with actually methodically building lasting wealth because they're not the same.

Brian: That certainly does make a lot of sense. I know in *The Secret* there was a discussion about health and how the Law Of Attraction can really help us to heal. Do you think there is an equal application there? What about someone who has been blessed with great health versus someone who has chronic health issues? What would you say about the Law Of Attraction as it relates to health?

Dr. Demartini: We don't want to exclude genetic backgrounds or environmental factors, but with all those things, without a doubt if somebody is living purposely and living inspired, their immune system, their epigenetic component is maximized. And whenever they are not, and they are feeling like they are banging their head against the wall trying to be somebody they're not, and trying to go after goals that are not really truly meaningful to them, they run into a low resiliency, a low adaptability factor which activates the autonomic nervous system and decreases the probability of having their immune maximally function. So the key is to make sure you're living authentically, living an inspired life, "tap dancing to work" as Warren Buffet said, doing what you love, delegating lower priority activities to increase the probability of having your immune system rally and do its natural job of normalizing physiology.

Brian: I am personally curious about this. Anytime I interview who has done something such as *The Secret* or getting to blog on Yahoo or Forbes, or do something that is relatively high-profile, I usually like to ask "How did this particular opportunity come to you? Did Rhonda Byrne seek you out? Did you hear about it and ask about it? What is it that brought this opportunity specifically to you?

Dr. Demartini: That was around 2006 or 2007, and I had a telephone call to our office from Rhonda stating that she was planning on doing a film called *The Secret*, and asked if there was any way I would be willing to be a part of that. I said "Tell me more about it", and everything about it sounded intriguing. And I said I was involved in the Transformational Leadership

Council that Jack Canfield initiated back in 2005, and I would be at that location on the date you are requesting. There will be a whole bunch of other educators there. She said she was aware of those people, and that's where she was headed. I said I would be there so why don't we get all done there. It turns out that she had 33 noted personal development specialists at one location, so she was able to interview 33 people in a matter of days, she worked day and night on this, and we were all in one location in Aspen, Colorado. We were there for a gathering to share ideas about how we could make a greater difference in the world.

Brian: That's wonderful, and I also wanted to ask—just knowing what I know about you and you do come from a place of serving, and you did say earlier about serving a massive number of people—from a branding perspective, projects like this can really catapult someone's business. Did you find that this project raised your profile exponentially and give you a greater platform to serve people as your mission is?

Dr Demartini: Well I speak pretty extensively. I was speaking before I got involved in *The Secret* I was speaking on average about 350 speeches a year. But that next 2 years I think we went over 400, then it dropped back down. Right now, I'm at around 350-360 and this year maybe 380 speeches, so it did definitely have a little bit of a spike. It did have a lingering effect with opportunities. I just had a call from St Petersburg, Russia, this morning asking me to present there, and it's because of *The Secret*. So there has definitely been a boost from it, and I am very grateful for that, but I can't say it was the only factor because I have been doing it for many years. This is my 45th year in speaking.

Brian: Wow! Well, it certainly has brought you a different audience, and an audience that had not been exposed to you before. We've been talking to Dr. John Demartini, author of many books and one of the featured experts in the book and movie *The Secret*.

He has a proprietary methodology called The Demartini Method. In my understanding, it's a very specific methodology based on your years of research to help people break through personal and business obstacles, and the process of helping people let go and moving forward. Is that a fairly accurate assessment of what this is about?

Dr. Demartini: Yes, that's great. I've been working on this since I was 18, and clinically been working on it for nearly 29 years with clients and attendees. What it basically is, as I stated earlier, is that the quality of our lives is based on the quality of the questions we ask. So the method is literally a very concise and precise set of questions that help awaken our mind to the hidden order of our daily events in such a way that we end up with gratitude and love in our heart, and certainty and presence on our mind. So it's basically a specific set of questions that allow us to see the other side of the equation that we don't see when we have emotional baggage, or when we have an event in our lives that we are upset about. It allows us to see things on the way, not in the way, see things as instructive, not obstructive, so we can become masters of our destiny and not victims of our history. It allows us to open our heart to life and to ourselves, and to the world around us, in a way that we are grateful. I was born on Thanksgiving Day in America, and I believe that is something to be grateful for. When we count our blessings, we get more to be grateful for. So the method is designed to leave a person in a state of awe and gratitude for whatever has happened in their life by allowing them to see the hidden order that's there.

Brian: That's great! On your website, you say that this is a tool that with 1000 uses. That makes it sound like a very comprehensive tool. I know you alluded to this just a little bit ago, but what are some of the specific things that people out there are hurting or have a painful past about? What are some things that this methodology can be used to help us with?

Dr. Demartini: First of all in our intellect, as far as our mental development, this tool is being used in educational settings. There are thousands of teachers in various countries who implement this for kids and even educators. It's helping students be "present" in the class where they're not manic or depressed, but they're present and living what's truly valuable to them, and linking whatever their curriculums are to whatever is truly highest on their values so they have awakening of their genius that's inside that every child has. So this method is used for education and activating genius and potential in children. Also, it's involved in honoring their individual values. Many times parents or teachers will autocratically—not democratically—impose values onto the children, and put labels on children, and end up medicating them because they don't know the art and science of respecting those values, and communication those values, and linking curriculums to those values. So that's one area.

In business, it has many applications: conflict resolution, overcoming phobias, sales intimidation factors. Any time there's shame or guilt about not living up to expectations or quotas, any time there is an anxiety about accomplishing within timetables, conflicts between anybody in business or departments in business.

Then there are areas in financial matters. It helps re-arrange value structures to assist people in really truly valuing money instead of fantasizing about it. It assists in maintaining a center instead of unstable or volatile emotions. It's a powerful tool allowing you to have self-governance. I commonly say if you are elated or depressed, you won't manage money. You'll do foolish things with it when you have extreme emotions, but you'll do amazing things with it when you have objective strategy. And the method allows you to maintain strategy with focus.

When it comes to relationships, it's one of the most powerful tools in dissolving conflict. There's a company called Fairway Divorce Solutions that utilizes it now throughout Canada, and it helps mediate emotions so you can respect and appreciate the person for who they are. Everybody wants to be loved for who they are, and whoever they are is whatever they value most in life. Learning the art of communicating their values is a by-product of using the method—and also resolving conflicts, because whatever you see in others you have inside you, even though you may be too humble or too proud to own it. And this tool allows you to own traits that you may not be able to own. In society, in social leadership and empowerment, we use it to allow leaders in various fields. When people own the traits of the greats and realize whatever they see in others is inside themselves by this method, they give themselves permission to play in a new field of possibility. So as far as owning greatness, I would say there is nothing missing in the individual, it's just that there are traits we are not honoring because we are not acknowledging them. This tool allows you to honor and acknowledge those, and wake them up—and give yourself permission to awaken their greatness.

And then physiologically, it normalizes physiological states by changing perceptions, and through your perceptions and neuroendocrine functions and epigenetic functions, we alter cell energetics and genetic expressions. Many diseases are regressions of genetic expressions in the physiology. In fact, in Toronto we had a gentleman who had 5000 oncology patients who is now learning the tool with the pathologists there to incorporate into the oncology. So it's being used. Psychiatrists are using it, medical doctors, integrative specialists are using it.

So it has a wide application, and I have spent many years attempting to refine it and help as many people as possible, and I am so grateful. I just finished training another 85 individuals here in Australia on the method, and they come from all walks of life.

Brian: I love what you just said a little bit ago about owning traits that you didn't know you have, and awakening your greatness, and honoring your greatness. Sometimes if people are experiencing worthiness issues, that is probably a really great place for your method to help someone "wake up" the greatness that they didn't realize they have that they were God-given. Does that sound right?

Dr. Demartini: Absolutely! Whenever we perceive that what we are doing is supporting our highest values we tend to build ourselves up. When we do things that we think are challenging our highest values, we put ourselves down. We have this bi-polarity mechanism inside our mind where we exaggerate or minimize ourselves, or create a superiority complex or inferiority complex, a high self-esteem or a low self-esteem. But the oscillating emotions that each of those provide oscillate around a center which I call the true self-worth. The more we deviate from the true self-worth or the center, the more we end up losing ourselves within these illusions that we think are ourselves. And the key with the method is to integrate those two polarities and get centered, focused, and empowered, and every time we do we raise the potentiality of our self-worth and expand it. Our self-worth is a reflection of how well we are able to see both sides of our true-center synchronously, and knowing how to ask questions that equilibrate the mind and bring balance to the mind liberates us from the bondage of the emotional illusions that most often run our lives. The Demartini Method is a very profound tool on raising self-worth. In fact, we are doing a whole project just on that topic because of it.

Brian: Well, let me ask you something. When you bring two people together who are having a conflict that's not resolved, do you find it helpful that both parties experience this method together, or do you find that there's value in having each of them complete this process separately and THEN coming together and debriefing both of them?

Dr. Demartini: Well, I've had the opportunity to work in all different scenarios. I've mediated divorce issues where two people are in literally opposite ends of the hotel, and I've mediated right in seminar rooms where they're sitting next to each other. I've also mediated in a hospital room where they're right next to each other. It doesn't really matter. Even if I am working with one side, because of the quantum entanglement like effect that this method has, the other person gets affected and our interaction with them changes. Every human being wants to be loved and appreciated for who they are, not for those fantasies we impose or project onto them. And the moment we open our hearts to them for who they are, they open their hearts back. It's really quite amazing. They want to be loved for who they are, and when you do they turn into who we love.

When you're finished with the method, every time, like science, you will end up with appreciation and love for this person because you will see things you never saw before—a hidden order in their daily chaos—and you'll sit there humbled for how much significance they have in your life and how much they have contributed to your life, and all you want to do is say "Thank you. I now see your important role in my life, there are no mistakes in it. Thank you!" When you do that and people get that, they respond back with "thank you".

Brian: That's great! Like I mentioned to you previously, I had the opportunity to go through this process with my friend Lynn Hope Thomas, who is one of your facilitators, and I found it to be an absolutely amazing experience. So I want to ask, if there are people out there, such as coaches or authors or counselors who really want to make a difference in other people's lives, you mentioned just a bit ago that you do a training that teaches people how to go through this either for themselves or in a coaching role with other people. How can people get involved with you if they are interested in learning more about going through this themselves, or going through the training so they can learn how to impact people's lives?

Dr. Demartini: All they have to do is contact www.drdemartini.com. Most people who are getting involved in the Demartini Method come to one of the seminar programs I present titled *The Breakthrough Experience*, which is one of my signature programs that I do about 43 times a year in various countries around the world. I've had the opportunity to present it in over 60 countries now. After they come to this program where I introduce the method and let them learn it and experience it, many of them decide they would like to incorporate it into their toolkit. Some people want to do it professionally, so they come to the Demartini Method training certification program. Now

I've been blessed to do the training program in France, Tokyo, Johannesburg, London, Sydney, Houston and different places around the world. So we have thousands of people who are now assisting me around the world. I'm working on getting 100,000 facilitators around the world to assist me in various walks of life. But all they have to do is come to The Breakthrough Experience or contact my website and they can read and learn more about the method and the event.

Brian: My very special guest this week is Dr. John Demartini, featured in the book and movie *The Secret*, and creator of The Demartini Method of helping us resolve conflicts and moving on from our past and a whole host of other things that we talked about. Now my friend Lynn told me that she was at your training that you just completed, and she said "Dr. Demartini has this HUGE gratitude journal, you must ask about that!" So tell us about your gratitude journal, what you do with it, and maybe enlighten us as to how we can make journaling more effective experience in our growth and development.

Dr. Demartini: On November 18, 1972, I met Paul Bragg and I was asked by him to document what exactly it is that I want to dedicate my life to, what my purpose is and what goals I have. He is the one who started me on this journey because I started this book back then. So that's 45 years that I've been compiling and daily updating this special book. I wrote out exactly how I wanted my life. I frequently say "Start with what you know, and let what you know grow." And in there, I have a very concise highly refined mission statement and 4000 pages of goals and objectives. And I also have in there—and now many volumes, what she saw was one of many—a list of the gratitudes that I have on a daily basis, so the gratitudes are every single thing that I get to experience in a day. I was taught by an Eastern mystic who had 6 PhD's at age 35. He was a very wise gentleman, who said that if you go to bed at night and you can't say thank you for whatever has happened—no matter what it is—you obviously aren't seeing it through the eyes of truth. So look back again and don't go to sleep until you can see everything that has happened as something that is "on the way" not "in the way".

So what I did is I started documenting whatever happened in the day as something that I had the opportunity to experience, and in a sense, reframe it in such a way that I could say thank you for it, then I would document that. In each day, it could anywhere from 6 things to 60 things that I document what was blessed to do, people I had the opportunity to meet. In fact, being on your show is in that book already. I put everything in there that I get the opportunity to do that's helping me fulfill my mission. So far as I'm concerned, wisdom is looking at your life and saying "thank you", not another alternative, and seeing that no matter what's happening whether it's supportive or challenging, it's on the way. It's something to be thankful for even though you may not see it. It could a year or 5 years later, it could turn out a blessing, but why wait when you can look right now for how it's serving you? So it's how you see it, and I document my gratitudes every single day, and I've probably got the largest collection of gratitudes of anybody I know.

Brian: So do these expressions come in the form of words and pictures, cards…?

Dr. Demartini: All of the above. This morning I received a request to speak in Germany and another one in St Petersburg, Russia, I had an opportunity to do something in China and also in Cape Town, South Africa. Then I had a chance to be on this show, and I have Woman's Weekly after this. Then I have an opportunity to fly and meet some people in Adelaide, Australia. So every day I get opportunities to do inspiring things. I had the opportunity to write an article last night for a magazine, I had another one today for Jet Set magazine. So I just document what I get to do, who get to meet, pictures of things I get to do. So anything I get to do on a daily basis, I document. I like to accumulate those things because if you are grateful what you get to do, you get more to be grateful for.

Brian: Absolutely! That is key right there. The more you are thankful for things you get to do, then you get more things to be grateful for, That's great! Is there anything else you want to say about your gratitude journal that might be helpful or impactful for us?

Dr. Demartini: Everything I have in that book, I document everything that I set out to do and put metrics on them. As I accomplish them I document them because it's one thing to set a goal, and another thing to actually accomplish it and confirm it in a time frame. I also have a posthumous biography. I was in Rome in 1999 presenting The Breakthrough Experience, and I had an opportunity to tour the city afterwards. I came across a square where Giordano Bruno had a statue. They were honoring him 400 years after burning him at the stake. Before he was burned at the stake, he was a heretic at the time and now they were honoring him as a genius. He wrote a posthumous biography of how he wanted his life to be perceived 500 years in the future, and 400 years later what he had written became reality.

So that night I wrote a posthumous biography of how I want to be perceived 1000 years from now. In the process of doing that—it's about a 26 page thesis of exactly how I want to be remembered and what I want to accomplish, and how I would love people will describe my life. I am now amazed, most people will say they are immortal souls but they don't write immortal goals. They write goals with timeframes that are miniscule compared to what their power and potential is. I commonly say unless you have a goal that's beyond your life, you probably won't get beyond your own limitations. So you have to have a posthumous biography to have an immortal legacy, and I'm a believer in that. And just a few years ago, I had the opportunity to speak in Vienna Austria and at the Melk Abbey in Mel Austria, and after my speech I had the opportunity to have my writings and The Demartini Method put in scroll paper, and locked and stored for 1000 years in the Infinity of Divinity library room at the abbey.

So I am a firm believer that we set goals and we create our reality, but they have to be concise, clear, and meaningful and congruent to become real. So you have to be true and know yourself if you're going to write goals that beyond yourself.

Brian: Wow, that is mind-blowing! Your Demartini Method was written on a scroll and stored for 1000 years. That is amazing. To wrap your head around something like that was probably amazing for you when they told you they were doing that.

Dr. Demartini: It brought me tears of inspiration because it gave me confirmation of how time is an illusion of the human mind. The mind adds space and time to the soul, and the soul extracts space and time from the mind. Whenever we transcend the mind with clarity of the soul, the immortal expression emerges spontaneously and we are able to do extraordinary things. That's what I'm interested in doing in The Breakthrough Experience. That's what the Demartini Method is designed to do, to give people permission to do magnificent lives.

Brian: We've got about 3-4 minutes left until the end of the show, so you've got a book coming out in a couple months called *The Values Factor*. Let's talk very briefly about that.

Dr. Demartini: Well, *The Values Factor* is being published by Penguin Books, and it is distilling the essence behind our existence. The thing that drives human behavior is human values. So by creating a treatise together on human values, it gives people probably the greatest most concise summary of how values work in a person's life, and how to set goals that are congruent with that to maximize potential in all 7 areas of life: our spiritual quest, our mental development and genius, our career fulfillment, our wealth, our family dynamics and intimacy, our social leadership, and our physical health. I believe that is the cornerstone of how to live a masterful life and I believe that everybody deep inside wants to be extraordinary and make a massive difference and become masters. So this book will help them do that. It will give them tools, practical applications, to live congruently and live and inspired life.

Brian: We are coming closer to the end of the show, so I have to ask the question that I ask everybody: Who inspires and motivates you?

Dr. Demartini: Well, you know I don't need motivation from the outside because I am pretty inspired from within. But what I've done is I've stood on the shoulders of giants most of my life. I've learned that you can't put your hand in a pot of glue without some of the glue sticking. So I've basically read every Nobel Prize winner and their speech since 1901. I've studied all of the great philosophers in the West and most of the Eastern mystics. I've studied the greatest religious leaders of the world. I've studied the people who are the biggest business leaders, and I've gone through most of the greatest financial leaders past and present. I've also looked at social and political leaders—anyone that has left any mark in history, I've tried to devour their biographies, look at their traits, own the traits, and stand on their shoulders and not live in their shadows. So they've all been mentors of mine. They've all inspired me, so I can't say there's any one. There are probably thousands involved in this.

Brian: OK, sounds great and one last time how can we get a hold of you and get involved with you, Dr. Demartini?

Dr. Demartini: The simple way to find out where I am and what I'm doing is to go to my website www.drdemartini.com or go to my Facebook page. By the way, they can download the Value Determination process to help identify what is truly important to them. There's tons of information on my website: radio shows, television shows, media, articles. There's so much there. Maybe they can join me for an evening event or maybe just chat and have a meal.

Brian: Sounds great, any final parting words of wisdom you'd like to share with us?

Dr. Demartini: No matter what a person has done or not done, they are worthy of love, and that if they don't see things ON the way they'll see it IN the way. It's wise to master the art, either through the Demartini Method or some other means, to help them see that no matter what they've done or not done, it's still part of their pathway and to be grateful for it. And know that the magnificence of who they are is greater than any fantasy they may impose on themselves, and give themselves permission to be themselves. If they do, they'll do extraordinary things on planet Earth.

Brian: That's great, it was absolutely wonderful, Dr. Demartini, having you on Success Profiles Radio this week. Thank you so much for being generous with your time and taking to us. I know you've got a plane to catch, and I want to thank all of you listening to the show this week!

LORAL LANGEMEIER

THE MILLIONAIRE MAKER

Brian: Hello and welcome to Success Profiles Radio. I'm your host Brian K Wright and it is an absolute pleasure to be here with you today. I am honored that you chose to spend part of your day with me here, and this is going to be a amazing show.

My guest this week is Loral Langemeier. Let me tell you a little bit about her.

Loral Langemeier is a money expert, sought after speaker, entrepreneurial thought leader, and best-selling author of five books who is on a relentless mission to change the conversation about money and empower people around the world to become millionaires.

The CEO and Founder of Live Out Loud, Inc.—a multinational organization—Loral shares her best advice without hesitation or apology. What sets her apart from other wealth experts is her innate ability to hone in on the skills and talents of everyday people to inspire them to generate wealth. She has created, nurtured, and perfected a 3-5 year strategy to make millions for the "Average Jill and Joe", and to date, the company has served thousands of individuals worldwide and created hundreds of millionaires through wealth building education keynotes, workshops, products, events, programs, and coaching services.

Loral's straight talk electrifies audiences and inspires powerful action from live stages and television programs ranging from CNN, CNBC, The Street TV, Fox News Channel, Fox Business Channel-America's Nightly Scoreboard, The Dr. Phil Show and The View. She is a regular guest-host on The Circle in Australia and has been featured in articles in USA Today, The Wall Street Journal, The New York Times, Forbes Magazine and was also featured in the film *The Secret* which is a movie that I really appreciate very much.

We will discuss all of this and much more on today's show. With all of that in mind, here is my guest, Loral Langemeier. How are you today, Loral?

Loral: I'm good, Brian. How are you today?

Brian: I'm doing fantastic, thank you so much for asking. Here's the first question that I always ask everyone. Just tell us a little bit about your background, your backstory, how you got started, what you overcame, what brought you to where you are now.

Loral: I grew up in a big farm family in Nebraska. I grew up in a big "work hard" attitude, and you know "rich people aren't great people". We didn't have any money conversations, and at age 17, I was given a book by Dennis Waitley. He gave me *Think and Grow Rich*, and it changed my entire thinking about money. I finally felt like I found a conversation that made sense, and so I switched my degree from going to law school to getting a finance degree, and figuring out why so few people can become wealthy. And you know what's interesting today, Brian. The statistics are moving very quickly. There's rarely, if ever, been more than 10% of a nation that becomes millionaires, and what's interesting is there's a whole formula so I started on that pursuit. I got a private education, and learned nothing about what I teach today which is pure entrepreneurialism. Because really, schools teach us to go get jobs and have occupational thinking. So from there I actually got a Master's in Fitness Physiology, and I spent several years building fitness centers across the world for Chevron and Union Pacific, and different places. I took my finance degree and I statistically analyzed how unhealthy people were costing companies a fortune. And in 1996, I met Robert Kiyosaki and Sharon Lechter, and I joined the Rich Dad, Poor Dad team as the master game facilitator so I traveled all over world putting together those cash flow clubs for Robert and Sharon.

In 1999 I became a millionaire, and real estate was my specialty. Then in 2001, I started "Live Out Loud" because I really had defined the formula and was making millionaires. Then fast forward, I wrote *The Millionaire Maker* book, had five on the New York Times best seller list, another one's in the works, with Kevin Harrington who's the original shark on Shark Tank, and we have a book coming out next year. So a lot iss going on and it's very exciting. What I do different is that I teach people how to make money very quickly and become millionaires in 3-5 years, and we have a whole system for it. It's not like a hope and a prayer, pixie dust and sip Kool-aid like some things. It's true entrepreneurialism and investing so it's really fun.

Brian: That's really great. We definitely will touch on that a little bit later. What I find really interesting about your situation, and for the stories of some of the people who have been on my show, what they started doing is nothing like what they ended up doing. What was your big epiphany for you?

Loral: Being an entrepreneur was all in the backdrop, but I never have a lot of models, so I think the big epiphany for me was probably being around the whole Rich Dad advisor group, and I also became really good friends with Dan Kennedy, Keith Cunningham, and being in that group of people who were already millionaires. I became one during that time, and really watching from their lifestyles from how they live, to who they spend time with, and their conversations. Modeling is your fastest way to become an entrepreneur. There are a lot of entrepreneurial schools right now, but obviously the fastest way to change your relationship with money is hang out with people who have it (laughs).

Brian: That makes a whole lot of sense, I've read *The Millionaire Maker* several times and I also spent some time in Nebraska, I lived in Lincoln for a few years back in the late 80's and into the mid-90's. So what part of Nebraska were you in?

Loral: That's funny, I was still there too. So I grew up in Mead, Nebraska which is out in the middle of nowhere between Omaha and Lincoln and out by Fremont.

Brian: I've heard of that, believe it or not. Lot of great folks out there in Nebraska, I had to move to Arizona because I just felt there were more opportunities out here for me, and that turned out to be true. I loved Nebraska, and I wouldn't trade that time for anything in the world, but everything we do shapes us. So let me ask you this because I put a question on Facebook yesterday and mentioned that I will be interviewing somebody who creates a lot of millionaires, but I waited until today to reveal who my guest is going to be. But I sometimes solicit questions from people on Facebook and one of the questions that was brought up was, "What is your biggest mistake that you have figured out how to overcome in your career or in your life?" Or maybe the most memorable one. I know we've all made a slew of mistakes for sure.

Loral: I would say there's a bunch, probably different phases too. So early on, I would trust teammates on their word and not doing enough due diligence, and now I dig really really deep into the background. Because the biggest financial mistakes are taking bad partners who don't have what it takes when the time gets hot.

Brian: Yeah

Loral: In the recession of 2008, I had partners that I needed to run our company because I've raised the money. We had a lot of money on the line and they couldn't do it. There are a lot of good entrepreneurs, Brian, who can run a company when times are easy. But there's very few that can do it when heat is on, and you have to produce cash for it to micromanage every move the company makes for growth. I'm a master at that. But you know at that time, you know it's during 2008 to 2011, we did a good job of keeping it together with some partners who I needed to do a deeper dive or I should've taken them out. I should have voted them off the island sooner.

So we could've put in new teams and then held stuff together. So, some of my biggest mistakes was in the partnership of people. But you know what? I still do it. I still preach that today and I will always, because you cannot do this game alone. Meaning…anything! You can't run a company alone, you can't invest alone, you can't minimize risk alone. So you've got to come up with formula and I think some of the most strategic teaching that I do is "How do you pick partners?", "How do you document your deals?", "How do you do it?", And you don't do it from a book.

And I love them. I will always do them but I think it's some of the most rigorous learning and experience that people just hesitate, especially women—women really hesitate jump into that.

Brian: Sure! I love that you brought up due diligence because that's HUGE! And I know that a number of listeners are in startup phases with their companies or have been running companies for a very short time. Let's talk very briefly about due diligence. With the internet, I would imagine it's easier, but do you do your due diligence by finding out who else they know that you know, or the internet, or looking at public records? How do you go about doing that?

Loral: You know I actually have a whole due diligence checklist and I have a whole set of gifts that I'm going to give people, it's not up there yet but I'm going add it.

Brian: Good.

Loral: I have a whole chapter in one of my *Millionaire Maker* books, my third book *Wealth Cycle Investing* book on how to do "Due Diligence". So I mean due diligence at different levels, including background checks. It might start with the referrals. You have to imagine the deal flow around here is crazy, the amount of deals people want me to look at, or sharks because we know a lot of sharks. So the deal flow is enormous but it starts with, "Is it a deal or an idea?" Have they monetized? We look at financials, we do background checks, we do referral checks, check with prior management teams and partners and boards. I mean, can they actually perform the way they say they can? Many times there's part of our due diligence, teams that will fly out to the sites and actually do really thorough onsite evaluations. Right now I'm really involved with a gas and oil company, and we did almost six months of due diligence before we jumped. I think this checklist can give people some sense of how to get started, so I will add that to this gift that we'll be giving people at the end of the show.

Brian: Yeah! That will be extremely valuable! Due diligence is so important and I think a lot of people fly by the seat of their pants, and they just go with their cousins or their uncle or their friends because they've known them all their lives, and they think they know them in and out, but you don't very often see people put in the kind of stressful situations that businesses can put you in, because people surprise you. (Laughing)

Loral: Exactly!

Brian: They can certainly surprise you. You know them more than anybody else. My very special guest this week is Loral Langemeier, her book is *The Millionaire Maker* and she got several other books including *Creating A Cash Machine*, and so many more. Loral, I want to ask you, because a lot of people I have on my show have written books, I always ask where the inspiration for this book came from?

Loral: Well you know what's interesting is, I was asked to do it. So I wanted to document my work so my first book before the big series was *Guerilla Wealth* with Jay Conrad Levinson and right after it came out, literally within a month, McGraw-Hill called me and said "Oh my Gosh! We are looking for a woman, there are very few women in the space, you actually have documented millionaires. We want you write about how to make millionaires." And I said, "No! I'm not going do that! I'm really busy buying real estate and staying a millionaire so I don't have time to write and I don't like to write, but thank you!" (Laughing) So I hung up!

Brian: Oh my gosh!

Loral: And then they invited me to New York, and so I went and thought, "I could do a free trip to New York". I love New York. And then they wined and dined me, and then we came up with three books of all the content and I just really taught them for a day with all the stuff that I do. And they said, "Why won't you do it?" and they said, "Is it money?" and I said, "Oh, no. I'll make you pay me a lot of money" and I said, "I really don't want to write— like, type, type, type, type, type." I said, "I rather chew glass than write." And then they said, "What if they get you a writer?" Well that sounded a better proposition. So anyway, the inspiration was being pursued. I was already doing it, I've love doing it, I love the conversation but I had NEVER considered being an author. It wouldn't even occurred me because the traditional way people think they become an author is you have to write a book, and the truth is I talk them. And now, I can crank out a book it five days. Because the truth is, Brian, the book is your information and the knowledge in your head.

Brian: Right.

Loral: Most people can't get it out of their head because they think they have to type it, and I tell all my students to get a book out of your head as fast as you can. Just be interviewed, any sort of interview, just talk into a recorder, transcribe it, have it edited and you have a book very very quickly. We crank out books very fast now because you already have all the knowledge, it's not like you get to research it.

Brian: Right.

Loral: So now I have a HUGE piece I encourage all my students. I waited too long to do it, but I had that little writing block going on.

Brian: Yeah. And I'm so glad you said that too because I recently started a book writing coaching program and one of things I tell them is if they don't feel like they have time, or they'll say, "I'm not a good writer", "I don't want to do this" Look, do you think Donald Trump sits on the keyboard? No! He talks! People transcribe! People transcribe the recordings, they transcribe their live conversation. His books are done just like that. I don't know how many books he's had, but I've got five of his books on my bookshelf right now as I'm looking at them. So, he didn't just sit on the keyboard so I'm really glad that you said that because there are other ways of making this happen other than just sitting on your keyboard and creating. God bless you if you love doing that.

I did that with my first book, but the some of my future books are going be based on contents on my show, and it sounds like exactly what you did. You just got your book out of your head, and on to the screen and on to the paper, or in someone else's computer, and boom! It gets done really fast. So that's really great, I'm glad you shared that. You talked in your book about how you can create a millionaire in three to five years and you did mention that earlier. Some people have this idea that a million dollars is so big! But, is it such a big number?

Loral: (Laughing) It's so little! Well, because millionaire status was made up in 1933 when all of the banking and all this whole system was really defined, and a million is not a lot of money. Because of the pay levels, people started entrepreneurial adventures thinking "I just want to replace my salary", so if you are making 80k, they are thinking that's enough, which isn't enough money. So people think it's still this unattainable number, but the truth is it's $4160 per day in a business and you know, I don't start a business unless I know it can be over a million. It's way too much work to do to start a company and not go for it. So what I find is that most people are not entrepreneurial trained, they are occupationally trained, so most my work is getting people to see there's a lane.

You know you can't listen to Suze Orman, Dave Ramsey, occupational people AND to entrepreneurial wealth builders. We are in different conversations, so we're not going to tell you to live debt free, or live within your means. We'll tell you to grow your means. We're going to tell you not to have a job, because it's fixed income. We're going to tell you to get an entrepreneurial venture. You cannot listen to Suze on Saturday and then listen to me and try to put our conversations together. It would be like "I want to be skinny and fat all in one sentence." You've got to pick a lane. I think a lot of people don't pick a lane, and it's not because they don't want to choose, they don't understand the distinction of the choice. If you're going to be an entrepreneur, you've really got to learn how to run a company—not be the best coach, not be the best chiropractor and interior designer. That's all important. But that's not where people fall down. Most people fall down because they don't know how to market, they don't know how to sell, and they don't understand cash flow. That's what I can teach at a very high level, how you run a company. And once you know how to run a company, you do it through corporations because companies make money and individuals get taxed. That's the worst kind of money. The worst kind of income is payroll money. It's W2 money and that's a worldwide problem. So everybody wants to go get a bigger job, that just means you are going to pay the most tax. So I teach people how to maximize tax strategy, how to make money inside your company. But the biggest mistake entrepreneurs make on that millionaire path is that they spent their money on a lifestyle. They don't put their money towards assets, because again they don't know enough about that. So I buy real estate, gas and oil, insurance products, I trade in the market—actively trade, not just passively. I have restaurants, I have a music store, I have hair salons. I own so many companies, but I know how to run the company, and I'm not doing the work every day. I run them at a very high level. So I love teaching people how to become millionaires, I help them to be a millionaire in 3 years. I have a client—one right move, one good financing, one good shark, and he'll be a millionaire in 3 years. He's dead broke, 4 kids, single dad and moving across the country to run his music store, and he will own it in 3-5 years.

Brian: Another one of my listeners wanted to ask: What is the greatest challenge entrepreneurs have on their way to the first million?

Loral: The first $100,000. The first $100,000 is your hardest money, because again you are trying to replace your salary, and what a lot of people don't realize is that you live on most of that 100K in your lifestyle. So then there's not enough money to hire the right people, so you have your nephew build your website. You're struggling to do your bookkeeping or have your significant other do it, so unless you really get that entrepreneurial venture to $100,000-$120,000 straight out of the gate…you have to go for it. That's what I teach people, go past that first $100,000, because you don't have enough people to hire the team, so you have substandard work. And worse there's not enough cash to hire the team, even home help. You don't have home help, so it's just intense to get people past the first $100,000. Once you get past the first $100,000 and you have set the business up right, going from $150000-$200,000 to 1 million is easy, it's the first 100,000 that's the toughest money to make.

Brian: Because you have to set up your system to accommodate going beyond that, am I right?

Loral: Yeah, and you are going to have to pay some money to get incorporated, you're going to pay some money for proper web design, so it really takes 5-10k to really get set probably. So if you are barely getting by just paying your bills, there's not enough money to hire the right people. So then you struggle building a Wordpress site all day, and then you struggle in your accounting, so you are trying to do everything. You're the entrepreneur, and when you need to be the one out marketing, selling, making money, your heads is down in the keyboard trying to figure out the business system. Over and over again I see it happening. I'd say 1 out of 10 can get through that quickly, and so I just show you how. I did this cool workshop—I just got back from Florida in fact—where in 3 days everyone is guaranteed to make money, and I teach them this exact conversation. So you set up a business, you learn the market and you learn to sell and everyone makes money. The winner of this show—she is a videographer—made $18,000 in 3 days, an image consultant made $15,000 in 3 days, a web designer made $12,000 in 3 days. I had a little teenager make $1000 in 3 days. So you can do it if you see the system. And what was cool about it too, if it's done right, which of course I'm biased on, you only have to learn once. Once you get it, you're thinking, "I wish you learned this a long time ago", but no one is teaching it properly, so what a lot of people are doing is using their occupational training and trying to fit in into this entrepreneurial box and they don't go together, does that make sense?

Brian: Absolutely it does, getting to the first $100,000 is the hardest part. That was not the answer I expecting, but it's so profound and brilliant, so thank you for that. I'm really glad I asked and I thank one of my listeners for offering that question up to me yesterday on Facebook. So in your book, you talk about turning what you know into dough, and your book demonstrates different case studies of couples and families who are struggling for various reasons. Maybe they are not making enough, or maybe they are making too much, but you know they don't have their system set up correctly or their corporation set up correctly, or their spending too much on this and not enough on that, and you do talk about turning what you know into dough, so how do we figure out what we are good at, that we can make money at?

Loral: Well, I do a skill set analyzer, and the questions there I always ask people are: what have you been doing to make money? What do you love to do? Not that what you love to do will make you money—if you love to sit on the couch and watch TV and eat bonbon's, that not going to make you money. So what gets you excited? I love teaching, I love marketing, I love sales, so I build everything that I do around those skill sets. So what are you really good at and how do you make money? For example, tutors—what's so interesting about teachers that hate teaching, they don't hate teaching. They love teaching, they hate the system of teaching and the paycheck of teaching and tutoring. In fact, I have a lot of students that have bought into Tutor Doctor. It's a great franchise. I have one student who was a teacher, in fact, he and his wife were both teachers. They're in their 50's and 60's, both wanted to retire from the school system and they had a lot of assets saved up and they bought—I don't even know how many at the time—I think 20-30 Tutor Doctor franchisees through the Midwest and they are making $100,000's. I haven't checked in with them in a long time, but they might be millionaires by now, but they bought a franchise doing the very thing they are doing.

Brian: This is Success Profiles Radio and my very special guest is Loral Langemeier talking about *The Millionaire Maker* and having conversations about money. I want to ask, because rich people have habits that are very different from habits that everyone else has. I've gotten that impression from a number of people who have been on my show, and I'd love to hear from you what you believe are rich people's habits?

Loral: What are rich people habits? We lead a lot, we don't do a lot. We're on more strategic thinking and relationships, and deal making. With that, we make more money to hire more people to do it, so we can also hire better people. So more specifically we're rigorous about putting our money away and make sure that is working for us. We make very quick decisions. We only hangout with very cool people who are in an abundant conversation. So even if they are not millionaires, but they're well on their way and they have a forward thinking direction of conversation, and not whining—we don't hang out with whining people or complaining people. You know another one that I learned from Bob Proctor early on, it's not that wealthy people don't take hits. In fact, I think our hits are a lot harder. So Bob used to say it this way, "When you get cut you don't get cut deeper, you don't stay cut long."

Brian: Hmmm.

Loral: Which means you're going take a hit, and you're not going drop in it for the next two weeks, that would be miserable. You get back up on your feet. So if something happens to me I don't ponder it around in my mind about it, because a lot of times your own mind is a very dangerous neighborhood to go to. So I might call on top people, my mentors and people that are in the same league, and go to their partners and we'll talk through it. We'll talk very strategically about what's coming, and how to either avoid it and take the hit, or don't have it last very long. Only have it last literally maybe an hour or two hours and you're back up. You have to stay in an enormously strong mindset, and you only get that through you really getting it. I would say most people have entrepreneurial wealth-building muscles somewhere in their body and most of them are atrophied. So one of the things I always teach people is how to get in shape, and it's rigorous. It's not casual and it comes with a lot of responsibility that I think of unfortunately too many people shy away from.

Brian: Yeah.

Loral: So what's your choice when I really get down in the nitty-gritty of it, stay poor or go get rich? And it's not to get rich just to get rich—it's to get rich to change lives. There has to be a mission beyond yourself. Live Out Loud's whole mission is to change this conversation about money, so we are in a more abundant and entrepreneurial conversation, not this occupational conversation that's still ruling most of the world.

Brian: Absolutely! And this is actually a really great question to bring up. You talked about having conversations about money. It starts at home and a lot of kids, I think, don't get to experience that conversation. I think that's why a lot of young adults—or even middle age or older adults—are really not-in-the-know as to how money should be working for them, instead of you working for money. So how should the money conversation go, and how can you teach kids to have a healthy conversation around money with adults?

Loral: Well the adult needs have it first. You know it's interesting you bring that up, because way back in the day, I did the Cash Flow game. Then I did when *The Millionaire Maker* book and now *The Millionaire Maker* game. It's a very comprehensive *Millionaire Maker* game, so it's like *Monopoly* on steroids, and people can get the game on our website. But it starts with reading. The parents needs to be educated, and they need to lead the conversation. I let all parents who are paying clients of mine bring their teenagers for free. So then we teach them how to have a conversation, and it starts with positive and forward thinking language. It starts with possibility instead of "you can't". You can get anything you want, you can have anything you want, and you can buy anything you want. Right now my son is a millionaire because I set his life up to be, and he was a millionaire at 10 and my daughter will be too.

Brian: Wow!

Loral: But now he is 15 and said "I want to do it by myself". He says it's been great that you did it for me, but I want to prove that I can do it by myself, and I want to learn to trade. So I found him a world-leading trader just this weekend, and I hired him to train my son. He'll fund the account with his Roth IRA, so it's his own money and he'll put $20,000 to work. And our goal in less than 5 years is to have Logan become a millionaire on his own by learning to trade and invest himself. So the conversation starts with me setting it. The parent has to set the stage for the child to perform in it, because legally the kids can't start their bank and credit card accounts in corporate structure.

On a simpler note, just talk about "What could the family do to make an extra thousand a month"? Put more cash in your pocket. What could do to make them $50 a day? Logan's got all sorts of things, he can tutor. He's a Math tutor. He could help people waxing skis, gives ski lessons and he does a lot of things. So as a family, just open a basic conversation as to what we could do to earn extra money? I have families that design jewelry together, I have family that actually host my *Millionaire Maker* game nights at their home and the kids make some money for selling my product. I have kids selling other people's books, I have moms just catering and doing something on the side. It just has to start, and that if somebody wants something, especially a child, my rule is if it's not something really big or it's a necessity, then we pay 50/50. So the question is how do you go and make the money? And then we just brainstorm, "What can you do to make the money? What are things you can do?" My daughter loves art. She makes bracelets, she makes little paper wallets, she makes posters, she does all sorts of art stuff, and now she's starting to cook a little bit. She's only 8, but she's really getting into it, and they can do anything that they want. We put the kids' money in a designated savings account with their name on it that can eventually go to a checking account.

Brian: Absolutely! That's great! And you mentioned a while ago asking yourself how can you make an extra $1000 a week? Here's what I want to ask. If someone needs you to generate some cash pretty fast what are some strategies that you recommend?

Loral: Pre-sell or deposits. So every time I do a book, I pre-sell my book. So as soon as Kevin and I are contracted with a New York agent, our publisher will start a website, pre-selling our book that won't be out for a few months. So pre-sell. Just this last weekend at the workshop down in Florida, people pre-sold gift deposits on websites. The videographer that made $18,000 was selling huge $5000-$10000 video packages, so people were giving $2000 down, and $3000 upon delivery of the video. So pre-sell. Book your time out appropriately. Get the deposits from pre-sales, accumulate the money upfront, and spend it very accurately. I have the whole checklist on how to spend money because most people get that money, and they start spending it. Then when it comes time to pay bills, or do what they needed to do, or pay vendors, the money is gone. So it's really being aware in the management of money, and it's not like a sophisticated skill set. Pay attention to what's coming in and what's going out, and document it.

Brian: That's a great answer. I think for a lot of people it may not occur to them that they can sell something that they haven't made yet, and it's absolutely true. I really appreciate that answer. So earlier in the show you talked a little bit about how you have alternative investment strategies. You talked about them in your book *The Millionaire Maker* and some in your other books, too. What are some alternative investment strategies that you use or teach, and how does one find them?

Loral: Read my book. So a book about a family that people should be reading is *Put More Cash In Your Pocket*, and go through it with the kids. It's not a high level book, it's the "lemonade stand" book, the "$1000 a month" book. If you want to learn about alternative investments, it's one of the only books in its category, and it's called *The Millionaire Makers Guide To Wealth Cycle Investing*. So I start by explaining the different kinds of alternative investments. So there's cash flow real estate, there's appreciated real estate, there's cash flow businesses, there's appreciated businesses, gas and oil, there's insurance products. There's trading in the market, there's private equity, there's all sorts of ways to do it. So what I tell people is to lean in to what you know the most. So if you bought a piece of property in the past, maybe real estate is where you should start. If you're actually running a company, maybe you partner with someone else and buy another company together and start some alignment. And I'm a huge fan of partnering up because somebody knows more about something than you do. If you go into an investment 100% by yourself and it doesn't work, you have a 100% of a problem. There are very few investments that I own solo, so I go in with very high-level people in that category. So my gas and oil guys, that's all they do. That's what they do 24 hours a day for decades. They're the best in class, and so they are my partners in that. Same with real estate—I don't do business with the beginners, and if you are a beginner, then find people who are more advanced and do business with them. So like we're back in the days with my first real estate, I found some of the best real estate investors in the country and I said "I'm going to get on your team. I don't have a lot of money, and I don't have a lot of experience, but I have time." And what people like us need are people with time that would be considered a bird dog, right?

Brian: Yeah!

Loral: Somebody's got to do the work and we don't have a lot of time. So you can earn your way on to teams by doing what we tell you to do.

That's really what my Big Table becomes, a lot of people needing to know what to do because they don't know how to do it, and it's a lot guidance. You know every pro athlete has a coach, it's shocking to me, Brian. That people who want to get rich in businesses don't have a coach. It's absurd to me, it's insanity to me. People would rather spend their money on a personal trainer before they spend their money on a business or financial coaching. Not that the personal trainer isn't important, but you've got to get them both right. And without money, I mean, how are you affording the trainer?

Brian: Exactly!

Loral: I see a lot of people do so many weird things out of order here and it's weird because they just don't know.

Brian: Exactly, they just don't know.

Loral: Yup! Yup! People can get my books on Amazon for 9 to 10 bucks at this point.

Brian: Absolutely! Tell us briefly where we can you link up with you, get on your list, and get your books?

Loral: Yup! So liveoutloud.com is my website but there is gift page just for you. So it is www.liveoutloud.com/gifts-thank-you

What I have up there is a Millionaire Road Map, a cash generating tool kit, how to quit your job in 120 days, and why do never pay your kid an allowance, and you can have a 30 minutes of free time with my team.

Brian: That's great!! My very special guest is Loral Langemeier, and her book is called *The Millionaire Maker*. I want to ask you about *The Secret* because I love this movie. I've interviewed Jack Canfield and Dr. John Demartini on the show previously, and I would like to get a few others in that family on my show at some point as well. How did that experience come to you? Did they pursue you, or how did this come to you?

Loral: So I was in Colorado with John Assaraf, Bob Proctor, and a whole bunch of folks having a big seminar in Aspen, and Bob called. He'd left for LA and I didn't know why, and then he called the next day you have to get to LA right now. It's one of the last days of *The Secret*'s recording you need to get in it. So getting a flight out of Aspen that day was like an act to Congress. So I got on a flight, flew in, spent the night in Beverly Hills, recorded the whole next day, flew back to Aspen. We recorded 5 to 6 hours, and I had no idea really what the whole thing was going to be about, and then it's just become this landslide of an amazing success story. So it's fun, blessed to be in it because a lot of people shot in that film were not in it. So again, if I wasn't in a mentoring and coaching relationship with Bob, I know that I wouldn't have been called. So, it's who you know, and who knows you, and how you asked earlier, "What's the one of the success habits of the rich?" I think was your question.

Brian: Yeah!

Loral: It's really staying connected to those who are connected.

Brian: Exactly!

Loral: And we do a lot of diligence staying connected to each other and supporting each other, and providing opportunities for each other. And if you're listening and you don't think that's how game works, it is completely how it works. It's the same with all the assets and the deals and the things that come to me. Why did so many deals come to me? People realize I know how to do them well, I know how to do due diligence. After lots of my failing teams, I know how to put together very high performing teams now. And I always say "I got my bruises already, I did everything wrong, so I can do everything right this round." (laughs)

Brian: Absolutely! And it comes from stepping out or it just getting yourself out. I mean, I can surely attest to that. I've gotten to meet so many amazing people because I have a show that I would never have an audience with. Perhaps at some point you and I would've had a chance to talk, but having a show accelerated that whole process. Having someone like Bob Burg come on my show, and Dr. John Demartini, Jack Canfield, Brian Smith, Ron Klein, Jeffrey Gitomer, Eric Lofhom, Sharon Lechter, and the list goes on and on and on. I get to talk to a lot of cool people because I have a show.

I got to go to Greg Reid's event and do red carpet interviews. I've have been invited to conferences. You just step out there and you get connected to the people, and it's amazing the opportunities that will show up and you have no idea where they came from or why. Just say "Thank you Universe, Thank You God", and just run with it.

Loral: Absolutely! Absolutely true!

Brian: So you talked about the Big Table a little bit, and you did talked about this in your book. This is your coaching program. Tell us a little bit about that and what we could expect to learn if we did decided to join up with your coaching program.

Loral: So, my business is pretty simple. I have a lot of books, a lot of programs, a lot of audio programs, and then what I'm known for is my signature 3-day workshop which is 9 years in the works called "3 Days 2 Cash", and you are guaranteed to make money in 3 days. I'll be in the LA area in July in 2 weeks. Next week I will be in Vancouver. So it's on my liveoutloud.com website under "Trainings", and so I'm known for that. Then my Big Table is really what's next.

So the Big Table is the millionaire plan where you learn. If you paid enormous tuition for 4 years to get a degree, give me 3 to 5 and I will give you the system to become a millionaire. So you have to do all the work. We are not a consulting firm, but we help you get your business up and running past 6 figures. My goal is 7 because anything less than 7 is a lot of work. Then let's move your business and make sure that your companies are set up right so you have high tech strategies and corporate structure, and then teach you how to look at alternative investments. So what would a portfolio look like? If you have a million bucks how would you invest? What ould you buy, how would you diversify, and how would you do the due diligence? You've got to know that I have an extraordinary rolodex of people that know how to teach you, and know how to introduce you. In June, we're taking whole bunch of my clients down to Texas on a gas and oil field trip, and it's real field trip. Nobody going to buy anything, they're going to learn about that asset class. When I was down in Florida earlier this week, I took some people down to Miami, show them how to look for fix and flip homes. So we really get in the streets with people because we do it ourselves very aggressively. I own a franchise company, so we take people on field trips, show them how to do stuff properly, how to find a team, how to do due diligence, and so that they can start doing it for themselves. It's really good. We are the only program in the world that does it.

Brian: Oh, really cool.

Loral: Yup! A lot of fun.

Brian: That's great. And you are very well connected and one of my favorite questions to ask to very well connected people is how do you connect to these very well connected people? For first step, of course, getting yourself out the there. Do you have a process or an agenda when you go to event to specifically meet people? Or does it just happen? How does it work for you?

Loral: Well, in the beginning I would just seek people out. I would go to their workshops, I hired them to coach me. I sometimes actually go to work for them and I contracted to them to support them with things that they need. But I gave first, "What do you need and how can I help you to go get it"? And so that's what I did in the beginning and now, people line up and I can't get to everybody. It's pretty intense (laughing) the demand for my time at this point.

Brian: Yeah!

Loral: And I'm really selective. Just last year I opened for private practice again, so I actually called it "Head Of The Table". So it's people who are in the Big Table that really want to go to the next level fast, and they hire me for an extra tuition for me to be their private coach. I have a small handful of people that I worked with in that category for those were ready to run and want to get it done. I opened my rolodex and really connect people quickly, and it happens so quickly if you allow it, and there's a part of this, Brian, that we really haven't talked about. There's a receiving part, and if you think, "I am not worth it" it's got to go at a comfortable pace. You've got to get over that really really quick because it goes really fast. You know people like to tell me, "When are you going slow down? I say, "When are you going to speed up? My pace is perfectly fine for me".

Brian: Yeah.

Loral: (Laughing) You know, it's interesting. If I would rewind 10 or 15 years that somebody told me that I'd be here, I wouldn't think it would have been possible. But this year alone, I've already spent 6 figures on my own tuition for other coaches and mentors. So I even get coached and mentored. I think everyone should always have a coach and mentors. There should always be someone ahead of you pulling you to the next place, and you should allow yourself to go to the next place—not because it's about all the money or the status or any of those things. In fact, I'm selling off a lot of stuff. But it's learning in very specific areas, and if you are really look at sustainable wealthy people we're avid learners. We love to learn, we collaborate a lot, we love being with other smart people, we love cutting deals. If you're hearing me say that, if you are listening right now, it wasn't always like this. You grow into it as you start spending time with the people who making it happen. You know there's 2 kinds of people in the world, the people who create and ones who consume, and I'd rather be on the creating side.

Brian: Yeah.

Loral: And, of course, I'm consuming in my economy and my town. I live in Lake Tahoe. It's a very small town, so, of course, we're consuming here. But I'm creating amazing commerce for this town as well by bringing mentors and students to my conference building and they stay in the hotels here, they eat at the restaurants here, they go gamble in casinos here. So you know there's got to be two sides to really be in an abundant economy. So what would you do to create? Of course, you know there always be a consumption side, but most people just consume and take.

Brian: Yeah. I understand and absolutely there are 2 sides of the table. There is consumer side and the producer side, and the people that they are making their money are those who are producing for other people. So that's something to really think about, if you are trying to build value in the world and your business creates something that people want, it's a win. So that's awesome. So let's re-visit your free bonuses again. I know you want to give gifts to our listeners which I really really appreciate. Tell us about that again and what we can get from you?

Loral: Alright, so if you go to www.liveoutloud.com/gifts-thank-you you are going to get 30 minutes of a free strategy test to one of my team members. You're going get the Millionaire Road Map that shows you the system of how to be a millionaire, a cash generating tool kit—which is one of my favorites—to teach you some of the fast techniques of how to make money quickly if you need it quickly, which most people do, How To Quit Your Job in 120 days, How To Never Pay Your Kid An Allowance, and I'm going put up my due diligence checklist there. So there are probably thousands of dollars worth of goodies. People can go to our page to opt in and get the download of all my goodies.

Brian: Sounds great! We've got 3 minutes to the end the show and I want to ask a question that I ask everyone at the end of the show.

Loral: I love it.

Brian: Loral, who inspires and motivates you?

Loral: Hmmm. So at this part of my life I would think God. All of my inspiration comes in, and I say that because I think as a content and thought leader—I think that a lot of people, even though you have may not have best-selling books, you're a thought leader at some level. But you have got to trust yourself to start delivering the message tucked inside of you. So I'm saying that more and more and more, because I see amazing new students that I get that have such brilliance. But because they haven't get out in their head, no one knows how brilliant they are and they can't change lives and are still stuck in their head. So if you're inspired and you have a message, share it as fast as you can. Other people in the world that are dear friends—as you mentioned earlier John Demartini is a very dear friend of mine. He's a huge inspiration to me and what I do. Richard Branson is world class in his business acumen. I think John Rutledge who's an economic adviser to the Premier of China, world leader in economics. So I like the guys in the finance space. I think Trump is amazing, he is ruthless and smart (laughing).

Brian: Yeah

Loral: I think Oprah is brilliant. So I follow them. You know, if they can do it, anyone can do it. It's a matter of finding the right formula, finding the right team and picking a lane and stop the confusion and the lack of the decision-making. Move! Move, move, move!

Brian: Yeah! Absolutely! Just, just go! Just do it! So we can find free gifts from Loral Langemeier at www.liveoutloud.com/gifts-thank-you, you can get a lot of stuff there. I'm looking forward to diving in to what's here. This is going be absolutely amazing, and we are reaching the end of the show. My very special guest this week has been Loral Langemeier. This is been one of my favorite interviews to date. Thank you so much Loral for being here, I am so grateful. Thank you.

Loral: Thank you, I appreciate being here.

DEBBIE ALLEN

THE HIGHLY PAID EXPERT

Brian: Hello and welcome to Success Profiles Radio. I'm your host Brian K Wright and it is a pleasure to be here with you today. I am honored that you chose to spend part of your day with me here, and this is going to be a fantastic show. I'll be introducing my guest shortly and I promise this will be a fun and informative hour. It will be great.

My guest this week is Debbie Allen. Let me tell you a little bit about her.

She is the expert of experts and she is a business and brand strategist, bestselling author of six books, a motivational film star and a mentor to business owners around the globe. She is an expert strategist in the fields of business growth, marketing and branding. She is also an award-winning entrepreneur who has presented before thousands of people in 28 countries around the world.

Debbie possesses the unique ability to instantly solve any business problem and leverage solutions and marketing trends that can earn you authority domination around your brand. With over four decades of business building wisdom, she easily understands the dynamics of making big money in any economy or with any business reinvention.

Her new book is called *The Highly Paid Expert*, and we will discuss all of this and so much more on today's show.

With all of this in mind, here is my guest, Debbie Allen. Debbie, are you there?

Debbie: I am, Brian, great to be here with you today!

Brian: Absolutely! I'm so glad to have you here too! The first question that I usually as everyone is, tell us about your background. Give us your backstory.

Debbie: So, I've been an entrepreneur my entire life. I've never applied for a JOB. I've never gone to college. Basically, I started out in a family business at age 19 and brought into the business as a part-owner then. I learned from experts all my life. That's really helped me just really grow my business and I never even would have considered I'd be an expert, I think like an entrepreneur. So, I built this whole business a little bit differently than just being a paid professional speaker, which I've done for 20 years. I really took it as more of an entrepreneur model. I've been doing this and helping people become experts for many years. So, I'm thrilled to finally actually get it out there to the world that this is what I'm doing. [chuckle]

Brian: That sounds fantastic! You know, there is something I do want to ask you and this is something that I think a lot have people have asked you. One of your great experiences has been being on the Howard Stern Show. The first time I heard you talk about this, you promoted it as you being one of the few women he's ever had on his show that managed to keep their clothes on during the interview. [laughter]

Debbie: That's what you've heard and really it is true, yes. I had my clothes on and I made a bestselling book out of it. Yeah, I mean that's a rare thing.

Howard is a brilliant marketer and I knew that when I went on the show. I do lots of radio shows, but you don't expect to do a show like that. It's not like I thought it would be "Oprah's Book of the Month Club", but it turned out to be "Howard's Book of the Month Club" because as you know the power of the media, the right people hearing it and somebody promoting it—it was a tough interview because at first he was beating me up. They're looking for looking controversy. I actually hired an expert who was on his show. So, I usually find an expert on everything and he was on his show and I said, "Can I hire you to be my mentor and teach me how to do this interview? How to be edgy? How can I be edgy and still be professional?" If you're on a show like that, it could be a train wreck. I mean, they're just looking to run you over and then back up and run you over again and make a fool out of you.

So, basically, I got a little sassy with him and called him on some of the stuff that he was doing. I also respected him a little bit and I gave him some funny stories, and we had a good time and he really turned the interview probably in two minutes because in the first two minutes they were really trying to beat me up. He then realized, "Hey, this chick, she's pretty tough. She's been out there. She knows what she's doing and we need to listen to her." So, that was cool.

Brian: That book you were promoting is called *Confessions of Shameless Self-Promoters*. Anyone out there listening, look that up and get that *Confessions of Shameless Self-Promoters*. It's a bunch of wisdom that Debbie put together that had helped her in her businesses and wisdom that other people have shared with her about how they've built their business shamelessly. You told Howard, "You're a shameless self-promoter," because he didn't say he was.

Debbie: Well, he said, "I'm not really shameless like other DJs. I have T-shirts and mugs." I said, "Howard, you're shamelessly fabulous because you're a great marketer and I see how people were turning you down all the time, getting fired all the time, and your wife and child on the way. You did not stop and for that I admire you, because all great successful people don't stop because they're going to run into some issues." So, I heard his head blowing up with the ego there, but then I slapped him down a little bit right after I finished telling him that. I said, "But I don't respect what you do to degrade women." I said, "That part I don't respect, but I do respect that you are shameless, and you have to admit it you are and that's what made you successful," and we went on the conversation from there.

Brian: Wow! That's great. So, how long was the interview supposed to be? And how long did it actually last?

Debbie: Well, the person that was my mentor had been on for 1.5 hours, and it went in lots of bad directions with him. He said, "You don't want more than five minutes or it will go in the wrong direction. Your goal is to get in there and get your book known, let the people know about it and you don't want more than five minutes." So at 4 1/2 minutes, I was starting to wrap up the interview. Then it went to Amazon Best Seller within two hours, it was pretty amazing.

Brian: Wow! That is really great and, of course, you were able to leverage that. I talk about this all the time when people tell me that they've been on Howard Stern or CNN or Oprah or whoever, I do say, "and you did leverage this going forward, right"? Of course, you did.

Debbie: Right. A lot of people say that, "I want to be on his show". It's all about leverage. Everything is about a goal. As an expert, you should be very,

very aligned. If you're very, very aligned as a credible expert, you're going be aligned and have a goal for every single thing you do or you don't do it, because you got to keep the brand integrity and you got to keep your expertise and credibility as well there.

Brian: Yes. So, talking about brand alignment and values alignment. Did you have some trepidation about doing this show considering this is not really who maybe you thought you were?

Debbie: Definitely. The reason I said yes to it was two reasons. One, I teach people to have gutsy goals and go for them. Whatever scares you makes you strong, I believe that. The other one, I'm a professional speaker. It's another story. I turned it into a really funny story because I basically told this exactly how it happened. It shocks people, I think that they don't think of Howard as somebody that actually will promote people and market people.

He is a great marketer. He definitely toned-down now. You see him in the show, *America's Got Talent*. He's a great host there, but back then, he was way edgy, way edgy. He stood up for me, actually. The other producers were putting me down a little bit and attacking me. He was standing up for me because he believed in it. If he believes in something you have, then that was it. I believed that he's a good marketer and I believe that what I had to share with him for this specific book would have been perfect.

Now, my new book *The Highly Paid Expert*, probably not the best fit for his show, but that one was. I could be edgier with it and I know I could have fun with it and he would like it.

Brian: Yeah. This book is coming out in about week or two, is that right?

Debbie: Yes. July 22nd is my big launch date on Amazon, *The Highly Paid Expert*. I got preview copies. I'm holding my new baby in my hand. It's awesome! I'm super excited because this is not just a book, Brian, this is a business plan. This is somebody wants to leave the corporate world that says, "I don't know what I want to do. I've got all this expertise and skills. I don't know how I could possibly build a business that could make me money as an expert and work the way I want to work to be financially free." I mean it's a step-by-step, walk-you-through-it, here's how you do it, or somebody that wants to take their business from just being a small business to say, "I want to be an expert and I want to blow my business up and get me a lot more money," and here's the blueprint.

Brian: Yeah, absolutely. We're definitely going be exploring the topics of your book throughout this show. So, I do want to leave with one question and this is about becoming a highly paid expert. What do you think an expert is? Can anyone be an expert, do you think?

Debbie: I think anybody can be an expert. They study into something or they have some skill set that they want to really expand upon. An expert is basically someone that's widely recognized as a reliable source for a specific skill, or passion or a body of knowledge that they have. An expert is known as the authority, not only by the public but also amongst their peers in any specific niche market. It's really important to be in a niche market. An expert can be somebody that's known for some advice that they've learned from having credentials with training and education, or could simply be from their own experiences and know the subject way beyond the average person. That's where I came from knowing the subject as an entrepreneur and being an expert who has reinvented themselves many times over.

Brian: Yeah, absolutely. You've been in a lot of different industries. Didn't your family get involved in the storage unit industry for a while?

Debbie: Yeah, I started in the car rental industry in Gary, Indiana, one of the toughest places to start a car rental business and repossessing cars, selling cars at 19 years old. Then we got into mini storage. Those were two of the first things I did.

Brian: Great! My very special guest this week is Debbie Allen. Her book is called *The Highly Paid Expert* and we are going to be talking for the rest of the show about how you can become an expert in your industry.

We've talked a little bit about the idea that anyone can be can expert. It's just a matter of knowing something well enough that you can begin down that path. So, let me just ask you, Debbie, how does someone begin if they really have no idea how to get started? They've got this expertise, they've got something that they're pretty good at, but they have no idea how to make themselves known. Where does someone start?

Debbie: First, I think it's a mind shift to say you are ready to step up to a bigger game because I believe the world is looking for what you have. I believe that everybody has an expert inside of them and they want to get that out. They want to share and help other people, and there's no better feeling than when you have some of that body of knowledge you can help people with whether that's personal or professional, whatever it is. On top of that, you're helping so many people and you get paid for it. I pinch myself and say that this is great. The world is looking for you.

If you're listening to us right now, think about what can you share that you can passionately share from your heart and your head to connect with other people because other people need your advice and your guidance more than you probably even have any idea about, and they're looking for what you have to share.

Really, Brian, there's no better time that I've ever seen to launch yourself as an expert than right now because we're able to do this online so much quicker. When it's done really well to begin with, you know your market, you know where you're going, you know that body of knowledge and then really launching yourself out there online, you could become an international expert in record time. When I launched my website in 1997, it was easy to get on the top of the search engines because nobody was there, right?

Brian: Right.

Debbie: Now, you get out there and people are looking. We are online every day searching for information. We're looking for experts on every kind of topic, everything you can think of. So, there's a lot of money we had in this business, and again people just didn't know how to get into it. They just thought, "An expert, that's too big, that seems too untouchable." But again, it's a different way of looking at business, and I believe that if you're out looking at the business today as creating an expert model, you're going have a lot of trouble competing in this new economy because there is money out there. But people are looking for the top people to do business with, they need to trust you, they need to know that you know your stuff if they're going hand you a lot of money.

Brian: Absolutely. In your book, you talked about what you called the Highly Paid Expert Pyramid and it's basically a step-by-step progression that one needs to go through whether it's a mind shift thing, whether it's taking the action. Talk about the Highly Paid Expert Pyramid that you discussed in your book. What steps are involved?

Debbie: Okay. So, that's a good way of thinking about it. As you said, Brian, somebody is just starting out. If you take a triangle and draw it like a pyramid, you see the bottom of the pyramid is really wide. That's where you start out as a "Novice" saying, "Okay, I'll learn about it, or I want to reinvent my business to just not be a business owner. I really want to create an entrepreneur model as an expert."

I'm going start from the bottom here because right now I'm competing with lots of people. So, when it's really wide, there's less money available to you because you're competing with way too many people. So, you have to move up that pyramid, and as you move up you start throwing off the competition. As you get higher and higher to the top, you become a "Money And Opportunity Magnet" because you move to the next level where people are coming to you for what you have to give to them. So, on top of the "Novice" level is you're starting to grow your business.

The next level above that is the "Skilled" level. At "Skilled", they know how to do stuff, they've got a better knowledge of what they can do, but they're not sure what to do with it yet. So, they're starting to move up. Then they start branding themselves and getting themselves known as the next level which is the "Specialist". So, the people are going to you for specific specialists saying, "This is the person who is the go-to authority for this."

Then you go to the next level. It starts going even more narrow. More opportunity and more money starts flowing to you. You go to the "Authority" Level.

Above the "Authority" level—because a lot of times people are authorities but they're still not making the money—the top level is "Highly Paid Expert". You are the go-to expert in your niche market. People know you. You are highly paid. You live a financially free lifestyle, and what that means is you create your day. Nobody creates a day for you. You decide where you want to go, who you want to work with, what kind of clients you want, where you want to work with them, how you want to work with them. It's where that wonderful financial freedom level is.

Brian: Yeah. That is freedom. Money freedom creates time freedom, and I think really deep down that's what we want. Like you said, the freedom to do what you want to do, when you want to do, and who you want to do it with, then just go wherever you want to go is the goal. Even if that means you can go to the beach and do an hour's worth of work there, and then just sit around and enjoy the rest of your day. If that's what you got going on, and you can automate all of that. We can talk about all that later, of course.

So, let me ask. If someone is looking to launch the new expert business or maybe they're reinventing a business they're already in, where would they start with that?

Debbie: Well, if they are looking at reinventing, there are two different ways looking at. There's the launch, I want to create a foundation as an expert and then launch myself, or I'm going to reinvent what I already have.

Now, Brian, you've known me for a while so I'm the queen of reinvention, and that's part of the entrepreneur for me, plus it also means I'm going another level, I'm doing something different and keeping it real all the time, keeping it fresh and going in a direction where I see the market heading.

So, as an expert, if you're going to a market where you see people need help. Basically, experts do two things—they find what the problem is in their niche market, and they solve the problem. Because you're solving problems, you're making the pain go away and people will give you money for that.

So, if you're just launching, you have to spend some really solid time creating a complete brand foundation.

So, I was talking with one of my clients and he said, "I don't know what I want to be an expert in." I said, "Okay. What have you done? What are your skill sets? We'll work through all of that. We'll create a business and a brand strategy that works together, and then we can get all of that built before we ever launch it." It means you don't market as an expert at all until you have all that foundation, the website built, and all the branding pieces are built, everything is done in your social media, everything is consistent—THEN you launch.

If you're going do a re-launch, it's a redo. Maybe it's a tweak from what you already have. Maybe it's getting deeper into the niche market you have. Maybe it's defining your value proposition statement better, and redoing touching up some of your brand work and some of your words on your website, so that is cleaner and stronger so that it will generate a higher value client.

Brian: Exactly. It seems like a lot of people want to do that backward. In other words, they just want to put something out there and see what sticks, and then if they find something that people didn't gravitate to, then they worry about branding and ask, "Why do people buy this?" So, it just seems like a backward way of doing it.

Debbie: Not only it's a backward way, it's a very, very costly way. The thing is once you've launched yourself out there and your launch bombed because you didn't have it effectively done, you got to re-launch again. So, it's time and it's money. Two things that everybody wants, two big excuses that anybody has, is time and money.

When you're a highly paid expert, you have more time, you have more money. You want to do it right and get there faster. When you launch you're going get there faster. You have to take the time to build the foundation or rebuild the foundation or there's going to be too many blocks in getting that specific target market.

A lot of times I've heard people saying, "I'm getting clients but they can't afford it, or I can't afford to raise my fees, or it's really hard to get people". Or there are all kinds of blocks in their marketing and there are all kinds of blocks in what they're putting out there as an expert, or they're not really positioning themselves effectively as an expert and that's why the money is not flowing.

Brian: Exactly. So, let me ask this, once somebody has picked a direction and they have that foundation in place, how then do you start dominating online? Because even though the internet has been around for a while and a lot of people are making money online, there are probably a lot of people who think there's still something really extremely mysterious about it and they wonder if they can succeed online too. So, how do you start dominating online?

Debbie: Well, it is a constant thing of relearning and learning. I've been studying internet marketing for 20 years, and still I'm not the expert of experts because there is social media stuff. So I hire experts to do the social media pieces, and then there are landing pages and there are a million things that I don't even know where to go first.

So, the thing is where to start. You need to find a brand direction or what are you going to be an expert at. You've got to be really clear, and when you are really clear, go out and you start grabbing as many domains around it as possible. If you're trying to launch a business model where you can't grab the .com and own brand domination on multiple domains around what you're doing, you already have a block. If there are too many ads around what you're doing, it's going be a block.

So, the first thing we do is when I work with a client is get very, very clear on it and start doing research. As I'm on the phone with them, researching Google what's out there, who are the other experts on that topic, where can I fit you, what domains are available, and we might get a dozen domains when we get the right niche and get all those domains and grab those up.

Here's a good example of a huge company, a huge organization that just made a big mistake. The National Speakers Association just had their convention in San Diego and during the convention, they announced—Wow! Out of nowhere!— "We're going have a new brand called Platform." Three-quarters of the audience said, "What? They've got to be kidding." I never heard anything about that, and all of a sudden they're going launch it and spend half a million dollars launching this brand.

So, the first thing I do is do what I do with my clients. I get online and think that they must have grabbed the .com. Let me see what else is out there around that word "platform". Oh my gosh! It was a nightmare. They didn't have the .com. They had the .net. They didn't even have the .org and there was another person that was really owning and dominating—Michael Hyatt dominated that word Platform. He has a book on that. He has programs on that.

Now the brand people in the National Speakers Association like myself and a number of others, we went a little crazy—this is nuts. You can't throw enough money to fight that brand. So, that's why that foundation is so critical is to have that right first. So, I put that out to all the top people, the top 5% of national speakers are certified speaking professionals. We have our own little private chat line. I said, "My prediction is that they're going to put their tails between their legs. If they really are leaders, they're going put their tails between their legs and say we've really screwed up and we're going go back to where we were." That's exactly what happened.

Brian: Yeah. Because I remembered when that announcement came out and I saw the buzz on Facebook, and Michael Hyatt is one of my Facebook friends and I follow him on Facebook and I'm thinking, "This is going be a catfight if this doesn't get resolved properly." So, I'm glad that they're retreating a little bit from this and hopefully, they do the research in the future, if they do decide to rebrand.

My guest this week is Debbie Allen and the book is called *The Highly Paid Expert* that's coming out in the next few days.

We're talking about brand domination, specifically online. So, Debbie, dominating a market online can certainly be a challenge especially if you have a career that is widely recognized. How do you help someone really stand out if they are in insurance, or a speaker, or an entrepreneur where space is already crowded enough. How do you help them get brand domination in a situation like that?

Debbie: Yeah, that is a little more challenging. A good example with that is one of my clients. He was actually speaking on leadership. Now, there are so many experts on leadership. There's so much out there on leadership, so you can think of any kind of leadership topic and it's gone. His name is Norm. He definitely is not the "norm" kind of person. We always joked about that. He likes to be out of the box and think differently. Even though he works in a corporate market, he wants to think and teach them leadership outside of what's normal. I said, "Oh my gosh, leadership outside the norm," and it perfectly fits his name, and we went with that. Then put some edgy spin on everything he did, so we can find something that he had and also find domains that he could launch that would work for him as well.

So, it takes a lot of research. The thing is, Brian, you're so close to your own stuff that it's hard for you to see it, and that's why experts hire other experts to get it for them. Even when sometimes I'm re-launching a brand or something I'm doing, I go hire an expert to work on it or bounce ideas, because I would rather throw a few thousand dollars on something versus months of time and it doesn't work. I want to know that it's right. Again, we are just so close to what we do, we don't see the most obvious things sometimes.

Brian: Yeah, exactly. So, once you've got this all figured out, what needs to happen next?

Debbie: Okay. So here is a case study of another client, I'd like to show what he did in 30 days. So, one of my clients is named Nev. Nev had three focuses because he had three loves. He did fitness, real estate investing, and diversity. Nev is all about diversity, because Nev was born in Europe. He moved to the US with no money at a very young age and started a business.

Actually, he got into real estate investing and started making that work. He was a woman and now he's a man. Talk about diversity!

So, it was pretty obvious to me when he told me about himself. I'm said, "You got to pick one path!" He was floundering for two years and making a little money here and there.

All we needed for Nev in 30 days was just pull out the diversity stuff and then we just blew that up. Believe it or not, I got him the domain DiversityForBusiness.com. I thought, "Wow! There's still so much need in there." He just didn't think there was enough money to be made in that market. I said, "Are you kidding me? There's so much in diversity. There are so many ways of doing diversity."

So, that was 30 days, he got re-launched and focused, and getting ready to redo his website, and now he's doing a live event—his very first live event that I'm going be attending as his guest this week. So, that's exciting because even though he had this, he didn't see it. So just refocusing somebody and then rebranding and pulling a piece out, that was 30 days.

Brian: That's wonderful.

Debbie: Yeah. Maybe if you really were focused and strong, you got another 30 days on a website and some other things. I mean he already had it. He had the base, right? And so his confidence level just soared and he took off. Once he had all these domains, and he's got this card and he's got this new identity even though it was there, it changed everything for him. He never would even have considered doing his own event.

I just finished working with him, and just a few months later, he's locked in and really being the expert out there. So, I think there's a level of confidence, too, when your audience embraces it, and you do know that you have all the right domains and you're locking things in.

One of the big things he is doing to lock in his domination online right now is video. Video marketing is just huge. It's a major opportunity for us with YouTube to have our own TV shows, have our own channel to be the experts. With the right keywords based around your expertise will get you noticed on Google very quickly. So, I love, love, love video. He's embracing all of that as well. It's just a game changer.

Brian: Absolutely. So, you've created an innovative system that's actually a step-by-step model called the Authority Domination Formula. How it's about that and how it works?

Debbie: The Authority Domination Formula is basically the step-by-step system that I share in my book. It's basically, this is what you're going do and then this is what you're going do, and the next thing and the next thing. So, if you are the authority in something, once you get past the branding, the next step is starting to build your coaching programs to where they are higher level where you've learned how to package them together.

You're doing speaking where you're learning how to sell. Basically, what you're doing is changing the marketing model that we know as traditional marketing and business, and moving that to what I call education-based marketing and education-based selling. So, there is no selling, there is no marketing, all you do is give up information. You're very, very generous with your information online with video communication. People need to trust, and we're seeing this videos or watching people. We're looking at video testimonials. It's so much online right now so you've got to give in a different way.

So, let's talk about funnels. The funnel of marketing now is getting somebody on to your site, giving them something. If you can give them an educational video and another educational video that goes deeper into what you're do in your expertise, the people are going start following you and they're thinking, "Oh my gosh! This person really knows," and then they start sharing your information on social media, and then people will go to your site.

So, this is how the funnel works, but they may come in directly from your website, they may come in from a video that goes to your website, come from the Facebook page, or YouTube that goes back to your website. Everything goes back. The whole funnel goes back to your website because no matter how great you are dominating online, if you're not getting them to your site and capturing their email database, you have no database list. As you know, social media can change any day.

I have a client whose business is called Wake Up Women. When she's started with me, we were trying to build it to a million dollar brand very quickly. She had 25,000 Facebook fans and I said, "That was a good start." We started building. She had no database list, no free gift on her site, and the process was we're just starting to get her out there. Somebody grabbed her Facebook page and shut that down, and she lost everybody. So, that was compromised and then she built it up again and somebody jeopardized it again. She's waking up women in other countries that don't want to woken up. So, those were not hers. Somebody can go in and grab all those and shut you down on social media, or social media could change in a day and have new rules, and they're not yours.

So, the whole idea of that is just getting in the funnel to get them to your site. Getting them to a landing page where they sign up or getting them to your webpage where they sign up.

Brian: Exactly. So, how can someone fast-track this process to start creating products that showcase their talent and who they are?

Debbie: So probably the quickest way to fast-track something is to do a teleseminar. You don't have to put up a PowerPoint together. You get on the phone and you talk, you record. You can do freeconferencepro.com and you can set up a time for a teleseminar, and people come in the call even if you got your best friend and their cat listening for the first time. I would suggest do it a series. You know, Brian, it takes time to build up the list.

The thing is when you do this even though it's a free conference call, you hit record and record it. You now have a product because it's saved. So, you can do a series of those based on your expertise, and I usually have my clients start with maybe a series of six teleseminars, very simple to do, it's free. They don't have to worry about the money. They've got a recording because a lot of the recordings now as we know—you've been going to seminars for a long time, you know we used to call this the thud factor when you walk out with the big workbook and 20 CDs. Now everything is downloaded or it's on a thumb drive. So, it's so easy for people to capture that information now. If you can pick up the phone and talk and push a button to record, you can get a great product fast.

Brian: Exactly. So, let me ask you this. That's a really great place for someone to start. How can someone create multiple streams of income with their business? I know there are a lot of different ways. We talked about teleseminars. We talked about having a list. We talked about doing books. How else can someone monetize what they're doing?

Debbie: As an expert, you're going to be a speaker whether you like it or not. You don't have to go on a stage in front of a lot of people. You can also speak online on a teleseminar or webinar, Google+, Hangouts, for example. So, those are some of the ways to be coming to a speaker, and there's a lot of money to be made through that.

Brian: Yeah, exactly. That's great! There are just so many different ways that I think depending too on your industry. The teleseminars are great. Coaching programs are fantastic. Books are fantastic. So what are the mistakes that people can avoid on their business?

Debbie: Well, basically, trying to do it on a shoestring budget thinking they don't need an expert to help them do it. You can't do a solo business, you need to invest in your business. So, when people come out and they want to become this expert, and they want to be this famous author and they want all these things, but they have no money to invest in their business, they're crazy. Any business takes money to invest. You have to have money to do this business right. Otherwise, it just going take you way too long or you're going try and do it cheesy, like a homemade website, and then it's going kill your credibility and your reputation. So, that's the biggest mistake I see that people wanting themselves in the expert business.

Brian: My very special guest this week is Debbie Allen and her book is called *The Highly Paid Expert*. Earlier, we were talking about different ways that you can create streams of income for your business. Of course, Debbie, you and I both know that speaking for groups and for other people and other organizations can be a very high leverage way of making some money. So, let's talk about how you built your speaking career as an expert?

Debbie: Well, I became an expert in a very specific niche market of retail because I built and sold numerous retail stores, so I became the expert in that. I wrote a book first because I didn't want to write a book, but I thought speakers needed to write a book to have credibility out there. I launched myself by doing that. By the first 10 years of my career, I had built up to be one of the highest paid women speakers in the world. I still do it occasionally but very seldom. My keynote fee was $8,500.

So, I went from there and the best thing that happened is the whole economy just took a massive dive, and what happened is 50% of the meetings in the US tanked. So, I quickly went internationally and spent most of my time internationally for the last three years of that paid speaking.

I realized there was another kind of business forming out there, people on stage selling. I said, "I need to learn how to do this," and I would try it and would bomb, then finally I'm said, "I think I got it." But everything is a system. You have to go with the right people that are doing it and you've got to learn how to do this system. I was determined to do it because I thought making $8,500 for 60- or 90-minute keynote was pretty cool until I learned how to sell from stage. It's basically educating from stage, and that's how I do it, educating from stage. I do it very smoothly transitioning to an offer, welcoming and inviting people to it and it's seamless.

The first one that I did went really well and I then took it to making six figures in 90 minutes on stage. So I said, "Okay, I'm really hooked on this." Then, I did a live event where did half a million dollars in three days and I said, "I'm totally hooked on this." There's a new model that I can use my expertise and my skills as a speaker, but I can also learn that there are other ways to use your speaking business, not only selling online with teleseminars and webinars, but doing your live events and creating your own stage where there's a lot of money and opportunity.

So, speaking definitely a critical way no matter how you want to do it. Most people that start out as speakers, they become broke really quickly because they go flying around everywhere and speak for free because they never learn how to educate and then sell people into the coaching programs.

So, that's why now it's so exciting to be able to share this with people and teach them this in my book. You can launch right away and start making the kind of money that I made as a top professional paid speaker, and this was never an opportunity in the past before.

Brian: Yeah. While I'm thinking about it, how can people get your book and how can they connect with you if they want to learn more about who you are and what you're doing at any given time?

Debbie: Well, they can go to www.debbieallen.com and you can get the book there along with some free gifts. Then, if they want to personally connect with me, there's a contact page on the website.

Brian: All right, that sounds fantastic! So, you have reinvented yourself a number of times. We talked about that at the beginning of the show. How does someone really do that? Because only a handful of business people that I can think of have successfully done that over and over again, and most of the people I think of are actors or musicians—Cher, Madonna, Tom Cruise, and people like that. They're up and they're down, they're up and they're down. John Travolta is another very good example. So, how do you pick yourself up when you're down and reinvent what you're doing? I'm sure a lot of people out there were hit very hard by the economy and they were feeling perhaps like they're having to start over and they just don't know what to do next.

Debbie: When that hit, I said, "How can I make the money?" I went internationally right away and it just took time to reinvent. Sometimes you do have to take a hit and you have to get knocked down pretty hard before you can get back up, but there's always an answer, and there's always another way of switching it around and paying attention if you're smart. If you're not a smart entrepreneur, you need to work with somebody who is. If you get into that mode, "I'm knocked down and I can't get back up," you need some help for somebody to give you some guidance and dust you off a little bit.

So, I've had this happened to me. When that economy hit with the speaking business, it knocked me down for about three months and that's it because I reinvented my website, and I really made myself an international speaker, and I just looked for only international opportunities. I was just online every day looking for them and I finally got booked. So, that was a pretty quick turnaround.

Then I met somebody when I was out there internationally, and I got on a three-year world tour with them. We were traveling and doing our programs together, even did a corporation partnership together. That worked very well for the time that it did. When the partnership ended, I got knocked down pretty hard. I reinvented myself, and then it took me about six months of reinventing and getting clients and doing okay, but not a big hit.

It took me almost a year to get my next big hit after that, and that's when I came up with *The Highly Paid Expert* concept. I said, "This is what I've been doing. How can I just repackage this and reword this? I'm going launch a book. I'm going to launch the products with teleseminar. I'm going launch a live event." and that's how I came back really, really bigger and stronger than ever.

So, sometimes, you don't have to completely start all over because you have the skills. Like you said, Brian, on our break. You said, "Things have to happen to you to have the skill or the knowledge to help people in a different way, or you come up with a different idea." We have to go through those periods to get better, to get stronger, so that we can keep going to the next level.

Brian: Yeah, absolutely. So you are a bestselling author of six different books. Most people would kill for one. So, tell us how you started out and how you've used your books to really use that as a platform to launch everything else that you're doing?

Debbie: Well, I think that my fifth book, my *Confessions* book, was definitely a hit. That definitely rebranded me and launched me in a great way so that was one of my favorite books.

This one is really my new baby. I feel like the best book I have ever written in six years because I'm giving somebody a business model. You read a book and you usually get a couple of ideas that you highlight. This is a business model. So, it took me awhile to get to learning how to teach that in a book.

When I wrote my first few books, I really didn't believe I was a good writer because I'm remembering high school English class, my teacher told me that I was going flunk English if I didn't pass the next test, so I didn't believe I was good or I can be ever a writer in my head.

So, I was good at interviewing like you are. I like interviewing people and I can put a little bit of my information in and I can interview people. So, I started out doing books with them, a collaboration of interviews. So I think anybody can do that if they like interviewing people and then you get to learn along the way. How cool is that? I mean, it's a bit of a lazy way to write a book. I interviewed people and put them on the book. I mean I chose really great people to be in my book though, like these are the people I want to learn from so I think that was critical.

Brian: Yeah, absolutely. On that note, you started out with your first couple of books self-publishing, but then you ended up getting an agent and major publishers working with you. How did that transition work for you?

Debbie: I wish I could say and give you a formula on that one, Brian, but I was really lucky on that. My New York agent found me on a Google search and that's what happens when you're the expert. You become very Google-able.

She contacted me to write a book on sales, how to close sales. I'm said, "Oh my God, I've read every book on closing sales." Joe Girard has the best book out there, the World Guinness record of car sales. I read each one of his books. I said, "I don't think we need more books on closing sales. You need a book on mindset and teach people how to think differently about sales."

So, she said, "I'll get back with you." She sold that to a publisher and that did okay, but I never really loved sales like I love marketing. I got a lot of business off of having that book—speaking engagements and consulting, but it wasn't my passion. I still want to go back to marketing.

So, then I wrote *Confessions of Shameless Self-Promoters* and then just self-published because I wanted it out there, and then when I had it done, I said, "Well, can you sell it to a major publisher now?" and she said, "Sure." McGraw-Hill picked it up and launched it in three months. It was no big deal.

Now my new publisher—I've worked with three major ones now—is Career Press, I love them. They've been amazing. They've hired me my own publicist and they're just really rocking it out. They get my message. They worked really hard to get me.

So, I had three publishers fighting over me over this book. So, I knew I was on to something good. It went with a lot of things in mind. It wasn't just what the royalty was, but how much they believe in your book and what they're going do. I mean if they're going take their own money and hire you a publicist, and they're going help you answer your emails when you respond in one day or less, and just be there for you, it's exciting. They understand the business model.

If you're getting a publisher, you need to get your book out internationally. Even when I self-publish, I get my book out internationally. I worked with an agent that took my book to the Frankfurt, Germany Book Fair. So, I asked my publisher, "Are you guys taking my book to Frankfurt and that's really important." They said, "Not only we're taking it to Frankfurt, we're taking to Beijing, and we're taking to London Book Fair and, of course, we'll be in the New York Book Expo.

So, again it all happened from just being online. That's why it's important that you dominate when somebody is there looking for you because you have media people and publicists, and you have book agents that are looking for people.

If you just go out there and try and get yourself, it's really hard. I actually tried that for this last book. I said, "Let me see if I can get an agent". Because

I'd like to go back to my same agent because she's been great, but let me see if I can get another agent just to have a conversation to compare. I just kept getting turned down and I'm thinking, "Enough of this, I got a great agent. I don't have to do anything."

Brian: Right. Wow! So, let me end on this. Let me ask you the question that I asked everybody as I get closer to the end of the show and it's simply, who inspires and motivates you?

Debbie: Richard Branson, hands down. I flew all the way to London to a VIP event just to connect with him because I just wanted to see him speak, and during the conversation, he talked about all the failures he had. He made fun of himself, and he was just so cool and so real. He's like a rock star, a freaking rock star.

Brian: All right. It looks like our show is actually over. I do want to thank Debbie so much for joining our show. Get the book when it comes out at www.debbieallen.com and join us next Monday at 6:00pm Eastern for another episode of Success Profiles Radio. Thank you for listening. Have a great week.

TOM ZIGLAR

BORN TO WIN

Brian: Hello and welcome to Success Profiles Radio. I'm your host Brian K Wright and it is a pleasure to be here with you today. I am honored that you chose to spend part of your day with me here, and this is going to be a fantastic show.

I am so over-the-top excited to have as my special guest this week, Tom Ziglar. Let me tell you a little bit about him.

Tom Ziglar is currently employed at Zig Ziglar Training Systems in the position of President. He was named to this position in 1996, when the company was created as the operations segment of Zig Ziglar Corporation.

Within the first six months after he began directing Ziglar Training Systems, production increased 40 percent with 30 percent fewer people. Prior to being named president, Ziglar initially began his career in retail and direct sales.

He joined the Zig Ziglar Corporation in 1987 learning every aspect of the company as he climbed from working in the warehouse to sales to seminar promotion to sales management. Ziglar shares the belief of his father, Zig Ziglar that "You can have everything in life you want if you just help enough other people get what they want."

He also embraces the following philosophies:

- To be successful in business, it takes honesty, integrity, hard work and wise counsel.

- You can't make a good business deal with a bad person.

- When negotiating: no secrets, no surprises

Tom graduated from Austin College in Sherman, Texas, with a bachelor's degree in political science.

We will discuss all of this and so much more on today's show. So here is my guest, Tom Ziglar.

Hello Tom, are you there? How are you?

Tom: Hello, Brian! It's great to be here. Thanks so much for having me.

Brian: You are very welcome. It's an honor and a privilege to have you here on the show, and I know we will be talking about your book *Born To Win* which you and you Dad co-authored together and it's amazing. I have several of your Dad's books and this ranked right up there with all of them. So anyone out there listening, the book is called *Born To Win* by Zig Ziglar and Tom Ziglar. Get it, get it, get it!

So Tom, the first thing I ask everyone who is on my show is to discuss your background: Where did you come from, how did you get to where you are, what did you overcome?" I'm sure it was very interesting growing up as a Ziglar. Very few other people have had that opportunity.

Tom: I'll tell you what, Brian, I am extremely blessed. Of course, Dad was an amazing speaker, author, and leader. He was an even better father, so I grew up really learning from the best and as good as he was on-stage, he was even better off-stage. When I was at Austin College, my goal and desire was to be a professional golfer. That didn't work out like I thought, so I came into the company while I was playing golf and I got hooked into sales. I discovered that I really had a love for selling, and I still love to sell. It's in my genes, I guess because it was in Dad's genes. Once I made that decision that I was going to focus full-time on what we do, I can honestly say I've never looked back and never regretted it. I'm glad I gave everything I had to golf, but I can't imagine anything better than what I'm doing right now.

Brian: Wow, that's really fantastic! So you wanted to be a golfer and your life took a detour. So let me ask you this. In your bio, I mentioned that you worked your way through the company. It's not one of those deals where your Dad said I'm just going to put you right here and you're going to learn in a really high position. You had to earn your way from the bottom like everyone else in the company, right?

Tom: (laughs) Yeah, when I started here 28 years ago now, we had our own warehouse, our own shipping, and our own production facility. So I was in the back packing boxes, moving inventory, and doing the things that make a business run at the foundational level. Then I moved into production—that was video, VHS and cassette tape duplication—packing our programs and doing that. So I got my hands dirty in the sense that I was moving dusty boxes all day long. But I learned the business from that perspective. Then when I moved into sales, I had the chance to work with our customers and go out to programs and big live events. I really fell in love with the business because I could really see how everybody in the business had a hand in delivering a life-changing product. There's nothing more satisfying than knowing that a message that you helped deliver—whether you're in shipping or sales or production, it doesn't matter—if you helped get it to the person whose life is changed, then you played a role in that. So for that reason, I've just loved working here ever since.

Brian: So as you were moving up in the company in sales, was it selling seminars, books and products, or selling tickets to your Dad's events? What was it exactly that you were doing?

Tom: It was a little bit of everything. When I first started, I was in phone sales, so back then you could actually call people and they would answer the phone, and you got say "Hey, I'm with the Zig Ziglar Corporation", and we had great customers, great lists. Dad's name was well-known. So people were always excited to get a motivational call from a sales guy, at least that's the way I felt about it. That's why I enjoyed it, I got to share what we did. And, of course, even then and today more than ever, people need hope and encouragement. So when you're selling hope and encouragement, there's usually a receptive audience on the other end because everybody needs a little hope and encouragement.

Brian: So let me ask you this. After 9/11 when everything went south all over the place, how did that affect your sales and your message? Did you stay busy, was it hard? What did you have to do to adjust to a bad economy?

Tom: Yeah, 9/11 was a very interesting time because, just for example, we had a large Fortune 100 client and we were scheduled to do a series of corporate trainings with them, and they called and canceled. Instead of having the corporate training, what they had was worst case scenario training. They had a bunch of oil refineries and they had to go secure and protect, because if you remember back then everybody was worried about where's the next attack going to come. This company had so much infrastructure. Our team would go out to Las Vegas 10-12 times a year, not for events that we were hosting, but just to be part of other people's events because that was a big convention area. And if you remember in Vegas, their business got cut by around 50% because everybody's travel budgets got cut like everything else. It was interesting because people needed the training, the hope and encouragement, the motivation, the things that we do more than ever, and at the same time they were pulling back on it because the economy had taken a nosedive and people's postures were really becoming defensive rather than growth-oriented.

Brian: So basically it involved re-positioning what you were doing somehow, right?

Tom: Right! And this is what we learned, and this is true of any economy we've ever been in and that is there are some companies and individuals who really suffer, and there are others who do really well. So what's the difference between the two? Dad used to say this: He said the economy is not really good or bad out there, it's good or bad between our two ears. That is so true, so what happened was there were companies who saw this as an opportunity. They knew it was tough out there, but it's even tougher for our competition. Now we can gain market share. Or, it's tough out there, but we can spend a little bit more time developing and training our people and going back to the basics. In every tough economy and every recession, there are businesses that do better than everybody else, and the difference between those who do well and those who don't is really a mindset or an attitude. And that's the strength of our business, that's what we teach more than anything else. So we had to re-trench for a few months, but after that the companies who were going and growing and seeing this as an opportunity were calling us. It wasn't fun, but we did OK during that time.

Brian: Great! So let's lay a very brief foundation for what this book is about. You split this book *Born To Win* into 3 separate parts. Those 3 parts are Plan to Win, Prepare to Win, and Expect to Win. How did you decide that as your overall foundational structure for the book?

Tom: Dad's original quote that he is famous for is this: "**You can have everything in life you want, if you will just help enough other people get what they want.**" You are born to win, but in order to be the winner you were born to be you must plan to win, prepare to win, and then and ONLY then can you expect to win.

So we took the book into 3 parts probably because he had said that quote thousands of times from stage. It's because it's true, you have to plan, prepare, and expect before you actually can win.

Brian: That's absolutely true! My very special guest this week is Tom Ziglar, son of the late Zig Ziglar who has always been one of my favorite speakers and authors. Tom co-authored a book with his Dad called *Born To Win*, and the first part of that book talks about how you have to plan to win. So let's spend this segment talking about some of the elements that go into planning to win. One of my favorite quotes from your Dad is the one we discussed earlier: "**You can have everything in life you want, if you will just help enough other people get what they want.**" I see it quoted all over the place. That is probably the quote he is most known for. How has that impacted your life and the way you run your business?

Tom: It's the motive the governs everything, and I know for a fact that today with social media, text messaging, and the instant communication world we live in, people can text somebody who is not transparent right away. We have radar out there for people who are putting on a mask. So if you go out into the world and say, "I'm going to help you get what you want", my motive is to serve you. Then everything in life that is worth having comes so much easier. So that whole quote is more true than it's ever been because people now can tell if someone is not being forthright and honest.

Brian: I think every successful company should have that as one of their major core values. I think things would be so much better if everyone thought that way. So let me ask you a question, and you do address this in your book, and I'm sure it's a question you get a lot: How do you achieve consistent and lasting success? Sometimes you see success and it happens for awhile, then bad things happen and people feel like they are on a roller coaster.

Tom: Well there's two things, and writing the book with Dad and asking him questions about it as we went through it really clarified some things. But #1—and Dad said this for years—the #1 reason for his success was his character and his integrity. So the key to long-term lasting success is you build a platform on character and integrity in everything you do. Now we say that trust is a by-product of integrity, and so if you want to be successful you've got to build trust. Seth Godin is one of our good friends, and he says that if you want to go out and be successful, his #1 focus and the thing that he focuses on more than anything else is the scalability of trust. In other words, so many people focus on revenue or profits or goals, but for Seth, he focuses on the scalability of trust.

Why is that?

In any relationship, if trust is growing, if I can constantly over time feel like I can trust you more, when I have something of value to offer you and you trust me, I've already done the hard part. The rest of it is easy. If you need it, you're going to buy it, right? So the key to long-term sustainable success is building everything on that platform of character and integrity.

And then I asked Dad in the book, after character and integrity being #1, what's #2? And he said the words "persistent consistency." I asked him what he meant. To give you the short version, that's the Ziglar definition of work-ethic. So what he really said was hard work is the key to success. You build on a character foundation, then you work hard but here's his uniqueness, the way he put it together: He said "persistent consistency". And consistency means you do what you need to do every day or as often as you need to do it.

So if you are in sales, you've got to make 30 calls in order to hit your quota. You make 30 calls every day, that's consistency. If you're trying to lose weight, what you do is you work out every day, that is consistency.

Persistency then is when you go a little extra. Persistency means that if you are in sales, then maybe the first day you make 30 calls, and then the second day you make 30 calls but you add a new question. The third day you make 30 calls, but you put in a new statement or a new feature or benefit. And you keep testing to see which one gets you a better result. So when you add that persistent consistency to character and integrity, then you've got a formula that works over and over again. Because like we learned in the economy and throughout time, what works today doesn't necessarily guarantee it's going to work tomorrow. Business is ever-changing. So if we build our relationships based on character and integrity, and we're constantly honing our skills and learning new things and testing new ways of doing it, and we're working hard on it every single day, that gives us the best chance for long-term stable success.

Brian: I love that. Let me ask you this. You talk about a three word mantra in this part of the book: will, skill, and refill. Talk about what that means in terms of planning to win.

Tom: Well, every time Dad would speak he had this formula that he didn't even realize that he had created, and the last three parts of that formula were "will, skill, and refill". So what he would say was that every single day, we need to work on our will and our skill, and then we need to refill it.

So "will" is simply the attitude, the heart, the desire, the want-to. What he's really saying is that every single day we need to listen to a recording, a radio show, or a podcast just like the one we are on right now—something that lifts us up, motivates us, and encourages us and gives us that power or information to have the right attitude, that desire to be, do, and have more. So every single day we need to work on our will.

But just because we have the right attitude doesn't mean that we have enough. We also have to have the right "skill". So whatever profession it is, whatever we want to do whatever business we have—if we are a business owner or we work somewhere—even if we want to be a professional golfer like I wanted to be, we've got to work on our skill. That's the aptitude, the how-to, the professionalism that says "I have a great attitude and look at this. I do things with excellence."

So if we work on our will and skill every single day, then we are always improving. It's when people get lazy, they let their attitude slide a little bit, or just because they did it well one time they think that they can rest on that. That's not the way the world works. Every day everybody gets a little better, your competition gets a little faster. So what you've got to do is sharpen your saw every single day, and that's what we mean by "will, skill and refill". Work on your attitude, work on your skill, and then do that again and again and again.

Brian: So let me ask you this. I know that desire is a foundational place to start. You can have a great attitude, but if don't really know what you want or you don't want something bad enough, that desire is not there. So if someone is stuck in a rut, if they feel stuck and don't feel all that excited about anything, how can you create a burning desire? How does that process work?

Tom: This is one of my favorite things to talk about. At leadership conferences and corporate environments, I'll say that the worst thing that's going on in business today, and it's an epidemic, is in America we're just inundated with zombies. Have you ever worked with someone who was like the Walking Dead?

Brian: Yeah, people who went through the motions and really didn't care, just putting in their time and hoping to get paid. Yes, absolutely!

Tom: That's right, instead of seeing where they are as a springboard to where they want to be, they see it as a sentence to be served. So they show up at the last possible minute and they leave as early as they can. When they go to a meeting, they don't offer to raise their hand, they don't talk about solutions, they don't even talk about problems, they think, "Don't pick me!" In a Gallup poll did a huge study on it—I use the word "zombie", they use the word "engagement"—and what they say is in the United States 70% of the people out there are what is called "disengaged". They don't care.

What I say is this: zombies don't care because they don't dream. So what really needs to happen is if we're going to get that desire back, we've got to dream a little bit. We've got to look out into the future and say, "What do I want to be, do, and have?" Do I want to be out of debt, go to Tahiti, do I want to get a new car, do I want to provide a college fund for my kids? What is it that I really want? What's motivating me, what would inspire me, what desire do I have to achieve? And then I've got to step back for a second and say "Wait a second here". If I go to work unmotivated just trying to get by, is that going to take me closer to my goals or further from my dream? So if I'm just coasting, obviously I'm not getting any closer to my dream, I'm getting further away. But if I go to work, and I'm working for a dream instead of a paycheck, then that changes everything. So until I know what my dream is, until I know and understand what my desire is, it's hard to make a commitment. But what I've noticed is every dream takes time and money to accomplish. So the reality is that the harder I work at whatever my job is, even if it's one I don't want, the faster I get my dream. Because when I work hard with the right attitude, I get a promotion, I get noticed by people who can hire me away. All kinds of good things happen when I work for a dream instead of a paycheck.

Brian: We're talking with Tom Ziglar, son of the legendary Zig Ziglar, and we are talking about their book *Born To Win*. Check that book out, read it, absorb it, it's fantastic!

We just talked about planning to win, now let's talk about preparing to win. Here's a really interesting question. The difference between planning to win and preparing to win—would you say it's the difference between having the inner game and outer game worked out?

Tom: Yes, that's a great way to look at it! I use a football analogy because that's what I grew up with. So planning to win is like you're the football coach and you're putting the game plan together. You scout the other team, you look at your own assets, you understand your strengths and weaknesses, their strengths and weaknesses. That's the plan. So you develop a game plan to go out and make it happen.

Preparing is you go to practice, you run the plays. You do the preparation, you do the drills, you do the physical activity. It's not mental anymore, it's actually going out and doing it. So that's the preparation.

Brian: There's something in the book that I was really intrigued by, and it's the idea that you can do more than you think. But a lot of people don't think and do more, why do you think people block their own potential?

Tom: There are a lot of reasons. One is they've never tried. Another one is they've never had someone who believed in them, and some people don't believe in themselves. So you've got to have the combination of stretching yourself, believing in yourself, and sometimes having a mentor or somebody you trust who believes in you.

I'll give you a great example that happened to me personally. There's a group of wounded warrior veterans called Operation Give Back. It's a group I've associated with and helped them raise some money. We run a race every year, the Ragnar Relay, which is a 200 mile race, and we do it in a team format. So on this team we've got amputees, wounded warriors, and then we've got other able-bodied teammates, and we run. So I'm running—and we're running from Miami to Key West—and I was running about 3 miles and I had another mile to go in my section. And I look up and there's a corner, and nobody can see me at this corner, but I know that when I come around the corner that my team is going to see me. I was really struggling, and so I'm thinking to myself, "I'm going to walk right here before I come around this corner" because I need to be jogging when I come around this corner so that everybody will see that I've been running. But I'm also hurting, it was 90 degrees and it's humid down in the Florida Keys. So just about the time that I'm going to walk, I look up and our team leader—his name was Jose—he comes jogging around the corner. And Jose was a Command Sergeant Major, he's a Chief Master Sergeant. So he starts jogging next to me, and he said "Ziglar, how you doing?" Of course now the Sergeant Major is there and I said, "I'm doing good sir!" So we're running and I'm huffing and puffing, and I'm sweating and dying, but there's no way I was letting this guy down. And we jogged together all the way to the finish line. So I ran further than I thought I could because somebody else believed in me. I had somebody else's expectations to live up to that were higher than my own.

That's why a personal development principle is that we need to find an accountability partner, or a mentor, or somebody who we really love and respect who sets a high standard for us, and then hold us accountable because we can do more than we think.

Brian: Exactly! And I love how you say in your book how making good choices improves your circumstances, which in turn leads to better choices being available. So it cycles upon itself, doesn't it?

Tom: Absolutely! Every positive decision that you make opens up a whole bunch of other doors for more positive decisions. The same thing is true every time you make a bad decision, the options aren't as good. We have fewer choices, and we can see that in life. You can see it with people who struggle with alcohol or drugs. You can make a decision to not drink, or to not do drugs. That means that you will have sobriety, then tomorrow you will be fresher and more mentally clear. You'll be able to do the things that you want to do, so it opens up those possibilities. If you start going down the wrong path, you start making things that limit your options.

So there's a principle that I learned from Dad, and that is where hope is born. You see, hopeless people don't believe that there's anything they can do to change the circumstance. They think they have no hope so why bother. And so Dad would ask this question. He would say, "How many of you here in the room today can make a decision in the next week that can make things in your family life, business life, or personal life worse?" Of course everybody raises their hand and laughs because of course we can make things worse. We could cut the tip of our fingers off. That would make things worse. Then he flips the question and says, "OK, how many of you here today in the next week can make a decision that make your family life, your business life, or your personal life better?" Everybody will raise their hands. And then what he'll say is this: Whether you realize it or not, you have just decided in your own mind that you have the ability to make things better or worse, and the choice is yours.

Brian: Exactly!

Tom: And that's an incredibly powerful thought to know that no matter where we are in our journey in our life, that right now this very second, we have the power to make things better or worse and the choice is ours.

Brian: What I sometimes hear from people who are struggling is "If I only had this opportunity…" Let's talk about opportunity. There are opportunities everywhere. Some people are really good at seeing them, and others can't seem to see them if they're sitting right there in front of their face. So how do we learn to recognize opportunities, Tom?

Tom: Well, there are a couple of things. One is we've got to have a brain that focuses on gratitude. Here's a simple thing: Most people see the world as dangerous, it hurts, bad things happen, I'm minding my own business and something bad happens and so we get negative. What we've got to do is train ourselves to be positive, and a great way to do that is to work on our gratitude. So every morning when you get up and you write down three things you are grateful for. Then the next day you review those three things you are grateful for, and then you write three more things. Then you do this every day for 30 days. At the end of 30 days, you'll have a list of 90 things you are grateful for. But here's the best part, your mind will be looking for things that you're grateful for all day long because you've trained it. There's another thing about opportunity. Rabbi Daniel Lapin, who is one of Dad's good friends and one of my friends, says that opportunity seeks out the generous. And here is what he means: Brian, if I had an opportunity and I brought it to you and said could you help me with this? And you realized it WAS a great opportunity but you couldn't do it—you weren't qualified to do it, it wasn't in your expertise—and I said who do you know who could do it? Your first thought is you would think of somebody. You wouldn't think of a miserly mean person, would you?

Brian: No, you would probably seek out one of the busiest people you know because they find time for stuff like that.

Tom: Right! You would find someone who was generous and well-qualified. We find the nice people we trust. So if you want opportunity to seek you out, then you need to give generously with your time. The more generous people are, the more opportunity knocks on their door, doesn't it?

Brian: Right!

Tom: It's a strange thing. It's really the way God created it. The more generous we are, the more people are trying to find us to give us stuff to do because they know they can trust us. And if somebody is going to win in this world, it might as well be a generous person.

Brian: Let me ask you something a little bit unrelated. It is in the same section of your book about preparing to win. Sometimes people don't like to hear feedback. They view it as criticism, or they are not trained to see it as something they can actually use. So how can we weigh whether the feedback we are receiving is valid or not?

Tom: So there are two questions there. How do we receive feedback, and then how do we know it's valid? First thing is there is a guy I love, his name is Michael Mayer and he has an acronym called L.I.F.E, and he talks about a stairway. Imagine the stairway going to the top and it's one of those circular spiral staircases. Each step has a letter on it, each one spelling out "LIFE" and then it repeats. What happens is we learn (L) something new, then we step up the stair and we implement (I) it. The next one is (F) and it stands for "fail". Guess what? There's nothing we do that's 100% perfect. So when somebody gives us feedback that says you can improve in this, we need to understand that failure is nothing more than new information. It's not who we are, it's just something we did that wasn't 100% perfect, and none of us do anything that's 100% perfect. So then we go to (E) and we examine it. What did I do wrong, what could I do better next time? We ask ourselves these questions, and then we take the next step. We learn some new things and we repeat the cycle. People who aren't climbing the stairway up to the top are stuck and they refuse to implement. They never examine, and they never understand that failure is nothing more than an event it's not a person. So the first thing you've got to understand is until we fail we can't grow.

Brian: We're with Tom Ziglar, who co-authored a book with his dad, Zig Ziglar, called *Born To Win*. While I'm thinking about this, Tom, where can we find and buy the book?

Tom: The best place is www.ziglar.com and we've got the book there. You can also find it at other places like Amazon, Barnes & Noble, and those kinds of places, but I'm partial to ziglar.com.

Brian: Sure, and it's a great site. You also have a free newsletter and you have assessments and different ways to help people and further their education with you, correct?

Tom: Absolutely, so when you come to our page we offer a few gifts. If you want to get our newsletter, one of Dad's greatest recordings is "Biscuits, Fleas, and Pump Handles" so there's an audio download of that. The newsletter comes out weekly. Just stop by and see what we have, we'd love to have you. And if you're on our list we do free webcasts all the time, so you'll be able to take advantage of those as well.

Brian: That's wonderful, so we talked earlier in the show about planning to win and then preparing to win. Then the final element is expecting to win. Now it's not just about positive thinking, you have to actually earn the right to win, so how do we really do that?

Tom: You know, it's amazing to me that people put in the work, and they go out and then for whatever reason they just don't expect to win. And that limits their ability to be the winner they were born to be. Sometimes they worry about the results, they don't get focused on all the good things that will happen. Instead they focus on what would happen if it goes wrong.

So you've got to get your mindset in a position of expecting to win. I've built my life on character, I've put in the hard work, the persistent consistency. I've done the planning and preparation—now I'm ready to go!

In the book, the example we give is if you go bowling, you do everything right. You hold the ball in the right place, you line up, you go down the alley and you release it. And once you release it, it's done. There's nothing you can do at that point, and the results are going to come. That's fine, that's what we should do is give it 100% of our effort, planning and preparation, and then we should expect to win. We should expect to get a strike. Then if we don't we get the next ball.

Brian: Right, because you have a chance to try again. That's not the only ball you're going to throw in the whole game. You got lots of chances in bowling. If you don't like your score you can play another entire game. So let me ask you this: In this section, you talked about cultivating an attitude of encouragement and hope. Certainly these are critical factors in expecting to win. It goes back to getting other people what they want first, right?

Tom: Yes, but we also have to be intentional about that, so it's good for us to have friends, family members, accountability partners, and people we love and trust who are encouraging, who lift us up and give us hope. If we have a goal or a dream that we want to accomplish, then we just share that with people who really truly want to see us accomplish that. So Dad talked a lot about Automobile University. This goes back to the will and the skill and the refill. We've got to put the good, the clean, the pure, and the powerful into our mind every single day. So we read the right stuff, we listen to the right things, but we also take time to cultivate friendships who we can just call on the phone and encourage them, and they'll do the same for us.

Brian: That's great, I love that! So you talked a little bit ago about not worrying about the results. We are a very result-oriented society, so that might seem really counter-intuitive to a lot of the people listening. But when you have a plan in place and you execute it—that really should be the thing you focus on, by focusing on the activities that get you where you want to go and the results will show themselves.

Tom: Absolutely. I did a study on Dad, and I was trying to figure out from God's perspective, what character quality did he have that was the most important to God? In our life, we're all trying to do the best we can and we want to be honest, we want to love—but from God's perspective what is the most important quality? A lot of people when you ask them, they'll say obedience or humility or love, and those are all really important—but I hit on this word, and the word was "brokenness". I started thinking about that, and that's exactly the attitude and quality that Dad exhibited. So when you dig into brokenness, it's very close to humility. So here's what a broken person is like. A broken person understands that there's nothing of eternal significance that they can do without God. In other words, if they are going to be eternally significant, God's got to be involved. And they only have to have two responsibilities.

The first responsibility is to have that vibrant relationship with God. The second is to share His truth and love. And so this was Dad's secret. He would walk out on stage, and his only goal was to share God's truth and love. That's it. What people did with it was totally up to them. He did not take any responsibility for how they received the truth and love. So because of that, he wasn't trying to make the front row of the audience happy. He was trying to please the person who paid him the paycheck. He was trying to please God, so he could go out there and be totally free to be himself. And so the responsibility he had was that he had to plan and prepare better than anybody in the world. That gives you freedom because in life, a lot of people think it's a popularity contest. We worry all the time about what people will think of us—will they like me, will they come back? But true freedom is when that's not your number one priority. Your number one priority is to share with people truth and love. Unfortunately, sometimes people share the truth but it's not in love, and there's nothing worse than that in my mind because you are sharing something that someone needs to hear but they know you're doing it as a sword instead of as a comfort.

Brian: Oh my gosh, you are so right. I have had people in my life who have done that. They tell me what they think I need to hear but there's not a spirit of humility about it—it's almost a spirit of "I'm saying this because I want you to feel hurt by what you've done.

It's interesting that you brought up the whole concept of worrying because when your Dad was up on stage, he was blessing others with the love of God and that's very liberating. And not worrying about things is also very liberating because when you worry about things, doesn't that make things a lot worse?

Tom: Absolutely! Dad said that worry is interest paid in advance on a debt that will never come due.

Brian: So there's no finality to it. It's something that perpetuates itself.

Tom: Right, there is no point to worrying. We have two things in our life. We have facts and we have problems. So when I ran that race with the Wounded Warriors some of them were amputees. The fact is they lost their leg—they can't worry about that anymore. Facts you have to accept. Problems, you can do something about. So the problem is it takes 30 minutes longer to get ready in the morning. You don't worry about problems either, you just plan for them. You get up 30 minutes earlier. Is it fair, is it right? Is it a horrible thing to happen? Yeah! But worrying doesn't change any of that. You accept facts, and you put a plan in place to overcome the problems. Worry has no part of it.

Brian: So we are coming to the end of the show, I can't believe how quickly this hour has gone. We've got less than 3 minutes, Tom, so I'm going to ask the question that I ask everyone at the end of the show.

Who inspires and motivates you? I think we all know what the answer to this question is going to be, but I'll ask anyway.

Tom: (laughs) Well, of course, my father, Zig Ziglar, has motivated and inspired me. I have a 19 year old daughter who is a sophomore in college, she keeps me going. Then the people I listen to and read every day are Dave Ramsey and Seth Godin. Those two guys have really had an impact on my life, and they are very different in what they teach and what they do. They have similar values, but they come from different ends. Between Dad and Dave and Seth, I get a daily dose of everything.

Brian: So tell us one more time: How can we find the book, how can we connect with you, and how can we be part of your community, Tom?

Tom: You can find the book at www.ziglar.com which is our website. We have all of our products and services there, our books, and many other books besides *Born To Win*. We do online webcasts and events on a regular basis, so you can get all of that information there. Another great place to check out is the Zig Ziglar fan page on Facebook. We got over 2 million likes there. We're growing by about 6,000 likes a day. We put out about 5-6 quotes, ideas, and concepts every single day and we've got literally hundreds of thousands of people looking at it, and hundreds of comments on every single one of them. So if you need a little check up from the neck up and getting rid of the hardening of the attitude, that's the place to go.

Brian: That's wonderful, and Tom, thank you so much for being on the show. I would love to have you back again someday soon.

Tom: You bet, thanks Brian!

WORK WITH ME

I will help you write your book!

Many people dream of writing a book someday, but most of them never get around to doing it. If you are one of those people, I can probably predict why that is the case:

- You hadn't thought about it before

- You don't think you have time

- You may not know how

- You might not believe you are a good enough writer

- You haven't clearly understood the benefits of having a book

When you are working with an experienced coach, these reasons go away because I will help you every step of the way.

As a published author, I can tell you that having a book of your own is critical to growing your business.

Here are some great reasons to have a book:

- It gives you added credibility in the marketplace. People automatically afford expert status to those who have written a book.

- All things being equal, you will stand out against your competitors who do NOT have a book. Let's say for simplicity that there are 20 businesses in your industry and market that compete for the same customers. If all of you are equally talented, how do you stand out? Being able to say to your prospect, "Here is a book that answers many of the common questions you might have about...." Wouldn't that make a difference? Absolutely it would!

- It can lead to added revenue. Authors can generate extra funds by selling books.

- It can lead to extra sources of revenue. For example, it can bring you new customers and referrals, it can lead to speaking opportunities, TV/radio interviews, blog posts, having your own radio show, coaching programs, and talks in your local community which could lead to them becoming new customers.

These are just a few of the ways that having a book can help your business.

As a published author of several books, I would love to be the one who helps you put this all together. Email me at brian@briankwright.com to begin the discussion.

ABOUT THE AUTHOR

Brian K Wright is the host of Success Profiles Radio, motivational speaker, author of multiple books, ghostwriter, and book writing coach for his clients. His mission is to motivate and inspire others to discover their unique talents and follow their dreams in life. This is so necessary because many people live far beneath their potential, and great leadership is needed now more than ever.

Having interviewed many world-class achievers on his radio show, Brian has taken the best lessons he has learned from others, applied them to his own life, and shares them with his audiences.

Brian grew up in Iowa and graduated from Iowa State University with a degree in Communication Studies, and holds a Master's degree in Adult Education from the University of Nebraska in Lincoln. He has extensive experience teaching and training in academic and corporate environments.

Throughout his career, Brian has been a top performer in the areas of sales, customer service, training, and has also written resumes professionally for students, working professionals, and executives. He is available to speak on the topics of motivation/inspiration, leadership, and book writing. He resides in the Phoenix, Arizona area.

Morgan James
Speakers Group

www.TheMorganJamesSpeakersGroup.com

We connect Morgan James published
authors with live and online events
and audiences who will benefit
from their expertise.